MW00565156

MY DOG
ALWAYS
EATS FIRST

MY DOG
ALWAYS
EATS FIRST

Homeless People and Their Animals

Leslie Irvine

LYNNE
RIENNER
PUBLISHERS

BOULDER
LONDON

Published in the United States of America in 2013 by
Lynne Rienner Publishers, Inc.
1800 30th Street, Boulder, Colorado 80301
www.rienner.com

and in the United Kingdom by
Lynne Rienner Publishers, Inc.
3 Henrietta Street, Covent Garden, London WC2E 8LU

Library of Congress Cataloging-in-Publication Data
Irvine, Leslie.
  My dog always eats first : homeless people and their animals /
Leslie Irvine.
      p. cm.
  Includes bibliographical references and index.
  ISBN 978-1-58826-888-4 (hc : alk. paper) 1. Homeless persons.
2. Animal welfare. 3. Human-animal relationships. I. Title.
  HV4493.I78 2013
  305.5'692—dc23

                                            2012030572

British Cataloguing in Publication Data
A Cataloguing in Publication record for this book
is available from the British Library.

Printed and bound in the United States of America

  The paper used in this publication meets the requirements
        of the American National Standard for Permanence of
        Paper for Printed Library Materials Z39.48-1992.

    5   4   3   2   1

Contents

Acknowledgments

This book originated in discussions with Andrew Berzanskis of Lynne Rienner Publishers, and I am grateful for his help and support along the way. I also thank Karen Williams, Karen Maye, and the other staff at Lynne Rienner Publishers, who helped in innumerable ways.

When I began this research, I had no experience with the homeless. A number of people helped me to get started. In particular, Lori Weise of Downtown Dog Rescue in Los Angeles gave me valuable advice on approaching homeless people about their dogs. Greg Harms of the Boulder Shelter for the Homeless and Genevieve Frederick of Feeding Pets of the Homeless also offered helpful suggestions.

I would like to acknowledge the debt I owe to those who made this book possible by helping me to gain access to homeless pet owners. My deep appreciation goes to veterinarian Ilana Strubel and to Maya DeNola, Allen Meyer, Beth Rittenhouse-Dhesi, Bess Touma, Bernadette Guirguis, and the other staff and clients of the San Francisco Community Clinic Consortium and Veterinary Street Outreach Services. I also thank Ilana and her partner, Michelle McAnanama, for their gracious hospitality during my visits to San Francisco. My thanks also go to Maya DeNola in her role with People and Animals Living Safely and to the staff and clients of the PALS clinic, to the staff and clients of the Homeless Youth Alliance of San Francisco, and to veterinarians Kelley Cayton and Morgan Weintraub and the clients of the Mercer Veterinary Clinic and Sacramento Loaves and Fishes. I learned a great deal during an inspiring conversation with the late Anneke Vos, founder of the Animal Emergency Services at Loaves and Fishes. I regret that she did not live to see this book in print. My gratitude also goes to Karen Mahar,

Eddie Gloria, Cliff Petit Homme, and the staff and clients of Camillus House. I also thank Pauline Clarke-Trotman and the residents of Better Way of Miami for their time and candor. I am grateful to Mark Rogers of Mark Rogers Photography for providing the photos that enhance the book. Royalties that I receive from the book will go back to organizations dedicated to helping the pets of the homeless.

The Department of Sociology at the University of Colorado provided sabbatical leave that allowed me to complete the writing of this book. A small grant from the university's Leadership Education for Advancement and Promotion program provided the gift cards for interviewees and travel support for the research. I received valuable research assistance from Kristina Kahl, Lauren Levin, and Jesse Smith.

And last, but by no means least, I thank Marc Krulewitch for many things, but mostly for being who he is.

MY DOG
ALWAYS
EATS FIRST

1 A Good Life for a Dog?

As I drove along a busy, four-lane street in Boulder, Colorado, one summer afternoon over a decade ago, I saw a young man and his dog standing on the median at a traffic light. By the man's age and appearance, I guessed him to be one of the countless people who camp on the National Forest land around Boulder, especially during the summer. They come into the city to panhandle for enough money to buy what supplies they need. They often have dogs with them. This particular man stood facing traffic, and he held a piece of corrugated cardboard with the words "Homeless, Hungry, Anything helps" scrawled on it in crude, black letters written with magic marker. He had two well-worn and overstuffed packs with him. Lying against them was a medium-sized, mixed-breed dog. Each time the stoplight turned red, another round of drivers reached out their windows to hand him money. The young man trotted over to each car in turn, leaving the dog to wait for him. The narrow median did not provide much room to maneuver. If either the dog or the man lost footing, they would fall into traffic. All the while, the summer sun beat down relentlessly on them both.

I saw a combination gas station and convenience store across from where the pair stood. I pulled my car in, parked, and bought a bottle of cold water. Then I went to the trunk of my car and took out a folding water dish that I kept there to use on hikes with my dog. I waited for a break in traffic and crossed over to the median. I stood in front of the man, but in doing so I inadvertently blocked drivers' view of his sign. Without acknowledging me, he shifted to the very edge of the median and held the sign out to the side of me. I offered him the water and the bowl for his dog.

"I don't need it," he said, keeping his eyes on the cars, with their potential donors.

"Your dog looks thirsty," I replied.

"He's okay," he said matter-of-factly. "I got plenty of water." He reached down and lifted the flap on one of the packs to reveal a gallon jug.

"Okay," I said. "Do you have food for him?"

"Yup," he said. Still no eye contact. He tapped his foot on the other bag so that I could hear the crunch of dog food. "Okay," I said, and I crossed back over to my car.

By this time, a woman I knew from my volunteer work at the local humane society had also pulled into the gas station. She was concerned about the dog, too. I told her what I had done, and about the man's response. She thought we could pool our money and buy the dog from him. Together, we came up with nearly sixty dollars, most of it hers. The guy should be happy to get some real money, we reasoned. After all, he was begging for change and we would offer dollars. We crossed over to the median together. My friend attempted some pleasantries and then said, "We'd like to buy your dog."

Without taking his eyes off the cars, he said, "You can't have my dog. Leave me alone."

I explained our logic to him. "You're begging for spare change, and we can give you more than you'll make here all afternoon. Your dog will have a good home."

"Get out of my face," he said. "I'm not selling my dog."

We persisted. We took turns telling him how his dog deserved a better life. *He* might have chosen homelessness, we said, but his dog had not. At this point, he looked straight at us and exploded. "You fuckin' yuppies! Why don't you mind your own fuckin' business? I take good care of my dog. He has a great life. He runs around in the forest all the time. He never has to be on a leash except when we come down here. He's got food. He's got water. He's had his shots. He never leaves my side. He's fine. Now get the hell out of here and leave me alone!"

We crossed back over to the gas station, where we shared our outrage and our frustration. We had one last idea. We would call Animal Control. Cell phones had not yet become ubiquitous, and I used the station's pay phone to make the call. When I reached the dispatcher, I told her about the homeless man and the dog on the median and gave the location. "Is he harming the animal?" she asked.

"No," I replied.

"Is the dog in distress?" she asked.

"No," I answered again.

"Does the owner have food and water for him?"

"Yes," I responded.

"Well, then, there's nothing the officers can do," she said. "He's not doing anything wrong."

I was not convinced. I thought he *was* doing something wrong. It was nothing I could put my finger on, no mistake that he could correct. Instead, the whole picture looked all wrong to me. My friend thought so, too. It troubled us that such a man had a dog. We felt sure that he could not provide proper care. We believed that the dog could have, *should* have, a better life. For us, that life would have meant four walls, a roof, and even a yard. It would have involved toys, crate training, and doggie daycare. For the young man on the median, a good life for a dog meant freedom, the outdoors, and constant companionship.

Over time, through my research on people's relationships with animals in other contexts and my volunteer work at an animal shelter, I realized that having a house did not imply that the dog—or cat—who lived there would have a good life. Long before I began the research for this book, I had begun thinking about the issues that animate it, such as what it means to care for and be in relationship with an animal, and the role of the animal in one's sense of self.

Another story; a pair of stories, really. In the course of volunteering at an animal shelter, I have seen many stray animals come and go. Most of the dogs' owners come to claim them; this is not so for cats, but that is yet another story. In this one, an animal control officer brought in a young, stray Shiba Inu. The breed originated in Japan. Shibas have small, compact, muscular bodies, pointy ears, and an upright, often curled tail. To my eye, they have a foxy look. Purebred puppies cost upwards of six hundred dollars, and a potential owner could easily pay over a thousand dollars. Originally bred for hunting, this particular dog had the alertness and independent streak expected of the breed. Fortunately, he also had a microchip, which allowed a staff member to contact the owner to notify him that he could pick up his dog at the shelter, and indeed had to do so within five days (after this, animals become the property of the shelter, potentially available for adoption). The owner explained that, during a fierce storm on the previous day, the wind had blown his fence gate open and the dog had run out of the yard.

The owner lived nearby, but it took him four days to arrive to claim his dog. A few weeks later, the dog reappeared at the shelter, having taken advantage of the freedom offered by the unreliable fence gate once again. Another phone call let the owner know his dog had arrived at the shelter. Another few days passed, and still the dog went unclaimed. The staff made follow-up phone calls, but no owner appeared. Finally, he relinquished the dog, saying that he found the dog's repeated escapes inconvenient.

Meanwhile, another man had also lost his dog. This man, the dog, and a second dog were camping in the mountains west of Boulder. The man had no address and no phone. During the same violent storm, thunder had startled the dog and she had run off. He had searched and searched to no avail. He came to the shelter every day to see if anyone had brought her in. He had no vehicle, so he walked. The walk took several hours. He made the trip both ways, daily, for weeks. More than one staff member saw him crying. He made signs about the lost dog and posted them, asking anyone who found her to bring her to the shelter. The staff eventually gave him a new pair of shoes because he had worn his only pair out trying to find his dog.

Which man provided better care? The one who lived in a house and who, by all signs, had plenty of money, or the one who wore holes in his shoes searching for his dog? Which dog would you say had the better life? Was it the one purchased for hundreds of dollars, whose urge to explore became inconvenient, or the one whose absence drove her owner to walk miles and break down in tears? When the question of whether homeless people can care for pets comes up, I think of these stories.

A Commitment to Stories

By beginning with these stories, I intend to call attention to the issues of relationships and care that remain salient throughout this book. But I also begin with stories to honor my commitment to the process that Art Frank calls "letting stories breathe." Stories breathe, Frank writes, like "the breath of a god in creation stories" (2010:3). They give life to people by establishing identities and situating experience within time. They endow us with a sense of self and give meaning to the relationships that surround it. They give us a way of experiencing what Jerome Bruner (1987) calls "lived time," which is to say that stories allow us to recount that first this happened, and then that happened. Stories also connect people. They make them characters in a mutual narrative and call out to them as members of a group who share a telling of the world. Stories are also resources, helping us understand and share what we find meaningful and what gives us purpose.

In this book I will explore the stories told by people who live, or have lived, on the streets with companion animals. I use both "stories" and "personal narratives" interchangeably to refer to "retrospective first-person accounts of individual lives" (Maynes, Pierce, and Laslett 2008:1). I gained these accounts through interviews with seventy-five homeless and formerly homeless pet owners. My interest centers on understanding how the stories that homeless people tell of their relationships with their animals enable the tellers to "be who they are" (Frank 2010:14). As I discuss more fully throughout the book, keeping a pet while being homeless involves an intense level of commitment and more than a little hardship. In surveys, homeless people report levels of attachment to their animals that may surpass those found among the domiciled public. They frequently refuse offers of shelter or housing that require them to give up or separate from their animals. Their circumstances shape unique relationships with their animals and unique stories of the self within those relationships.

The literature on human-animal relationships, including some of my own work, has demonstrated that close relationships with pets involve intersubjectivity and the mutual construction of identity (Alger and Alger 1997; Irvine 2004a, 2004b; Sanders 1999, 2003). Scholars have come to understand a great deal about the dynamics of human-animal relationships, but thus far the research has focused mostly on how they occur in middle-class contexts. We know little about how these relationships occur at the margins of society, among those who live not in houses but on the streets. In some ways, we might anticipate finding no differences. Regardless of setting, animals do not judge us by the same yardsticks used by our human friends. As Clinton Sanders has written:

> In an important way, the distinction between relationships with humans and with animal-persons is central to the special character of the human-animal bond. Because they are not human relationships, those with companion animals are constant rather than contingent. The animal's response to his or her companion does not depend on the latter's appearance, age, economic fortunes, abilities, or the other vagaries that, for good or ill, constrain human-to-human relationships. (2003:418)

Animals, unlike humans, cannot be "fair-weather friends," and so we would expect to see many similarities among these relationships, regardless of the social status of the owner. Indeed, some of what I offer in the following pages will sound familiar. Yet some of it occurs in what will seem like another world. In this world, people must protect their dogs from being confiscated and even shot. They must sleep with their dogs tied to their legs at night. They face numerous risks and confront fears with only their animals as company. In this world, the roles animals play often differ from those they play in the lives of the domiciled. Therefore, the stories homeless people tell of those relationships—and of the selves embedded in those relationships—differ from those the literature already documents. These stories from the margins of society can provide a fuller, more critical insight into the lived experiences of homelessness, relationships with animals, and selfhood.

This combination of interests led me to draw on various literatures. The social scientific research on the narrative shaping of identity and the self has had an obvious influence on my thinking (e.g., Berger 2008; Berger and Quinney 2005; Bruner 1987, 1994; Goetting 1995; McAdams 1993, 2006a, 2006b; Rosenwald and Ochberg 1992).[1] Since approximately the 1980s, this growing body of work has examined narrative identity from various disciplinary perspectives.[2] The field has been so prolific that even a cursory review would fill an entire volume. Instead of attempting a summary, I will call attention to two key features of the research on narrative identity that figure heavily in this book, beginning with a definition. As Dan McAdams explains, "Narrative identity is the internalized and evolving story of the self that a person constructs to make sense and meaning out of his or her life. The story is a selective reconstruction of the autobiographical past and a narrative anticipation of the imagined future that serves to explain, for the self and others, how the person came to be and where his or her life may be going" (2011:99). As I have written elsewhere, the narrative concept of the self "is not so much a matter of people making up stories as it is of stories making up people" (Irvine 1999:2). Consistent with this understanding, I have made an effort to honor how the people I interviewed construct the stories they tell about themselves and their relationships with their animals. In other words, I let the tellers have their say. Because narrative research provides "a methodologically privileged location from which to comprehend human agency," it has the unique ability to capture subjective experience (Maynes, Pierce, and Laslett 2008:3). To tap into this advantage, a narrative researcher must allow tellers to tell authentic stories—those they hold as true—without insisting on verifiability. To give an example of what I mean, I present in Chapter 7 the story of a formerly homeless woman I call Donna who tells about how her deceased dog Athena sent her a new dog from the afterlife. For Donna, this explains why her new dog shares a similar disposition and many other characteristics with her deceased dog. It also explains why, according to Donna, the new dog has a mission: to keep her clean, sober, and alive. If you ask Donna how she quit a lifetime habit of using drugs, she will say, "Because of Athena." As Donna tells it, after Athena died, Athena sent the new dog to continue her work in Donna's life. I honored Donna's telling by listening to this story without saying, "Oh, come on now. You don't really believe that." I let Donna have her say, and I listened for how the story connects her to her dogs and to her past, present, and future. I kept Frank's words in mind: "The stories we tell ourselves about our lives are not necessarily those lives as they were lived, but these stories become our experience of those lives" (1995:22). For Donna, and others, I wanted to understand the dog's role in how the story became her experience.

I let the tellers have their say, but at the same time, as a sociologist, I also wanted to understand the influence of social structure, institutions, and culture on their narratives (Irvine 1999, 2000). People may engage in what McAdams (2011) calls "selective reconstruction," but they do not simply make up stories out of thin air. They anchor them in time and circumstance. As Mary Jo Maynes, Jennifer Pierce, and Barbara Laslett put it, "The stories that people tell about their lives are never simply individual, but are told in historically specific times and settings and draw on the rules and models in circulation that govern how story elements link together in narrative logics" (2008:3). In this light, I focused my analysis on realizing how stories reveal the social embeddedness of subjectivity. A story such as Donna's, for example, like most others in the book, could circulate only in a time and place that honors stories about closeness between humans and dogs. It could exist only when and where narrative models grant dogs supernatural powers, or at least do not rule them out. And, as I discuss at length later, Donna's story depends on the discourse of redemption, through which even a life that seems hopelessly out of control can change for the better.

In addition to the literature on narrative, I draw on the research on homelessness. I have sought guidance from the vast and interdisciplinary research on the subject, but have relied heavily on ethnographies of the lived experience of those on the streets. In particular, I have drawn inspiration from David Snow and Leon Anderson's *Down on Their Luck* (1993), which examines the strategies that street people use to survive materially and make sense of their situations psychologically; Jason Wasserman and Jeffrey Clair's *At Home on the Street* (2010), which investigates community among street people; and Teresa Gowan's *Hobos, Hustlers, and Backsliders* (2010), which focuses on the homeless subculture built around recycling.[3] My book shares with these titles an interest in the creation of meaning and self-worth among those on the margins. It differs from these other works in methodological approach. I did not eat at soup kitchens or sleep in shelters or encampments, as Snow, Anderson, Wasserman, and Clair did. Nor did I work alongside the homeless or become friends with anyone on the streets, as Gowan did. My contact with people on the streets took place through interviews and observation.

Within the literature on homelessness, in general, animals are mentioned only occasionally, in the context of pet ownership. An exception to this is Lars Eighner's autobiographical *Travels with Lizbeth* (1993), which details over two years of homelessness and hitchhiking with a dog. This richly chronicled book provides a vivid personal narrative, but Eighner did not intend it as a study of pet ownership among the homeless. Within the research literature on homelessness, animals have not yet entered the analysis. I can suggest two reasons for this. First, one could argue that pet owners constitute a small portion of a population that already has highly diverse needs. Although no precise figures on the number of homeless pet owners exist, the National Coalition for the Homeless estimates it at around 10 percent of the total homeless population. In some areas, social service providers put the figure closer to 24 percent. The estimates vary because pet owners constitute a hidden population among the homeless. Some pet owners remain secretive about their animals out of fear that the animals will be taken away from them. In addition, homeless pet owners do not appear on counts taken at shelters because most shelters do not allow pets. Even getting a meal at a soup kitchen requires having a dependable pet sitter, if only for a few minutes. As Eighner said of the predicament of pet ownership among the homeless, speaking about his own dog, "Lizbeth had her disadvantages. I could not go some places with her. Usually I had no safe place to leave her. Individuals and institutions who might have helped me alone could not consider the two of us" (1993:xiii). Viewing homeless pet owners in this way—as people whose needs go unaddressed—gives their numbers significance in a practical sense, if not a statistical one.

A second reason for the invisibility of animals in the research on homelessness has to do with the historical failure of the social sciences to recognize the importance of animals in human society. Scholars who study human-animal relationships find this puzzling because much of what constitutes "society" includes or depends on animals. For example, what we think of as a "household" includes more than just people. Over 70 percent of US households include dogs, cats, and birds, and nearly half consider these animals family members (AVMA 2007). The presence of animals also challenges our definition of "family," as more children grow up with pets than with siblings or fathers (Melson 2001). Animal products—including meat, eggs, and dairy products; leather, wool, and silk; and ingredients for cosmetics, toiletries, and medications—play important roles in our economy. We live surrounded by products that contain substances obtained from animals, such as drywall, linoleum, paint, and adhesive for wallpaper and carpet. Our language contains countless animal references, such as "pony tail," "lame duck," and "barking up the wrong tree" (see Bryant 1979; Smith-Harris 2004). Throughout history, animals have plowed our fields, served as transportation, and helped us wage war. They help people see and hear, alert them to impending seizures, and even detect undiagnosed cancer. Finally, animals figure heavily in many of our social problems, including hoarding and abuse (Arluke 2006), illegal activities such as dog fighting (Kalof and Taylor 2007), natural disasters (Irvine 2009), and debates over endangered species and conflicts between humans and wildlife (Herda-Rapp and Goedeke 2005).

Animals also provide companionship, which leads back to the issue of homelessness. Although animals are largely absent from the major works on the topic, there is a body of literature that examines pet ownership among this population. Scholars have explored various issues, but most have assessed the bond that homeless people have with their animals. Beginning with the first published study of homeless pet owners (Kidd and Kidd 1994), researchers have consistently found very high levels of attachment to pets among the homeless

(Baker 2001; Labreque and Walsh 2011; Rew 2000; Singer, Hart, and Zasloff 1995; Taylor, Williams, and Gray 2004). In the first study, Aline Kidd and Robert Kidd established "attachment" qualitatively, inferring it from phrases such as "best friend," "only thing I love," and "only thing that loves me." A majority of those interviewed identified their pets as "their only relationships with other living beings" (1994:720). Later, Randall Singer, Lynette Hart, and Lee Zasloff (1995) expanded on these efforts by administering the Lexington Attachment to Pets Scale, in addition to the use of qualitative assessments (see Johnson, Garrity, and Stallones 1992). This allowed them to compare measures of attachment found among the homeless with those in other populations. Homeless men and women had significantly higher attachment scores than did those in the standardization group (the domiciled), with homeless men scoring higher than women. A later study by Heidi Taylor, Pauline Williams, and David Gray (2004), using the Companion Animal Bonding Scale developed by Robert Poresky and colleagues (1987), also found significant differences in attachment scores when comparing the homeless with the domiciled.

Some research examines the benefits homeless people claim to receive from their companion animals. Lynn Rew (2000) focused on the emotional and health benefits that homeless youth attribute to their pets, including suicide prevention. The majority of the youth interviewed identified canine companionship as one of two main coping strategies for loneliness, along with the company of friends. Two studies found lower levels of criminal activity among homeless pet owners (Rew 2000; Taylor, Williams, and Gray 2004). Oswin Baker (2001) found a lower rate of drug use among dog-owning homeless people than among their non-owning counterparts, although Taylor, Williams, and Gray (2004) found no statistically significant differences.

Despite the common belief that animals are good for people, which I examine in Chapter 5, some research has found a downside to pet ownership among the homeless.[4] For example, Baker (2001) found that more homeless pet owners than non-owners admitted to having an alcohol problem. He also found that twice as many owners as non-owners suffered from mental health and social issues, such as anxiety, aggressive behavior, and isolation. Homeless pet owners also reported experiencing more loneliness and more frequent panic attacks than did their non-pet-owning counterparts. Taylor, Williams, and Gray (2004) found that fewer homeless dog owners than non-owners used medical care facilities. They also found lower health scores among the dog owners, indicating that the lower rates of use stemmed not from better health but from lack of access to facilities, most likely because of the dogs' presence.

Research has also examined the obstacles pets pose for homeless people seeking permanent housing. Baker (2001) found, as I did, that very few people had lost their housing because of pets. Once people become homeless, however, pets present a significant barrier to re-housing. Singer, Hart, and Zasloff (1995) found that although a majority of those they interviewed wanted to get off the streets, most had been refused housing because of their pets. Baker found similar results, with a majority having been denied accommodation in a wide range of housing options, including hostels, shelters, and private and public rentals. Singer, Hart, and Zasloff then considered whether pet ownership prolongs homelessness, but concluded that the emotional benefits outweigh the hardships. Along these lines, Jennifer Labreque and Christine Walsh (2011) found that a majority of the homeless women they interviewed in six Canadian cities had had to relinquish pets because of their circumstances. Some women found homes for the animals with friends or family, but many had surrendered them to animal shelters, even knowing that the animals would be euthanized. Labreque and Walsh write that "those who had given up pets in exchange for shelter spoke of the pain, trauma, and negative effects that relinquishing a pet had on themselves and their children" (2011:90). The authors emphasize the need to design homeless shelters to accommodate pets.

These studies of the homeless have included approximately equal numbers of men and women in their samples of pet owners. Using another approach, Courtney Cronley and colleagues (2009) analyzed data from 4,100 clients of a network of Tennessee agencies that provide services to the homeless. Between November 2004 and January 2007, the agencies' intake forms included a question about animal caretaking. This allowed Cronley and colleagues to assess the demographic differences between pet-owning and non-owning homeless clients. Their analysis revealed that 5.5 percent of the homeless population in the area was caring for animals. Euro-American, married women who were homeless for the first time were more likely than their male, non-Euro-American, unmarried counterparts to have pets. In addition, pet owners reported histories of domestic violence in

Photograph by Mark Rodgers, courtesy of San Francisco Community Clinic Consortium's VET SOS project.

No matter where this homeless San Franciscan goes,
her dogs go with her.

their prior living situations more often than non-owners did. The authors suggest that intake measures incorporating questions about animal caretaking can help providers meet the unique needs of these homeless clients.

In sum, the extant research literature on pet ownership among the homeless has documented that people claim to feel an intense bond with their animals, exceeding in measure the scores reported by the domiciled. The research has also acknowledged that people claim to benefit from relationships with animals. In addition, the research has noted the obstacles and restrictions faced by those who have pets while homeless and in their efforts to reenter housing. In this book, I will reintroduce some of these themes, building on them to provide deeper portrayals rather than reproducing established results. For example, although variations on the theme of attachment run through several chapters, I examine the concept through the roles homeless people assign to their animals, rather than through a numerical assessment. But I also introduce much that readers will find new and perhaps even surprising, learned through listening to voices that typically go unheard.

Organization of the Book

In Chapter 2, I discuss the methods I used in this study. In many ways, homelessness constitutes a subculture, a world to which most of us lack access. Pet owners make up a hidden population within that world. Although it sometimes seems that homeless people appear on every street corner, in terms of research one cannot access them through the means typically used to study homelessness. Through organizations that provide veterinary services to the pets of the homeless, such as Veterinary Street Outreach Services (VET SOS), in San Francisco, and the Mercer Clinic, in Sacramento, I gained access to far more homeless pet owners than I ever could have approached on my own. Also in Chapter 2, I outline the typology of homelessness that I use throughout the book and expand on my approach to the analysis of narrative. The term "narrative" has different meanings for scholars from different camps, and the methods they use to analyze narratives as sources of data vary as well. As Frank has written, "any book on narrative that seeks to deploy all the definitional distinctions that fill the literature on narrative will find itself unable to get out of the thicket in which it has embedded itself" (2010:17). In Chapter 2, I try to clarify my approach without falling into this trap.

In Chapter 3, I return to the issue raised in the stories that open this chapter—namely, what it means to take care of an animal and whether a homeless person can do so. I examine how homeless pet owners provide for their animals, as well as how they respond to criticism about not being able to do so.

Beginning with Chapter 4, I explore how the experience a person has with homelessness, among other factors, matters for the kinds of stories she or he tells. Each chapter focuses on a particular role narratively assigned to a companion animal and on the self that emerges from that story. This provides critical insight into the relationship between social structure and narrative. I analyze four aspects of this storytelling (see Frank 1995:76): plots or themes; the affinity that particular types of stories have for particular types of homelessness or other circumstance; how stories of relationships with animals also serves as self-stories; and the power and limitations, strengths and pitfalls, of each type of story.

In Chapter 8, I conclude by highlighting what the study of homeless people and their pets can tell us about social phenomena beyond the realm of pet ownership and homelessness, such as identity and stigma management. I suggest avenues for further investigation and discuss the implications my conclusions have for the literature and policy on homelessness.

On Writing About Animals

Stories about animals often face criticism based on what Marc Bekoff (2002) calls "the dreaded A-word": anthropomorphism. The term, which refers to attributing characteristics considered human to nonhuman animals (and inanimate objects), usually suggests sentimental and inaccurate projection. Critics often use the charge of anthropomorphism to dismiss claims about animals' capacities. But the charge has two related flaws. First, we do not anthropomorphize *only* when we talk about animals. We do it all the time. As Kenneth Shapiro points out, "all understanding is anthropomorphic (from *anthropo,* meaning 'man' and *morphe,* 'form' or 'shape') for it is partly shaped by the human investigator as subject. However, since this is a perspective or 'bias' inherent in all experience, it is not an occasional attributional error to which we are particularly prone when we cross species' lines" (1997:294). In short, we cannot escape our human perspective. By recognizing this, we can dodge the second flaw, which involves overcorrection by avoiding anthropomorphism altogether. Instead, we can take a middle ground between its "unconstrained use" and its "total elimination" (Bekoff 2002:49–50). Scholars have called this middle ground "critical" or "interpretive" anthropomorphism (Burghardt 1998; Fisher 1991; see also Mitchell, Thompson, and Miles 1997; Sanders 1999).[5] These types of anthropomorphism respect the "natural history, perceptual and learning capabilities, physiology, nervous system, and previous individual history" of animals (Burghardt 1998:72). For example, using critical or interpretive anthropomorphism, I have no qualms about describing a dog's alertness or a cat's interest, or attempts by either species to solicit attention. These fall within the range of canine and feline capacities, and using phrases such as "the cat wants attention" describes an action well. Attempting to avoid anthropomorphism altogether would require a tedious detailing of the movements of muscles in the face and ears, rather than simply explaining, "the cat wants attention." Throughout this book, when I have written phrases such as "Tommy's dog did a little dance," I do so because it conveys a sense of an action better than saying the dog "lifted his front paws alternately."

In some cases, language that appears anthropomorphic might involve a process known as "speaking for" animals, or giving voice to animals' thoughts or feelings (Arluke and Sanders 1996:51–61). In numerous instances throughout this book, I allow pet owners to "speak for" their animals. Doing so is a common aspect of pet ownership, often undertaken to promote an animal's best interests. "Speaking for" also helps establish the identity of the animal, without which there can be little interaction, much less a relationship. In "speaking for" a dog or a cat, the guardian "gives voice to what he or she understands to be the [animal's] thoughts or perspective" (Arluke and Sanders 1996:67). The guardian thus actively constructs the animal's identity. This phenomenon of "interlocution" also appears in interactions between caregivers and Alzheimer's patients (Gubrium 1986), people with cognitive disabilities (Bogdan and Taylor 1989; Goode 1984; Pollner and McDonald-Wikler 1985), and babies (Brazelton 1984). These studies reveal how caregivers give voice to the subjective experience of the other and thereby construct him or her as having preferences and a self-conscious sense of intention, and thus construct them as persons.[6] Characterizing the accomplishment of personhood in this way allows for the admission of companion animals into its ranks, if in a virtual sense. Rather than dismissing interactions with animals as "just" anthropomorphism, the act of "speaking for" animals represents a way of making them minded coactors in social situations (Irvine 2004a, 2004b; Sanders 1993).

Finally, I use the terms "pet" and "owner" interchangeably with "companion animal" and "guardian" or "caretaker." I use the former set of terms despite their subtext of human power over animals—and despite having taken a stance against their use in previous work (Irvine

2004a). I use all four terms for either convenience or consistency with their use in interviews. I found that, even in Boulder and San Francisco, where legislatures adopted "companion animal" and "guardian" in official city language, "pet" and "owner" remain in wide use. In addition, I sometimes found it cumbersome to write "the companion animal of a homeless person" when just "pet" would suffice.

Notes

1. Additional works that have influenced my approach include Josselson 1996; Josselson and Lieblich 1993, 1995; Neisser and Fivush 1994; Polkinghorne 1988, 1991; and Plummer 1983, 1995.

2. See Maines 1993 and Maynes, Pierce, and Laslett 2008 for discussions of the factors that influenced both the interest in narrative analysis and some of the directions narrative research has taken.

3. Other works I have found influential include Dordick 1997; Liebow 1993; Pippert 2007; Wagner 1993; and Wright 1997.

4. See Harold Herzog's (2011) research on the hypothesis that pets are good for people.

5. I have used the term "sentimental" anthropomorphism to indicate a type that verges on silliness and insults animals' dignity (Irvine 2004a:68–76).

6. This contrasts with the dehumanizing treatment the disabled often receive in other circumstances (Bogdan et al. 1974; Taylor 1987).

2 Accessing Homeless Pet Owners

Late on a Friday afternoon, Maya, the VET SOS project assistant, drove the blue van through a labyrinthine neighborhood of warehouses, auto repair shops, and storage units on the eastern edge of San Francisco. I rode shotgun. Dr. Strubel, a veterinarian, and her volunteer technician sat in the back of the van, propping up stacks of supplies, as Maya turned left, right, left again. We encountered little traffic on the streets. The daytime activity had begun winding down for the weekend and soon the area would seem abandoned. We eventually pulled in to a dead-end at the base of a scrubby hill that supported the entrance ramp to an elevated freeway. The Bay created a cove in this part of the city, and in the afternoon light the water provided a serene, shimmering contrast to the asphalt, concrete, and metal all around. Several large concrete piers jutted into the water. Plastic bags, bottles, scraps of wood, and other accumulated junk clotted the shore. Multicolored layers of graffiti decorated the freeway supports. An eight-foot-high chain-link fence surrounded the area, and scrubby vegetation grew up around the fence. We walked through a lopsided opening in the chain link and continued along the length of the freeway. The commuter rail passed close by, deafening us as it ran its route. When it had roared on, the noise from the traffic on the overpass seemed a relief by contrast.

The sloping ground we walked on consisted of fine, black dirt, almost powdery in texture. Every kind of trash imaginable created a postapocalyptic chaos. Cans and bottles mixed with broken furniture, mangled electronics, milk crates, single shoes, and torn clothing of all kinds. VHS tape pulled from a cassette strangled a one-armed doll. Several old campfires marked the sites of nighttime revelry. The

17

pungent odor of urine mixed with that of exhaust fumes from the cars above us. On our right a large pipeline, about five feet in diameter, ran the length of the freeway and disappeared into the ground somewhere near where we had entered. Years of accumulated litter formed a slope against the pipe. We walked along, taking care to avoid broken glass and dog feces. After a short distance, when the ground leveled off, we passed another set of freeway supports. As with the others, graffiti covered every reachable inch. Just then, a large, black pit bull came charging along the top of the pipe, obviously accustomed to running on this balance beam. As he barked at us, the hackles rose on his back. Almost immediately, two other pit bulls on the ground also ran toward us.

We had come to check on these dogs, along with a fourth one absent from this opening charge, and to see what their owners needed in caring for them. Maya and Dr. Strubel began calling the dogs by name in friendly, high-pitched voices. Within seconds, the dogs had visibly relaxed their bodies. As they settled and began greeting us, their entire hindquarters wagged along with their tails in that "wiggle butt" way that pit bulls have. The technician and I hung back to give the unfamiliar dogs some space, but within seconds they had detected the treats I carried in my pocket. Fortunately, I had enough for all three dogs, and, friendships thus cemented, all seven of us walked along. The amount of trash increased the farther we went, until the ground consisted entirely of broken televisions and radios, discarded batteries, whiskey bottles, beer cans, frayed rope, old chairs, rags, and twisted pieces of metal. I found it impossible not to step on something no matter where I placed my feet.

Soon, a thin, middle-aged, white man came out from behind a freeway stanchion, drawn by the racket from the dogs. He scrambled along the mountain of trash and greeted Dr. Strubel, who introduced Maya, the technician, and me. The man smiled warmly, revealing several missing teeth, and shook hands all around. His hands were thickly callused and dirty. While he talked with Dr. Strubel, a woman wearing a headlamp peeked out of a vent panel above us, on the underside of the freeway. The scene reminded me of *Pee-wee's Playhouse,* where characters would pop down from the ceiling. She peered at us for a few seconds and then lowered herself onto a teetering stack of old furniture that served as a ladder. She quickly made her way to the ground. She had been getting dressed, and she worked a belt through the loops in her jeans before walking over to meet us.

She wore black, and by this time my clothes were so dirty that I wished I had done so, too. She removed her headlamp as she approached. She had a broad smile and bleached blond hair. Her weather-beaten skin pulled over angular features, and when she introduced herself, her voice revealed years of smoking. She joined the conversation about the dogs.

As Dr. Strubel talked with the woman and the man, the fourth dog appeared, limping. Dr. Strubel asked what had happened. Some steel cable had apparently fallen on the dog's paw, and Dr. Strubel suspected a fracture in addition to a visible cut. She worried about him recuperating in that environment, with the dirt and the obstacles. The dog belonged to a man named Don, who was out working at the

Photograph by Mark Rodgers, courtesy of San Francisco Community Clinic Consortium's VET SOS project.

The Veterinary Street Outreach Services (VET SOS) van.

time. Dr. Strubel left word for Don to call her to arrange for treatment, free of charge. Meanwhile, Maya would return later with medication for pain and inflammation, also free.

When Dr. Strubel had invited me to tag along on a house call to "the people who live under the freeway," I imagined an outdoor encampment. I had never thought enough about road construction to know that freeways even had vents, which I later learned the residents call "boxes," much less to consider that people would live in them. On another visit, I interviewed Don, who owned not only the injured dog, but one of the others, too. He had lived under the freeway for fifteen years. I asked him to describe a "box."

"It's only about maybe four and a half feet high," he said, "and you can't stand up in there, but it's eight or nine feet wide, and it's about sixty feet long. All those hatches that people go up into, they're all individual boxes. They're not interconnected in any way. Once you go up inside you can't go from one box to another box. Once you're inside, you're in your own room."

"And your dogs, do they sleep up there with you?" I asked.

"Oh, yeah. I lift them up," he said, reaching down to demonstrate. "They jump up on the tubing [the pipe] and I lift them up."

I imagined having to haul my dogs through a hatch into a box in the ceiling each night. "I saw one woman wearing a headlamp," I said. "Is that how you have light in your space?"

"Yeah. We have two or three generators over there, so we have electricity. About the only thing we're missing is running water."

"So what do you do about that?"

"We just get five-gallon bottles . . . and we go down and fill 'em up at the tap." He pointed over toward one of the businesses.

"What's it like living here?" I asked.

"Depressing," he said, without any hesitation. "Like being stuck in the mud. But we make do. We do the best we can. Everybody that lives down here, we're just basically trying to stay out of the way. I've been to prison and I didn't enjoy that, and I enjoy my freedom a lot more."

As we continued to talk, I learned that ten people and four dogs lived in that particular area at the time. "Do you see yourselves as a group or a family or what?" I asked.

"We interact," he said, smiling. "There are times when people don't see eye-to-eye and things get a little heated but we all kind of take care of each other. And we look out for each other and, yeah, we kind of act like a family, like a normal family would, you know, we have mom, dad, we have the mayor, and the postmaster, whatever."

"So what's your role?"

"I'm the CEO," he said, with a grin and a twinkle in his eye. "I've been down here the longest out of anybody and people know I'm here, and if they come to interact, they usually get ahold of me. But we just all try, when we can, to put in for the good of everybody. Like with food. The food, it's all general. We don't take food and put it out and keep it from the other people. We put it out so that if they're hungry, they can eat, you know, and it's not like we tell people, 'You can't be here,' you know, 'cause we don't want anybody telling us we can't be here. And people will drift through and whatnot, and they're welcome. It's not like we're trying to keep people out. There's people sometimes that get thrown out of their place or they're arguing with whoever they're living with, and they don't have anywhere to go, and we go out of our way to put 'em up if that's what they want to do. It's like a family."

We went on to talk about the dogs, and my head spun as I tried to keep track of all I had just learned. People were living in crawl spaces under the freeway. Some had lived there for over a decade. They worked, and they had phones. And they had dogs.

* * *

Don's story continues later, and he reappears throughout the book. But I begin this discussion of methods with this "house call" story for three reasons. First, it highlights the importance of "gatekeepers" in gaining access to homeless people. Second, it points out the variety of living situations that can characterize homeless people's experiences and the subsequent challenges of defining what it means to be homeless. Third, as part of my commitment to "letting stories breathe," I let the story do the work of *showing,* rather than having me *tell.*

Accessing a Hidden Population

The bulk of the data I draw on comes from interviews with seventy-five homeless pet owners in Boulder, Colorado; Berkeley, Sacramento, and San Francisco, California; and Miami, Florida.[1] In Berkeley, Sacramento, and San Francisco, I conducted the interviews at street clinics for pets of the homeless, with the help of veterinarians and veterinary students.[2] I cannot overstate their role in helping me gain access to a sample of homeless pet owners. Research on the homeless, including attempts to estimate their numbers, often takes a point-in-time approach, counting or surveying people in shelters or on the streets on a single night.[3] Ethnographers can often meet and talk with homeless people by hanging out in shelters. However, most homeless shelters do not accommodate animals because of safety and health concerns. Some, such as the one in Boulder, provide outdoor kennels for dogs, but a woman in Boulder voiced a view I heard from others when she said, "I won't stay there, would never stay there, because I'm like, 'Well, [my dog] is my best friend, and if he's got to stay outside, I'm going to stay outside.'" A man in Boulder agreed. When I asked if he ever stayed at the homeless shelter, he said, "No, because they want to put people's animals in the kennels outside. I can't deal with that. I can't sleep. I

Dogs are not the only pets of the homeless.

Photograph by Mark Rodgers, courtesy of San Francisco Community Clinic Consortium's VET SOS project.

don't sleep well without my dogs. They're my family, and they help me sleep at night, to even get the hours of sleep that I get." Thus, the absence of homeless pet owners from the shelters ruled out one of the usual methods for recruiting a critical mass of interviewees for this research.

When I began this research, I approached homeless people I saw on the street with their pets. Whenever I set out to look for pet owners, with voice recorder and notebook at hand, I found no one. But when I was on my way to some destination, with no time to spare, homeless people appeared on every corner with their pets. When the timing was right and I approached a homeless man or woman who had a pet, I found it hard to assuage their suspicion of me. Accustomed to criticism, they were quick to assure me of the health and safety of their animals. They showed me bags of food and jugs of water. In addition, I often encountered them as they panhandled, and I was a distraction from their work. Moreover, as the vignette that opens this chapter shows, not all homeless pet owners live on the streets.

Through online research, I learned that San Francisco and Sacramento have well-established veterinary clinics for the pets of the homeless. VET SOS operates as a component of the San Francisco Community Clinic Consortium. Veterinarian Ilana Strubel started it in 2001, with encouragement from Pali Boucher, a formerly homeless pet owner. The pair met when Pali brought her dogs to the veterinary clinic at the San Francisco Society for the Prevention of Cruelty to Animals (SPCA), where Dr. Strubel worked. Pali had grown up on the streets in San Francisco, with a drug-addicted, mentally ill mother.[4] Her mother died when she was ten, and she lived first with her father, and then in foster care, but soon ended up back on the streets. She evaded Child Protective Services to stay out of the foster care system. She was homeless for twenty years, and along the way became addicted to drugs and alcohol. Pali credits a dog named Leadbelly, along with a drug program, with saving her life, a theme I explore in Chapter 7. Now in her forties, clean and sober, and living with HIV, she runs the nonprofit Rocket Dog Rescue, which saves homeless and abandoned dogs from euthanasia in overcrowded shelters.

Pali had known about the medical services provided by the Consortium's Street Outreach Services, which provides healthcare for the homeless. She had also seen homeless people try to treat their pets' injuries and illnesses themselves out of fear that a visit to a veterinarian might mean having their animals confiscated. While a client of Dr. Strubel's, Pali asked her if she would consider creating a version of SOS for the pets of the homeless. Dr. Strubel had noticed that veterinary emergencies made up the majority of cases involving the pets of the homeless, and she knew that providing preventive services could reduce those numbers. After two decades on the streets, Pali knew where all the homeless people lived and hung out. The two made a perfect team. The San Francisco Veterinary Medical Association provided volunteers and supplies, and the Consortium's nonprofit Street Outreach Services provided use of a van. On the first day out, Dr. Strubel and VET SOS treated fourteen animals. "It was humbling," she said, "seeing a homeless vehicle encampment and realizing that even getting water for their pets is a challenge."[5]

Dr. Strubel gradually realized that holding clinics at set locations would allow her to see more animals. So on the second Friday of each month, VET SOS takes a van filled with medications, vaccinations, leashes, charts, and pet food and supplies to scheduled locations for "clinics without walls." I interviewed clients at three of these clinics. Veterinary technicians and volunteers told clients about my research as they conducted intake discussions. They made a list of the names of those interested, and I worked my way down the list, interviewing clients as they waited for the veterinarians to see their animals. The clinics took place in different parts of the city, and they included one at the Homeless Youth Alliance on Haight Street, which gave me unique access to this especially wary population. And, as the opening vignette shows, Dr. Strubel still conducts "house calls" too, visiting areas where homeless people with pets live, as she did in the early days of VET SOS. By bringing me along on some of these visits, I could observe a realm that I would not have otherwise known about, much less ventured into alone.

In Berkeley, Maya DeNola founded People and Animals Living Safely (PALS) to reach homeless pet owners in the East Bay area. Berkeley Animal Care Services and the East Bay Humane Society provide vaccinations and other supplies. Maya made it possible for me to interview clients at a PALS veterinary clinic held at Youth Engagement, Advocacy, and Housing (YEAH), Berkeley's seasonal shelter for homeless youth. As at the VET SOS clinics, Maya and other PALS volunteers told clients about my research during intake and created a list of those interested. In Sacramento, veterinary students and faculty have held the monthly Mercer Clinic for the Pets of the Homeless since 1993. I visited one of these clinics, where a veterinary student introduced me to clients as they waited for their animals to be examined. Clients soon began creating their own snowball sample, introducing me to friends who also waited with their animals.

As I continued searching online for services to homeless pet owners, I learned that Camillus House in downtown Miami had begun construction on a three-acre campus that would include kennels for pets in its array of services for the homeless. I arranged to visit. The staff understood the importance of animals in the lives of their clients, and they helped me gather data in two ways. One staff member who had done street outreach for many years drove me to places where homeless people tend to camp and congregate. People on the street knew and appreciated him, so they willingly talked with me after he provided an introduction. Another staff member arranged for me to interview residents of Better Way of Miami, a program that provides housing and supportive services for homeless people with histories of severe substance abuse who might also be HIV-positive or suffer from chronic mental illness. Many of the residents have pets, and I spent an afternoon in the portable building that serves as Better Way's community center talking with some of them about their relationships with their animals.

In sum, when I made connections with organizations that provide services to homeless pet owners, the door opened to a sizable number of people. The gatekeepers also vouched for my research, which helped to minimize suspicion on the part of the homeless. The one exception to this strategy was in Boulder, where I interviewed several street people, and some in a downtown area that attracts large numbers of homeless people passing through with their dogs, especially during the summer. A shady area of a park along the Boulder Creek serves as a gathering place for these nomads, and some of them agreed to talk with me as they passed the time of day. The interviews I conducted in Boulder took advantage of this convenience sample and provided a rough comparison with those interviewed at veterinary clinics.

Sources of Data

The interviews that constitute the majority of the data I draw on in this book ranged in length from twenty minutes to over an hour. The animals made perfect icebreakers. After introducing myself, I began most interviews by asking the people if I could pet their dog or see their cat. I then asked about the animal's history, starting with how the pet had come into the person's life. As Clinton Sanders has pointed out, "acquisition stories" come easily to caretakers (2003:417). Most, including homeless people, eagerly talk about how they found, adopted, or purchased their animal companions. I gradually segued to other questions. Everyone who completed an interview received a gift card redeemable for five dollars at local pet food and supply stores. To avoid incentivizing participation, people did not learn about the gift card until after the interview. Word about the gift cards could have spread, but I did not notice a coincidental surge in participation at any sites after giving the first few interviewees their cards.

I found the homeless pet owners more than willing to talk. Many of them made statements along the lines of "no one's ever asked me that before" or "I don't get to talk about this very much." Scholars who conduct interview-based research often find that people like talking about their lives and they open up quite readily, but three factors made this especially so in this research. First, most of the people I interviewed had little else to do while they waited for the veterinarians to see their animals. Some chatted with friends, but most sat alone with their animals and consequently welcomed the opportunity to pass the time. Second, the technicians and clinic volunteers had "preselected" interviewees during intake for their appointments, when they told the clients about my research and invited them to participate. In other words, I interviewed only those who were already inclined to talk. Third, and perhaps most important, receiving attention provided a welcome change for many of the people in this study. Homeless people are "routinely ignored or avoided by the domiciled" (Snow and Anderson 1993:199). They suffer from what Charles Derber called "attention deprivation" by virtue of being "regarded as less worthy of attention in relationships with members of dominant classes" (1979:42). Thus, the interviews provided at least a brief opportunity for them to feel they had something of value to say.

In addition to the interviews, three other sources of data inform my arguments. A survey of 147 domiciled citizens on their attitudes toward homeless people who have pets factors into the discussion in Chapter 3. In addition, I draw on field conversations I had with a range of people who provide services to homeless people and their pets, including veterinarians, animal control officers, and homeless-shelter staff members. Finally, I also rely on field notes I took after the interviews, during clinics, and following "house calls." I transcribed all interviews and notes, then coded and analyzed the data using NVivo software (QSR International, Doncaster, Victoria, Australia) and the inductive practices well acknowledged in qualitative sociological research, particularly that informed by the grounded theory tradition (Charmaz 1983, 2000; Glaser and Strauss 1967).

Analytic Perspective

As mentioned in Chapter 1, stories constitute the key to this research. The approach I take has been characterized as "personal narrative analysis" (Maynes, Pierce, and Laslett 2008) and "socio-narratology" (Frank 2010). I do not claim to have captured histories of entire lives. What I sought in the interviews was both more focused than and not as comprehensive as a full life story. I wanted to learn how homeless people narrated the slices of their lives that involved a relationship with an animal. The relationship constituted an aspect of each person's overall, emergent, evolving life story. Indeed, for many homeless people I interviewed, their attachment to their animals and the constant companionship they shared made the relationship the primary theme in their lives. Much as another kind of interview might elicit high and low points in life, turning points, earliest memories, and so on, these interviews posed the animal as the medium for the construction of the story. In this way, the interviews constituted what Robert Zussman (1996, 2000) has called "autobiographical occasions," or instances that require people to give accounts of themselves. Zussman's examples include résumés, photo albums, medical histories, confessions of various sorts, and divorce hearings—all of which highlight the extent to which stories are embedded in and shaped by social structure. In this case, my research interests prompted the stories, and rather than telling stories of entire lives, the narrators told stories with animals in the cast, often as main characters.

By situating my work within the analysis of narratives, I must point out that I have less interest in narrative as a *mode* of analysis than as the *object* of analysis (see Zussman 2000:6). This preference builds on a long-standing fascination with how people create meaning, especially the meaning of selfhood (e.g., Irvine 1999, 2000, 2004a, 2004b). As mentioned in Chapter 1, I draw on the body of literature that examines narratives as the primary way we know about our world, including our sense of who we believe ourselves to be. As Arthur Frank writes, stories are "the self's medium of being" (1995:53). We shape our memories, hopes, and experiences into compelling tales and thus make and remake our selves by telling stories. The outcome of this—the narratives themselves—can be studied in many ways. Some scholars engage in formal analysis, showing how the semantic components of narratives work together to accomplish meaning (see Barthes and Duisit 1975). To the extent that I engaged in formal analysis, I strove to locate the general narrative themes or archetypes through which homeless people talk about their relationships with animals. These provide evidence of the person's experience of that relationship and, simultaneously, evidence of how society "speaks itself" through people's lives (Rosenwald and Ochberg 1992:7; see also Berger 2008; Frank 1995; Goetting 1995). By this, I refer to the vocabularies or discourses available and acceptable for talking about relationships with animals. In any narrative, the discourse used demonstrates a historically specific context (see Maynes, Pierce, and Laslett 2008:45–51). In the narratives recounted in this book, the portrayals of animals would have been unlikely in another time or place. Human-animal relationships have a history, and only relatively recently have we humans elevated animals to the status of friend or family member, for example. In some cultures, it would be unthinkable to speak of a dog in these terms. Thus, the narratives recounted here describe individual relationships as people tell about them *and* reveal aspects of the overall state of human-animal relationships in the twenty-first century.

Because much of my interest lies beyond the formal aspects of narrative genre, my analysis concentrated on a somewhat functional dimension of narrative. I aim primarily to understand how narratives produce selves. Consequently, I searched the transcripts to discover how a certain narrative of relationship with an animal existed alongside certain life circumstances and produced certain stories of selves. As Frank writes, "People's access to narrative resources depends on their social location: what stories are told where they live and work, which stories do they take seriously or not, and especially what stories they exchange as tokens of membership" (2010:13). Put differently, I wanted to understand how social structure shapes and requires particular kinds of stories. Finally, I let homeless people "have their say," but in the analysis I remained mindful of my "authorial" obligation to make sociologically informed sense of their stories (Berger and Quinney 2005; Gubrium and Holstein 1999; Holstein and Gubrium 2000). In processing the raw material of people's narratives, their factual accuracy yielded to the meanings embedded in the accounts. Thus, in making sociological sense of personal narratives, I transformed what people said into concepts and insights they would scarcely recognize. This transformation points out the extent to which the construction of meaning represents a collaborative act. In telling personal narratives, tellers created meanings that held significance for them in the context of the interview. In analyzing those narratives, my task involved appreciating their storied quality while examining them from angles that would reveal other possible meanings and significance. The analysis thus did not capture the one "true" version of the stories, but instead tapped into how the stories worked for their tellers through their symbolic and emotional power.

The Sample

My sample of seventy-five homeless pet owners comprises forty-three people from San Francisco and Berkeley, eighteen from Sacramento, nine from Miami, and five from Boulder. Coincidentally, California and Florida, along with New York, have the highest rates of homelessness in the country (Department of Housing and Urban Development 2010). Both states have high rates of unemployment and foreclosure and high housing costs combined with shortages of affordable housing (Sermons and Witte 2011). Indeed, the people I interviewed gave these as main reasons for their homelessness. Thirty-three had lost housing because of foreclosure or eviction, usually because a landlord had defaulted on the mortgage on a rental property. Another eleven had lost their jobs and could no longer afford housing. Only two people said they had lost housing because of their animals. In each interview, we discussed what would need to change for the interviewee to live in a physical home again. Each person said that he or she would accept housing only if it accommodated pets. A few people had already turned down housing opportunities because their animals would not be allowed.

In terms of gender, the sample comprises forty women, thirty-four men, and one transgendered person (male to female). This differs from the homeless population overall, where single males constitute the majority. I attribute the slight predominance of women in my sample to their willingness to engage in interviews when invited to do so by a veterinary technician during the animal-intake process. As for race, the majority of people in the sample are white (fifty-four), ten are African American, and five are Hispanic or Latino/Latina; the race of the remaining six is undetermined (these people did not discuss or identify their race).[6] By comparison, a 2009 point-in-time count of the sheltered and unsheltered homeless conducted by the Department of Housing and Urban Development (2010) found that minorities comprised 62 percent of the homeless population nationally. I attribute the racial composition of my sample to a combination of the regional dynamics in which I did the research and the relatively low rates of pet ownership among minorities. According to research conducted for the pet food industry, "minority groups remain sorely underrepresented as pet owners. As of fall 2010, the household dog/cat ownership rates were at 40% for Hispanics, 20% for Blacks and 23% for Asians, compared with 58% for White Non-Hispanic households" ("Market Report" 2011). A study by Courtney Cronley and colleagues (2009), mentioned in Chapter 1, found that race/ethnicity predicted pet ownership, with those who identified as "Euro-American" more likely to own pets than their "non-Euro-American" counterparts. Finally, for my Boulder survey of domiciled citizens, the majority of people in the sample (81 out of 147) are female and white.

Most of the homeless pet owners I interviewed had a single pet, and dogs outnumbered cats. Thirteen people had cats only, and four had both cats and dogs. Eleven had two or three animals, and six people had more than three. Those in the latter category, and those with cats, stayed in places not intended for housing, such as an abandoned building, a storage shed, and a school bus, rather than on the street. Most people said they had always liked animals, and only four had not had pets prior to acquiring their current animal. The animals I observed were in reasonably good health, although a few had serious issues such as cancer that were most likely unrelated to their living situation. I noted a few cases of ear mites and upper respiratory infections. Most of these homeless pet owners had brought their animals to the veterinary clinics for routine examinations and the vaccinations that would allow them to obtain or renew pet ownership licenses. With one exception of a house call, the cats were all in carriers and their demeanor varied according to how well adapted they were to such confinement. Most of the dogs, due to the around-the-clock company of their guardians, were relaxed and attentive; most had received some training and knew at least the basic commands, such as "sit."

All of the clinics where I conducted the interviews have spay and neuter requirements, meaning that owners must have their animals fixed to obtain services and food a second time. Both clinics provide free spay and neuter surgery. VET SOS transports animals to the San Francisco SPCA, which provides free surgery for animals that are less than six years of age. The Mercer Clinic has a mobile spay/neuter hospital. Consequently, I encountered mostly spayed or neutered animals, and a few were scheduled to have the surgery immediately following the clinics I attended. Most of the homeless pet owners agreed with the policy and appreciated the access to free surgery. The exception to this was among the homeless youth, a phenomenon I discuss in Chapter 6.

About half of the dog guardians had obtained "service tags" for their pets, and many who had not said they intended to do so. The majority of guardians in San Francisco had such tags for their dogs, and one had them for her cat.[7] The tags designate animals as "companions," legally able to accompany their owners into public buildings and on mass transit. And should the owner of a registered companion animal find housing in a building with a "no pets" policy, the tags entail a waiver of that policy under the Fair Housing Amendments Act of 1988. The issue of extending the status once reserved for service animals to companion animals has aroused significant controversy. The Americans with Disabilities Act (ADA) defines a "service animal" only as one specially trained to perform a task that the guardian cannot do for him- or herself. Seeing-eye dogs constitute a familiar example. As of 2011, the ADA designation includes only dogs, with a special provision for trained miniature horses.[8] None of the homeless pet owners I encountered had service dogs in the strict sense of the definition. Rather, they had "companion animals," "emotional support animals," or "assistance animals." These animals have no special training. In this respect, they can be just like any other pet. They provide companionship and comfort. Yet some state and local laws give such companion animals the same rights as those accorded to highly trained service animals. A physician provides documentation that a patient needs the companionship of his or her animal, essentially "prescribing" the emotional support the animal provides. In San Francisco, a guardian takes the doctor's letter to the SPCA to obtain the aforementioned tag, which identifies the animal publicly (although the ADA does not require these tags) and grants the animal access to places it would otherwise be prohibited from entering. Controversy has arisen because of the proliferation of animals, both domestic and exotic, that people use as companion or assistance animals. Some users of specially trained dogs claim that this has produced confusion about what true "service animals" actually do and what constitutes a reasonable accommodation to a legitimate disability.[9] Changes in the ADA intended to provide clarity on this issue took effect in March 2011, and only time will tell whether they will have an impact on homeless pet owners.

Defining Homelessness

Other scholars have pointed out the problems posed for research by the task of defining homelessness and distinguishing among types of homeless people and their circumstances (see, e.g., Barak 1991; Blau 1992; Kusmer 2002; Shlay and Rossi 1992; Lee, Tyler, and Wright 2010; Snow and Anderson 1993; Wasserman and Clair 2010). As well-known scholar and homeless advocate Kim Hopper put it, "Definitional quandaries have long plagued discussions of American homelessness" (2003:15). Indeed, these quandaries have existed at least since sociologist Nels Anderson conducted the first census of the homeless in 1923. Researchers now distinguish between "old homelessness," the skid row era from the 1940s to the 1970s, and the "new homelessness" that emerged in the 1980s (see Bogard 2001, 2003; Hopper 1991; Rossi 1989, 1990). The "old homeless" were primarily single men, past middle age, who drank heavily and stayed in the many inexpensive, single room occupancy hotels and "flophouses" that were once plentiful in urban neighborhoods such as Manhattan's Bowery (see Bahr 1973; Bahr and Caplow 1974).[10] The men of skid row "were technically not without housing; they had addresses and places in which to sleep. . . . [S]ocial researchers called them homeless because they were adult males who lived outside normal family life" (Shlay and Rossi 1992:131; see also Rossi 1990). Nor were they destitute. As Hopper wrote, "though poor, such men were not penniless. A good number of skid row men (between a third and a half, depending on the local labor market) worked, typically at menial jobs" (1991:765; see also Bogue 1963). To the extent that skid row was an issue—its separation from "better" areas of the cities made it invisible to many non–skid row residents, and thus its presence brought no public outcry—it was not so much a social problem as an individual one: the men of skid row were considered responsible for their plight. Purportedly, those on the streets did not end up there because of a shortage of low-cost housing, or even necessarily because of poverty. Rather, they landed on the streets because of problems labeled "disaffiliation" (Bahr 1970, 1973) and "social maladjustment" (Bogue 1963).[11]

Then, during the Reagan era, homelessness increased dramatically in the United States.[12] Cuts to social services, intended to reduce the size of government, eliminated many programs for the poor. Urban renewal did away with much affordable housing. Gentrification largely put skid rows out of existence. The resulting "new homeless" differed from the men of skid row. The new population included families, women, children, and minorities. They slept in doorways, on sidewalk grates, on park benches, and in bus stations, and they moved about openly in public spaces. The debate about the role of individual character persisted, although with fewer adherents than it had had in the skid row era.

Most often, scholars and policymakers conceptualize "new homelessness" as a social problem associated with poverty and a lack of affordable housing.[13] But this has not made matters of definition easier. For example, in a widely cited study, Peter Rossi defined homelessness as "not having customary and regular access to a conventional dwelling," but he went on to question what "customary and regular access" and "conventional dwelling" meant (1989:10–11). The McKinney-Vento Homeless Assistance Act, the federal law that provides funding for a wide range of programs, defines the homeless as those who "lack a fixed, regular, and adequate nighttime residence" and extends this to include emergency shelters and places "not meant for human habitation." The definition also includes those who will lose their housing within a week, unaccompanied youth, families with children, and those escaping domestic violence.

As Rossi noted, "the line between homelessness and having a home is fuzzy" (1989:10). This became clear to me as I met people who slept on the streets, in their vehicles, in shelters, on friends' couches, and even in crawl spaces under freeways. According to research in 2008–2009 by the National Alliance to End Homelessness, nearly four in ten of the homeless did not stay in shelters but in places "not intended for human habitation" (Sermons and Witte 2011:1). This seems clear enough, but during my research I encountered people who called such places "home." I also encountered people who said, "Home is wherever I lay my head," and defined themselves as "houseless, not homeless."[14] Fortunately, for my purposes, the veterinary clinics made the decision for me, by screening clients and verifying their status as homeless using established procedures.[15] In Miami and Boulder, I asked people where they slept. Table 2.1 lists the range of places and Table 2.2 lists the length of time homeless.

Because I wanted to understand how circumstances shaped homeless people's relationships with their animals, I found that I needed a way to describe and compare the various experiences of homelessness, despite the difficulties posed by trying to do so. Within the research literature, scholars have developed typologies that characterize homeless subgroups in various ways. For example, using measures of time homeless, size of social network, and level of functioning, Charles Grigsby and colleagues (1990) arrived at the "recently dislo-

Table 2.1 Where Homeless People Were Sleeping

	Number of Interviewees
In a shelter	4
On the street/outdoors	28
With friends	9
In a vehicle	11
In temporary housing (single room occupancy)	4
In transitional housing/treatment program	8
In a vacant building	4
In a subleased room or apartment	3
In a junkyard	3
Other	1

Table 2.2 Length of Time Homeless

	Number of Interviewees
Less than 6 months	11
6–12 months	12
1–2 years	7
2–4 years	16
More than 4 years	13
Not currently homeless (stably living)	16

cated," the "vulnerable," "outsiders," and the "prolonged." Using measures of community living, depression, aggression, psychoticism, and substance abuse, Carol Mowbray, Deborah Bybee, and Evan Cohen (1993) identified the "hostile/psychotic," the "depressed," the "best functioning," and the "substance abusing." Dennis Culhane and Randall Kuhn (1998) referred to the "chronically," "episodically," and "transitionally" homeless. Most typologies either rely on quantified measures (e.g., Grigsby et al., Mowbray et al.), aim at targets outside the scope of my study (e.g., Mowbray et al.), or draw on data from shelters (e.g., Culhane and Kuhn), which, as mentioned, prohibit pet owners. In addition, none of these categories captured the range of homelessness I encountered. Consequently, I used a typology loosely based on the one used by David Snow and Leon Anderson (1993). I identified four discrete types of homeless people and two subtypes based on a combination of factors, including length of time on the street, lifestyle dimensions such as sleeping arrangements and daily routines, and orientation toward getting off the street.

The Recently Dislocated

This category comprised seventeen people. As the name indicates, these people were experiencing homelessness for the first time and for a short while. Most (ten) had been homeless for less than six months. Some were "couch surfing," or doubling up with family or friends, while others slept on sidewalks, camped in more private settings, or lived in their vehicles. The Recently Dislocated were still finding their way through the vast network of agencies and social services that Teresa Gowan (2010) aptly refers to as the "homeless archipelago," which can open the door to General Assistance (the welfare programs for adults without dependents), Supplemental Security Income (SSI, the federal income supplement program for the disabled), Section 8 housing (the federal rental assistance program), or other benefits. In addition, those on the streets for the first time must learn where and when to find food, safe places to sleep, or parking. Many had recently become disabled, become unemployed, been evicted, or some combination of the three. Most (eleven) were female.

Straddlers

This category also comprised seventeen people. As the name suggests, these people were experiencing homelessness for the second or third time, and some had bounced between housing and the street numerous times throughout their lives. Their sleeping arrangements included vehicles, a junked shipping container, a pet-friendly shelter, a van, and various outdoor settings such as tent camps. Some saw other housing opportunities in their future, and some had made it onto lists for Section 8 housing, for which people often wait years. Most Straddlers had learned to cobble together various sources of support, and their daily routines and survival strategies were often highly complex and time-consuming. They might eat meals at various soup kitchens on particular days of the week, obtain a few nonperishable items at a food bank, collect SSI because of disabilities, hold sporadic unskilled jobs, and accept monetary donations from the public through panhandling. Women just slightly outnumbered men as Straddlers.

Outsiders

This category comprised twenty-five people. Outsiders are homeless people "for whom street life has become taken-for-granted" (Snow and Anderson 1993:57–58). They are "Outsiders" in the sense that they live outside of mainstream society, including most of the service agencies intended to help the homeless, with the exception of those intended for animals. Their daily routines focus on accomplishing what they need to do to survive. I distinguished two types of Outsiders.

Settled Outsiders. Nine of the twenty-five Outsiders were "chronically homeless," having lived on the streets for five or more years. However, those in Culhane and Kuhn's "chronically homeless" category came to use emergency shelters as their permanent homes. In contrast, many of those I interviewed said that they could not imagine themselves ever sleeping indoors. Nevertheless, Settled Outsiders have carved out more-or-less permanent living situations, sometimes in remarkable places, such as the vents under a freeway, and a junkyard, where they lived in abandoned trailers and gutted school buses, obtaining water from nearby businesses or industries and power from generators. Many Settled Outsiders received SSI because of mental or physical disabilities. Some earned income through recycling cardboard or metal. As with Straddlers, women slightly outnumbered men among the Settled Outsiders.

Travelers. The remaining sixteen of the twenty-five Outsiders held the same marginal ethos as that of the Settled Outsiders, but moved around frequently. I refer to them using the term they used for them-selves: "Travelers." Although technically homeless, many instead defined themselves as "houseless." Many in this group were young adults under age twenty-five, and entrenched in street culture and life on the road. Many supported themselves through "spanging," slang for "spare changing," or "flying a sign," both of which refer to pan-handling. Some Travelers occasionally returned home to live with family for short periods before traveling again. Most Travelers (twelve) were male. In equal numbers, they had spent two to three years or more than five years on the streets. They avoided the "home-less archipelago," seeing it as full of older, alcoholic, or addicted street people.[16] They did use some of the services specifically cater-ing to youth, especially those with harm reduction policies, which refer to programs that attempt to reduce the negative effects of behaviors such as drug and alcohol abuse while taking a nonjudg-mental approach to those behaviors.

Housed/Stably Living

This category comprised sixteen people, including nine people who lived at Miami's Better Way housing program, mentioned previously. It also included several people who had been in residential addiction treatment programs for such a short time that they still qualified as homeless and thus brought their pets to the veterinary clinics, and some who had only recently found housing. I included this group of people in the analysis for several reasons. First, all of them had expe-rienced homelessness for at least a year, and one man had lived on the streets for twenty-three years. Second, they had animals while on the streets or they attributed much of their ability to stay off the streets to their companion animals. Third, I wanted their insight into what might help homeless pet owners get off the streets.

* * *

In keeping with the standard practice in interview-based research, I have used pseudonyms for the homeless people and their pets who appear in this book. Prior to beginning the interviews, when I men-tioned that I would change all names, most people shrugged or laughed and said they had nothing to hide. This contrasted with pre-vious research I had done among people higher up on the social ladder, who expressed concern about how they might appear in the published work. Whether because of having little left to lose, or because they might have liked the idea of their names appearing in a book, the homeless people I interviewed cared little about anonymity. Despite their willingness to be identified, I have used pseudonyms, but I remain struck by the transparency wrought by marginality.

Notes

1. I interviewed seventy-seven people, but did not include interviews with two men in Miami whose mental state was such that they wandered from my questions into delusion.

2. This research received approval from the University of Colorado's Institutional Review Board in accordance with federal regulations, university policies, and ethical standards for the protection of human subjects.

3. For a brief, concise summary of methodological approaches to and problems with counts of the homeless, see www.nationalhomeless.org/fact sheets/How_Many.html, accessed July 25, 2011.

4. Pali appears several times in this book. She graciously gave me permission to use her real name. For more information on her and her organization, Rocket Dog Rescue, see www.rocketdogrescue.org/about-us/our-founder, accessed March 1, 2012.

5. See Pullen 2006.

6. These figures are not representative of the overall homeless population; representation was not a goal of this study.

7. For more on the controversy surrounding San Francisco's service-animal laws, see Eskanazi 2009 and Zimmerman 2001.

8. Miniature horses provide an alternative to dogs for those with allergies or phobias, or those whose religion prohibits close contact with dogs. Advocates point out that guide horses live much longer than guide dogs, are not easily distracted in crowds, and exercise excellent judgment.

9. Because of the range of conditions, both visible and invisible, that can constitute a disability, and because of the prohibitions about asking for proof of the disability and the need for the service animal, some people have pushed the limits of this issue, either intentionally or mistakenly. For two views on this matter, see Eskanazi 2009 and Zimmerman 2011.

10. Other classic studies of skid row life depict Chicago (Anderson 1923; Bogue 1963) and Philadelphia (Blumberg, Shipley, and Shandler 1973).

11. Nels Anderson (1923) stood out as an exception to the disaffiliation perspective. He made the prescient insight that many homeless people have social relationships that are unseen by the domiciled public.

12. Michael Harrington (1980) offers an excellent discussion of the economic policies of this era. Jason Wasserman and Jeffrey Clair (2011) provide insight into the impact of recent gentrification on the urban homeless.

13. The public, and certainly many public officials, continue to see homelessness as an individual problem of deviance, addiction, and mental illness (Bogard 2001, 2003; DePastino 2003; Wasserman and Clair 2011).

14. The use of the term "houseless" rather than "homeless" could constitute "associational distancing." See Snow and Anderson 1993:chap. 7.

15. See the rules from the US Department of Housing and Urban Development at www.ncsha.org/blog/hud-releases-proposed-rule-defining-homelessness, and from the Social Security Administration at www.ssa.gov/pubs/10100.html#homeless, both accessed February 6, 2011.

16. This represents another example of "associational distancing."

3 Confrontations and Donations

Tall, willowy Linda leaned against the side of her van with her arms folded across her chest, waiting for the VET SOS clinic at Dolores Park to begin seeing clients. Her dog, Doc, a Great Dane, was first on the list. Linda's long, straight hair and flowing clothes accentuated her height. She had slid the van's side door open a crack, and every few minutes she reached inside to reassure Doc. Linda was a white, middle-aged Straddler, homeless off and on for the last seven years, Doc's entire life. "Wherever I've been, he's been," she said. "But as far as living in an actual house, that just has not happened." Over the years, she had held various unskilled jobs, mostly making only enough to feed Doc, herself, and other animals she'd had along the way. Her most recent job loss and subsequent eviction had forced Doc and her into the van. She described the logistics of sharing close quarters with a Great Dane. "He's got a bed and I've got a bed," she said, and with a laugh, added, "and you can guess where he ends up."

Parking posed another challenge, as it does for anyone trying to live in a vehicle in most cities.[1] For a long time, Linda had parked in a lot where the attendant knew she and Doc slept in the van, but looked the other way. After she lost the part-time job that paid her a little money under the table, she could no longer afford the space in the lot. She spent much of her time looking for a free, legal place to park—a daunting task in San Francisco. VET SOS provided Doc's food, but Linda's diet suffered. The inability to keep food cool and fresh led to a steady menu of peanut butter sandwiches at best and, at worst, a case of food poisoning when Linda took a chance on other things, as she recently had done with milk. I shuddered at the thought

41

Photograph by Mark Rodgers, courtesy of San Francisco Community Clinic Consortium's VET SOS project.

Doc waits with Linda for his examination.

of enduring food poisoning without bathroom facilities, but Linda took it in stride.

Great Danes have short life-spans relative to most breeds. At seven, Doc was already old for a Dane, and along the way he had developed two types of cancer. "So far, he's beaten the odds," Linda said, "and he doesn't know he's sick. He walks and bounces around and he's just a very happy dog. And very crazy about other dogs. A gentle giant." VET SOS saw to Doc's needs, but on the list of hardships, Linda included facing constant criticism about having a dog at all. She felt that judgment "just constantly," she said. "I get this, 'You should have gotten rid of him.' I'm so sick of that phrase."

"Who says that to you?" I asked.

"Everybody," she responded.

"Just people walking by, or what?"

"Everybody, from my ex-husband to strangers walking by. There's nobody who hasn't at some point. I mean, my ex-husband said it. They think I'm crazy for keeping him. They can't understand that you make a commitment to animals for their whole lives, the same as you would for children. There was just never any question."

When Linda could park in a lot, she and Doc attracted little attention. Now that she had to park on the streets, she and Doc were exposed. One cannot easily conceal a Great Dane. She felt constant scrutiny. "I got a note on my van yesterday," she said, "about keeping my dog in this 'prison of a vehicle,' and how they're going to call the police and the SPCA and do something to my van. And pretty much every place that I go to in San Francisco, I've got what I call a 'humaniac' against what I'm doing, and that's a constant problem." "Humaniac" is a derogatory term for people who devote themselves to rescuing animals, but as Linda pointed out, Doc did not need saving. He ate well and received regular veterinary care. Moreover, he enjoyed Linda's constant companionship. "He's utterly devoted to me," she said, stroking his broad head. "He's had such a strange life that he's very dependent on me, and I'm very dependent on him, and our lives have just become very focused on each other."

The criticism and Linda's response piqued my curiosity. As the research continued, I found that most homeless pet owners had heard comments or criticism of this sort. I knew that many domiciled people doubted the ability of homeless people to care for animals; after all, as a certified humaniac, I had once had similar doubts. And although homeless people in general endure frequent stigmatizing assaults on their character, having a pet makes one especially vulnerable. In this chapter, I explore how homeless pet owners' responses to these assaults add to the understanding of how discredited persons or those of low status attempt to salvage a sense of self-worth and dignity (see Anderson and Snow 2001 for a review).

Stigma and Identity

In *Stigma,* Erving Goffman outlined the strategies of "passing," in which the discreditable person conceals a stigma through "information control," and "covering," whereby he or she "makes a great effort to keep the stigma from looming large" (1963b:102). Building on Goffman's work, scholars have examined the processes of passing and covering in various contexts (e.g., Anderson, Snow, and Cress 1994; Charmaz 1991; Herman 1993; Nack 2008). When neither strategy will work, or when one has reached the limits of patience and tolerance, defiant behavior becomes an option. The stigmatized then engage in "reactive, entailing actions and verbalizations meant to reject humiliating moral assaults or ridicule" (Anderson, Snow, and Cress 1994:134). These "actions and verbalizations" can take "open" and "contained" forms (Goffman 1961). Open acts of defiance can include yelling, disobedience, and other gestures that challenge the prevailing order in "an overt and directly confrontational" way (Anderson, Snow, and Cress 1994:134). Acts of this sort provide momentary relief from humiliation, but often only perpetuate the stereotype associated with the stigma. Contained defiance might involve grumbling under one's breath or complaining to peers.[2] Contained or hidden forms of defiance can relieve humiliation backstage, but ultimately do not challenge the conditions of stigmatization.

Drawing on the interactionist emphasis on role-taking, one might conclude that the experience of stigma would result in a degraded sense of self. In this view, which Viktor Gecas and Peter Burke (1995) term the "reflected appraisals" approach, the perceptions of others have a significant influence on self-concept. However, "the reflected appraisals process does not operate all the time or under all conditions" (Gecas and Burke 1995:51; see also Kaufman and Johnson 2004). The self is "not simply a passive sponge that soaks up information from the environment; rather, it is an active agent engaged in various self-serving processes" (Gecas and Burke 1995:51). Faced with the appraisals of others, people engage in interpretation (see also Strauss 1969). When the evaluations of others contradict one's own perceptions, the interpretive process leads one to decide whether to accept or reject the views of others, or to take a position somewhere in between. As Leon Anderson and David Snow argue, even those who face constant affronts can reduce the impact of those affronts on one's sense of self:

> No automatic reflected appraisal process connects status affronts, on the one hand, with self-concept and self-esteem, on the other. Rather, the social actor's cognitions and activities are critical in determining the impact of stigmatization or subordination. The imputation of a negative social identity does not automatically translate into the acceptance of that identity, no matter how denigrated or demeaned the social status and the self implied, because the actor may assert a strong contrary view. (2001:401)

Of the numerous conditions and circumstances that can result in stigmatization, homelessness ranks near the top of the list. The domiciled often treat the homeless as what Goffman (1963a) called "nonpersons." Moreover, homelessness constitutes a "master status" that affects all areas of experience (LaGory, Fitzpatrick, and Ritchey 2001). Even so, studies reveal considerable variety in the quality of life among the homeless. Scholars seeking to understand how some homeless people create a reasonable sense of meaning and well-being despite their lack of resources have arrived at answers that vary widely. These include the combined effects of "life chances and choices" (LaGory, Fitzpatrick, and Ritchey 2001; see also Jencks 1994), a sense of community (Wasserman and Clair 2010), and social movement activism (Cress and Snow 1996; Snow and Mulcahy 2001; Wagner 1993; Wright 1997).

Snow and Anderson (1987, 1993) focus on the construction of positive personal identity among the homeless. Their analysis begins from the premise that all social interaction requires that the actors situate one another as social objects, and that doing so entails establishing the identities at play within the situation (see also Stone 1962; Turner 1968; McCall and Simmons 1978). In this construal, identity can take a *social* form, when imputed by others based on clues acquired from appearance and behavior in the setting. It can also take a *personal* form, when asserted or claimed by the actor him- or herself. Social and personal identities can correspond or conflict. For example, when a passerby shouts to a homeless person, "Get a job, you lazy bum," the target of this slur might say, "That's right, I am a bum." In doing so, he would embrace the social identity attributed to him, making it consistent with his personal identity. But another person might see that social identity as inconsistent with his personal identity and instead distance himself from it, declaring, "I ain't no bum" (Snow and Anderson 1993:214).[3] The avowal or disavowal of implied social identities through distancing and embracement brings personal identity to the fore. Even those who have few resources with which to assert personal identity nevertheless strive to do so in a positive manner. As Snow and Anderson point out, "The presented personal identities of individuals who are frequent objects of negative attention or attention deprivation, as are the homeless, can be especially revealing, because they offer a glimpse of how those people deal interactionally with their pariah-like status and the demeaning social identities into which they are frequently cast" (1993:214).

People construct personal identity through various activities that Snow and Anderson call "identity work." The list includes (1) the procurement or arrangement of physical settings and props; (2) cosmetic face work or the arrangement of personal appearance; (3) selective association with other individuals and groups; and (4) verbal construction and assertion of personal identities (1993:214).

Snow and Anderson argue that of the four types of identity work, "talk is perhaps the primary avenue through which [the homeless] can attempt to construct, assert, and maintain desired personal identities." Lacking "the financial or social resources to pursue the other varieties of identity work," homeless people rely on identity talk to either embrace or distance themselves from negative social identities (1987:1348).

I argue that homeless pet owners engage in a form of identity work that minimizes stigma by combining identity talk with what I will cautiously describe as a form of props. The "props" of interest here are pets, or companion animals, hence my caution.[4] To be sure, the homeless consider their pets far more than "props," but I use the term in an analytic sense. Dogs, in particular, because they appear with people in public more often than cats, serve as "badges" that announce "some characteristic of the possessor that is usually unavailable to the public but that, once displayed, becomes a resource for focused interaction and conversation" (Gardner 1995:93). As when one is carrying a popular book, or wearing a "message" t-shirt, strangers will initiate a conversation with a person accompanied by a dog whereas they would not do so with a person alone. Dogs become "social facilitators" in interactions between people (see Messent 1983; Robins, Sanders, and Cahill 1991; Sanders 1999; Irvine 2004a). However, "mixed contacts" between the homeless and the domiciled can cut both ways (Goffman 1963b; see also Lankenau 1999). On the one hand, interactions with the public can result in gestures of goodwill, such as a contribution of pet food. On the other, interactions can also mean confrontation: an attack on the homeless person's character that deems him or her unable to care for the animal and therefore undeserving of animal companionship.

Pet Ownership and Inequality: Historicizing Stigmatization

The experience of homeless pet owners offers a unique lens on stigma management because the combination of poverty and pet ownership reveals how inequality manifests itself "both materially and symbolically in the course of everyday life" (Anderson and Snow 2001:396). The criticism faced by homeless pet owners represents an interactional manifestation of inequality. Pet ownership has symbolic power obscured by the ordinariness it enjoys today. A long history of stigmatization and even prohibition exists regarding pet ownership among the poor. Although a review falls outside the scope of this book, a summary will make the point.

The first signs of class-specific norms about dog ownership appeared in Western Europe during the early Middle Ages (Cartmill 1997; Menache 2000; Serpell 1988; Thomas 1983). By this time, hunting had become a sport among the nobility, rather than a necessity for survival. Dogs improved the likelihood of a successful hunt, and consequently became a status symbol incorporated into a "socioeconomic, cultural equation of nobility = hunting = dogs" (Menache 2000:55; see also Cartmill 1997). Among the poor, however, hunting remained necessary for subsistence. To maintain the noble character of hunting, and thus to ensure that it stood as a "projection mechanism" for the upper ranks of society, laws in England and France began to prohibit the "indiscriminate ownership of hunting dogs" (Menache 2000:50). First, laws outlawed the ownership of greyhounds among the poor (defined as any "mean person"). Violators incurred fines, and the dogs of those owners who could not pay were confiscated and destroyed. The law did allow the poor to keep small dogs, seen as useless in hunting. To avoid fines, pets had to fit through "dog gauges" consisting of seven-by-five-inch oval metal rings.[5] Then, gradually, hunting became off-limits to the poor, to preserve forest areas and game for nobles. Additional laws made it unlawful for the poor to own mastiffs and spaniels, in addition to greyhounds. The poor could own mastiff-type dogs for protection, but only if they were "expeditated" (see Derr 1997). This cruel practice, which originated in Denmark, involved chopping off the two middle toes of the front paws so that the dogs could not pursue deer, the emblem of the nobility.

The laws established during the Middle Ages gradually softened, but traces of the underlying discrimination remained well into the modern era. For example, the British elite considered the dogs of the Victorian-era poor the "living emblems of the depravity of their owners" (Ritvo 1987:177). Until scientists understood, in the late nineteenth century, how rabies was transmitted, upper-class French and English blamed the disease on "poor people's dogs" and "the squalid habits of working class life" (Kete 1994:111; see also Ritvo 1987). Although the practice of pet-keeping became democratized in the early twentieth century (see Irvine 2004a), the experiences of the homeless suggest that pet ownership among those at the bottom rungs of society remains stigmatized.

Confrontations

As mentioned, part of this research involved an informal survey of domiciled citizens about their attitudes toward pet ownership among the homeless. The analysis revealed approximately even responses (76 out of 147 in favor).[6] I wanted primarily to examine the reasons offered by those who opposed pet ownership. Many of the comments took the form of "they should not have a dog if they can't take care of themselves." Having a physical home also figured heavily, with "they shouldn't have a pet if they don't have a home" appearing often. In another common response, people said that any money a homeless person comes across should support his or her own needs, and that using that money to care for a pet was irresponsible. Some claimed that the homeless were selfish to have pets. These respondents held the opinion that it was not fair to the animal to be "made homeless" by living with a homeless person. They made statements such as, "The animal doesn't get a choice. They shouldn't have to be homeless just because a person is." More cynically, some claimed that the homeless have pets only to gain sympathy when panhandling.

Most of the homeless pet owners had encountered some form of criticism from domiciled citizens about their right or ability to have a companion animal. This occurred far more often among people with dogs, for the obvious reason that people and dogs appear in public together, whereas those who had cats did not typically move about in public with them. People who had been homeless for longer had heard more criticism. Straddlers and Traveling Outsiders heard criticism most frequently, because they encountered the domiciled more often while panhandling or just hanging out. For instance, I met Doug, a young, African American Straddler, at the PALS clinic in Berkeley, where he had brought his already-spayed dog for her vaccinations. He showed me a large bag of dog food he carried in his backpack. Doug had lost his job and could not seem to find another one. When his money had run out, he had lost his apartment, too. He said he looked for work every day, and had a friend who would dog-sit once he found a job. When not job hunting, he sat on the sidewalk on the same Berkeley street reading, while his dog lay at his side.

The pair slept at YEAH's seasonal, pet-friendly shelter and Doug did not panhandle. Nevertheless, he said, "I see people in the street that tell me all the time, 'You shouldn't have a dog if you don't have a place to live.'" Similarly, Megan, a white woman in her mid-twenties who had drifted to San Francisco with her boyfriend and their dog, told me, "People are just mean. They're like, 'You don't deserve a dog. You shouldn't have one. You can't take care of him.'" We met at the VET SOS clinic, where she turned down a donation of dog food because her boyfriend had a twenty-pound bag in his pack.

Homeless pet owners reported that domiciled people occasionally offered to buy their dogs, as my friend and I had once done. For example, Chris and I talked while he waited at the VET SOS clinic at the Homeless Youth Alliance in San Francisco. At twenty-two, he had spent several years traveling the country with two dogs, who now lay calmly beside him. When he recounted the time a man tried to buy his blue-nosed pit bull, I listened sheepishly.

"I got offered [money] by this rich guy for him in Vegas. He said, 'My daughter wants that dog, and money's not an object.' He kept going up and up, and I just looked at him and said, 'Would you sell your daughter, even for half a million dollars?' And he's like, 'No.' And I said, 'Okay, then. I'm not going to sell my kid to you for any amount.'"

Another Traveler at the Youth Alliance had this experience several times. "That's something you deal with a lot," he said, "people trying to buy your animals off you 'cause they want to give 'em a better home, and this and that."

Pet ownership is considered nearly a birthright in contemporary Western societies. In most people's everyday lives, the right to animal companionship and the ability to provide care go uncontested. The homeless are likely the only group criticized and stigmatized for having pets. They use several strategies to defy accusations from domiciled strangers.

Homeless Pet Owners Respond

Open Defiance: Cursing

Cursing was the response of choice for many Travelers, mostly youth whose history of homelessness spanned from three to five years. Men and women seemed to curse equally. For example, I met Ronnie, a young Traveler who appears again in Chapter 6, at the PALS clinic in Berkeley. He had been on the road for four years. He grew up in Florida and became homeless at eighteen after losing his job and apartment. He lived on the street for a while, but then hit the road, often hopping freight trains. For the last year, he had been traveling with a pit bull/Labrador mix named Dozer. While on the road, Ronnie had stopped at a drop-in center to take a shower, and a woman was sitting outside looking for someone who could take the dog because she could no longer care for him. "We're inseparable," Ronnie said. During the interview, when I asked, "Have you ever had any people say to you something like . . . ," he finished my sentence by adding, "'You're homeless. You don't deserve a dog.'"

"Exactly," I said. We both laughed, and I added, "So how do you respond?"

"With a big 'F-You'! I've had people say, 'I'm calling animal control and having your dog taken away from you,' and I'm like, 'Yeah, yeah. Whatever.' Because animal control's going to come and see a healthy, happy dog and be like, 'You have a nice day.' [laughs again] They're not going to take Dozer from me. For what?"

Red-haired Toni is a Traveler who, though not yet twenty-five, has lived in Golden Gate Park on and off for six years. She spends her days on Haight Street among the street kids, whom she refers to as her family. She has a pit bull she refers to as her "road dog." She answered without hesitation when I asked how she responded to those who said she should not have a dog. "Fuck off!" she said, laughing loudly. "'Scuse my language," she added, "but that's what we tell 'em. They don't know anything." Similarly, Melanie, a Traveler who brought a four-month-old puppy to a VET SOS clinic for vaccinations, described a recent encounter: "[A woman] told me, like, I'm a bad person for having my dog on the streets and just because I'm homeless doesn't mean my dog wants to be homeless."

"So how did you react?"

"She said it in her car and she drove off, so it was like whatever. You know. They don't know me. They don't know my dog. So fuck 'em."

In some instances, the response is still a curse but without profanity. For example, I asked Ike, another young Traveler in San Francisco, whether anyone had ever said that he shouldn't have a dog. "Uh huh," he said, nodding.

"How do you react to that?"

"I tell 'em that they shouldn't have a life!" he exclaimed, laughing.

One could easily dismiss the act of cursing as irrelevant, but doing so disregards how people use language to achieve emotional and social goals. The kind of cursing that homeless pet owners engaged in consisted of wishing strangers harm (e.g., "fuck you," "fuck off"). The main intention of emotionally harmful curses "is to lower the social status of one's opponent" (Jay 2000:159; see also Jay 2009; Želvys 1990). Their use points to interactional advantages and disadvantages associated with social rank (see Branaman 2003). As Goffman (1955, 1967) has argued, two rules of social interaction ensure that people can "maintain face" in most situations. As Ann Branaman notes, the rule of self-respect "calls for individuals to maintain the face they have been given, typically on the basis of various social attributes ascribed to the person by others in the situation and by the wider society." The rule of considerateness asks them "to exercise tact with respect to the feelings and faces of others in social situations" (2003:93). Typically, the combined effects of the rules favor high-status persons. In this case, however, cursing violates both rules and thus disrespects those with higher status. To be sure, cursing does not challenge the social order, but it allows one to "express detachment and implicitly affirm the dignity and value of the self" (Branaman 2003:117). An act of open defiance such as cursing might provide some temporary satisfaction, but it can "reinforce others' negative perceptions of the homeless" (Anderson, Snow, and Cress 1994:135).

Contained Defiance: Ignoring

To an extent, most homeless people ignored some of the negative comments targeted at them, perhaps understanding that they could not change the minds of those launching the assault. For example, Stan, a white Straddler, had been homeless—this time—for about a year. He had been evicted for turning a two-bedroom apartment into a three-bedroom place by subletting one of the rooms to a couple he knew. He had a Section 8 housing voucher, but the eviction on his record had made it especially hard to find a landlord willing to take a chance. There were so many other, less risky, prospective tenants on the market for rental housing. In any case, housing authorities in San Francisco were forecasting no openings for several years.

Stan's tan-and-white dog, Roxy, had been his companion for most of her ten years of life. The pair had camped in San Francisco's

Presidio Park for several months. Before that, they had slept in a trailer at a construction site for a while, where the site manager had paid Stan to serve as unofficial temporary night watchman. They had even spent a few nights in a dumpster. Although the thought of this made me cringe, Stan simply shrugged and said, "It was a shelter over our heads in the bad weather."

A disabled Vietnam veteran, Stan was receiving SSI and sometimes help from friends. "We don't ask people for money," he said, "but people will sometimes give me twenty or thirty extra bucks here and there. So I get a little extra." When we met, he had saved up enough money to stay in a single-room occupancy hotel for a while, just to enjoy a bed and hot shower. He also kept an emergency fund in case anything happened to Roxy. When I asked whether anybody had ever criticized him for having a dog, Stan nodded immediately and recalled: "Oh, yeah. Yeah. When I first became homeless, everybody said it was really selfish to keep her. They said I should give her to someone, and everybody had suggestions as to where I could give her up, then it would be easier for me to get a place like a shelter or something like that. . . . It was very hard at that time. So a lot of people criticized me."

"And how did you respond when they said that?"

"I just ignored them," he laughed. "It's just, most people would think that probably it makes it a lot harder and it's not worth it, but that's because they don't have a dog. For me, it was never an option to give her up. It just wasn't. I couldn't do that. I love her as much as people love their children."

Stan ignored criticism because he knew that others did not understand what Roxy meant to him. Other homeless people had other reasons for ignoring comments about their dogs. Trish, another Straddler whom we will meet again in Chapter 7, regularly panhandled with her dog at her side. She brushed off the insults she regularly encountered from drivers who yelled that she did not deserve to have a dog. "I usually don't say much," she said. "Everybody's entitled to their opinion." Others who ignored the insults saw them as based on ignorance about how the homeless live and how they care for their companion animals. Sandy, nearly thirty and living in an abandoned car in Sacramento with her cat, had had comments hurled at her the morning we met. As she brought her cat to the Mercer Clinic in a carrier, someone told her she could not take care of a pet. "I ignore it," she said. "It affects me, sure. But they don't know. People just don't know." Jason, a young Traveler, gave a similar response. He hitch-hikes around the country with his girlfriend and their two dogs. A Californian by birth, he had made his way back and we met at the PALS clinic in Berkeley. Although only in his early twenties, he pointed out that his ability to ignore comments came with time and experience. "I don't respond," he said, then added, "now, at least. At first, it wasn't so good. I had to really, like, think about that one and work on it. Sometimes when I'm not thinking, I still respond pretty bad. But, it's sheer ignorance on their part, though. My dog is well loved and cared for."

Other scholars have noted attributions of ignorance as a stigma management strategy. For example, in their study of African American women with HIV, Aaron Buseh and Patricia Stevens found that women who attributed hurtful comments to ignorance could "understand why and how [stigma] existed. . . . They could identify with people's fears and hostility" (2007:12). Similarly, homeless pet owners who ignored the insults were relatively gentle in doing so. They either had developed thick skin on the streets or assumed ignorance on the part of others, but overall they framed their responses in a self-protective manner.

Redefining

Most homeless pet owners responded to affronts by redefining pet ownership to incorporate what they do in the course of caring for their animals. As a strategy, redefining blurs the boundary between open and contained defiance. It involves responding openly to verbal assaults, but doing so in a way that indicates a rejection of the values behind those assaults, rather than simply a defense against humiliation. In this way, the homeless make positive moral sense of their pet ownership.

The alternative definition of pet ownership has three components, which appeared alone or in combination. The first component emphasizes the importance of making sure that one's dog eats first and eats well, and that the owner will sacrifice to feed the dog. For instance, when I asked Don, the man who lived in the encampment under the freeway in San Francisco, if he had ever encountered any criticism about keeping dogs, he said, "Yes. Quite a bit, actually." He continued: "They say, 'You can't take care of yourself, how do you expect to take care of your animal?' It's not that I can't take care of myself. I think I do a pretty good job of taking care of myself, considering that I eat every day, three times a day if I want. It kind of bothers me. They don't know what I do, or to what extent I will go, to make sure my dogs eat every day. They come first. Off the top, they come first, you know. And so there's no way they could tell me that I don't take care of my dogs."

Pete, a recently dislocated white man in his late forties, had been camping in Sacramento with his two large dogs after losing his job, his home, and then his truck in five short months. Nevertheless, he said, "These dogs eat before I do. They'll eat before I do, period. They eat well." With a chuckle, he added, "And they eat as much of my food as I do anyway."

Others echoed the theme of never letting their dogs go hungry, and even putting the dog first. Toni said, "My dog eats before I do. Way before me. She comes way before me." Jerry, a Settled Outsider with two dogs, put it this way when we talked in Boulder: "Some of us out here take damn better care of our animals than ourselves," he said. "When I don't have any money sometimes for food, I'll give 'em what I'm eating and go without food, 'cause I won't see my animals go hungry." Like Jerry, a young man in San Francisco had also gone without food so that his dogs could eat. As he explained, "It gets hard sometimes because you gotta feed them before yourself, so sometimes you're going hungry a little bit for them." Likewise, Karl, on the road with his dog and his girlfriend, said, "I make sure that my dog gets fed before me. If I gotta starve for a day so that she can eat, I do. She can't go out and ask somebody, 'Hey, I'm hungry. I need some food.' I can. So every day, I make sure my girlfriend's fed, make sure my dog's fed." Stan said about his dog, "I make sure she gets good food. Even though I'm homeless I just make it a point, you know. She has a pretty good diet. And she's never missed a meal." Portraying the sacrifice in somewhat therapeutic or perhaps spiritual terms, another pet owner said, "The dog isn't starving, you know, because I will always feed the dog before I feed myself, which is strange in the sense that you're supposed to love yourself before you love anybody else, but I do feed the dog before I feed myself."

The second component of redefined pet ownership involves constant companionship. Many tellers extolled the fact that they seldom, if ever, leave their dogs alone. Some made this into a moral critique in which holding a job, and thus keeping a dog at home and often alone all day, constitutes improper care bordering on abuse. For example, Ike could not conceal his disdain when he "condemned the condemners" (Sykes and Matza 1957): "They put their pets in their houses and then go to work all day, and they barely see their dogs. And when they come home, they're too tired to spend any time with their dogs, so their dog's kind of like a floor item, just off to the side. Just some 'thing.' It's their pet. It's not their kid. It's not their son or daughter like these guys are. It's their pet."

Toni reinforced this when she said, "It really pisses me off when the yuppies are like, 'You don't feed your dog' or 'You don't take care of your dog right.' You know what? All they do is leave their dog in their apartment for twelve hours out of the day. That's not fair."

"So what do you mean, 'yuppies'?" I asked.

"You know, it means all the people that walk up and down the street."

"So, people who have jobs?"

"Yeah."

"So everybody who doesn't live on the street is a yuppie?"

"Not everybody," she said. "But the snooty people with that personality that think they're better than everybody else? That's what we call yuppies. Just mainly everyone talking shit to you."

Buzz, a Traveler whom I met in Boulder, held a similar view:

> People think because you're homeless, you can't take care of a dog. Being homeless, that's not the point, okay? Even people that have houses abuse and mistreat and neglect their animals, so that has nothing to do with it, whether you have a house. Certain people should not own animals, okay? I totally agree that there are some people on the streets, that are homeless, and I mean, there's no way they can take care of a dog. I understand it completely. But it goes the same way with people that got houses and jobs. You ain't got the time to spend with the animal, 'cause you're busy at work trying to keep that house that you have and pay your car payments, that your dog is neglected and doesn't see you but when you come home, and when you come home, you just want to eat and go to bed. That dog, that's mistreatment, too.

Not all tellers engaged in a moral critique of those who must leave their dogs alone. Some emphasized the benefits of constant companionship for the dogs. For example, Paula, a white woman nearing sixty, said, "Dogs of homeless people are incredibly lucky dogs, because they get 100 percent of the people's attention. [They are] normally more well behaved, more well rounded socially."

The third component of redefined pet ownership emphasizes freedom. For example, Devon, a Straddler who sometimes lives indoors during cold weather, claims his dog prefers their homeless spells. "He gets to play, and he's out in the trees," he said. "He sees more dogs, and he's not cooped up in the house." Similarly, Don said, referring to his dog Ace: "That dog is happy. He's healthy. He has fun every day. He has a gigantic field that he can just run and romp in. He don't have to worry about cars, you know? And he's behind a fence so there's no outside interference [he gestured toward the fencing around the entrance to the San Francisco freeway encampment where he was living], and he's happy. So what am I doing wrong?"

Cory, whom I met at the Homeless Youth Alliance clinic, suggested that his dog repaid him for the freedom he provided her: "She gets plenty of exercise chasing sticks all day. I give her that, and then, in return, she gives me companionship. She won't leave me. I could take her off the leash and run down the street, and she'll keep right up with me. She does not want to be apart from me, and that's really cool. It's unconditional love on both our parts, both sides of it."

Kaz, a young Traveler whose two dogs rested quietly by his pack during our interview, incorporated all three components when he redefined pet ownership this way:

> They tell me that "you can't take care of a dog on the street," and I tell them that they're crazy, because I spend 24/7 with my dogs. My dogs don't leave my hip. They eat way more than I do. They eat before I do. They get plenty of water. Plenty of food. They get way lot of attention. They get 24/7 attention. I go to parks with them. They get to run around and have fun. They get to see new things every day and they're exploring nature like they were meant for. They weren't born to live in a box. That's why, when you see a dog in a house, they're freaking out because they want to go outside, 'cause that's their natural habitat, you know, they don't even like it in the house, so I get 'em through the woods and all that. And I take 'em to dog parks. They exercise more than anybody. I mean [laughs], look at their muscles!

Whereas many of the domiciled see animals as deprived if they do not have a house, and see homeless people as unable to take care of animals by virtue of being homeless, these statements cast a different light on the situation. For the tellers, responsible pet ownership involves feeding their animals first and the sacrifices they make to do so. It also involves a combination of freedom and constant companionship that the circumstances of homelessness make possible. By redefining pet ownership, homeless pet owners express their values in ways that resemble what Katherine Edin and Maria Kefalas (2005) found among low-income, unmarried mothers. Whereas middle-class women put education, career, and marriage before childbearing, low-income women (and girls) saw children as a way to prove their worth. For them, children provide more certainty than marriage does. They put motherhood first, with marriage possible only once they have their careers and lives "set." Likewise, homeless pet owners reversed the typical sequence, in which the house and yard come first, and then the dog. Most homeless pet owners aspire to having a home, but many find it difficult to reach that goal. Having a pet provides a sense of meaning in the present. Just as the unmarried mothers in Edin and Kefalas's study redefined the value of marriage to reflect their structured experience, homeless pet owners redefine pet ownership to reflect theirs.

The Positive Side of Interacting with the Domiciled

Not all interactions between homeless people and the domiciled public result in stigmatizing accusations. Much of the interaction that dogs spark takes a friendly course.[7] For example, I met Austin, a white, gay man in his thirties, at a VET SOS clinic. He described how much attention his tiny poodle mix attracted. "People are always stopping and going, 'How cute your dog is!' People will interact with you because you have a super-cute dog. It's so weird. They'll stop you on the street and say, 'What kind is it?'" The same day, I also spoke with Darrell, a Straddler in San Francisco, who described similar experiences with his dog, Buddy. "Everybody wants to stop and say hi to Buddy and talk to him," Darrell said. "He's cute and he's friendly, so people come up to us all the time. He keeps me kind of social I guess." Similarly, Stan said that people constantly came up wanting to pet Roxy as the two of them sat in public. "We've made a lot of friends," he told me. "People ask about her all the time. She makes me mix with other people, you know, because they talk about her, and she's just a catalyst for getting out among the world. Otherwise, I tend to isolate."

I did not find it surprising that Austin's dog attracted admirers. The dog is a friendly ball of white fluff, with alert, shining, brown eyes and a button nose. But Darrell's dog, Buddy, is a massive pit bull, and Darrell himself is bearded and burly. He and Buddy made a formidable-looking pair, and Roxy, Stan's dog, is a sweet but unremarkable, tan-and-white mixed-breed. That all three men reported that people approached them regularly complements existing studies of dog-facilitated social interaction.

Austin's, Stan's, and Darrell's dogs all had light-color coats. Research suggests that people find black dogs less approachable than dogs of lighter color (Wells and Hepper 1992; Leonard 2011). But when I met Gordon and his dog, Radar, at the Mercer Clinic in Sacramento, Gordon said that Radar, a large, mostly black German shepherd, "gets friends everywhere. People smile when they see him," he said. "Everyone knows him. Everyone always has treats for him. They take his picture. All kinds of stuff. They always remember his name," he said, then laughed and added, "They never remember my name. They just call me Radar's Dad, and sometimes they even call him Gordon!" I heard similar stories of social facilitation from other owners of black dogs. Although this evidence is anecdotal, coat color does not seem to deter strangers from approaching dogs.

The experiences of the homeless pet guardians support the findings of another study in which the "effect of having a dog present persisted even when the appearance of the dog and/or experimenter was less appealing" (McNicholas and Collis 2000:68). In this particular research, the authors used both yellow and black Labradors, and both male and female handlers. But they also altered the appearance of the handler and the dog. In one condition, the handler appeared neatly dressed and the dog had a matching collar and leash. The authors referred to this as "smart" handler and "pet" dog. In another condition, a "scruffy" handler wore torn jeans, scuffed work boots, an old t-shirt, and a stained work jacket, while the "rough" dog had on a studded leather collar with a frayed piece of rope tied to it as a leash. The experimenters could then examine six conditions: "smart" handler with "pet" dog, "smart" handler with "rough" dog, "scruffy" handler with "pet" dog, "scruffy" handler with "rough" dog," and each of the two handler types alone, without a dog. Regardless of appearance, handlers experienced increased interactions when accompanied by dogs, but the "rough dog" attracted *more* interactions than did the dog in the "pet" condition. The smartly dressed handler with the "rough" dog attracted the highest number of interactions, followed by the "scruffy" handler with the "rough" dog. The "scruffy" handler with "rough" dog condition described Darrell and Buddy as well as Gordon and Radar. Although the study used Labrador retrievers, one of the authors had personal experience handling a dog from one of the "bully" breeds, and noted anecdotally that this did not deter people. Thus, if measured quantitatively, dogs such as Buddy and Radar might well attract more attention than dogs like Austin's "super-cute" ball of fluff.

Donations and Enabled Resistance

In the course of these animal-facilitated interactions, many members of the domiciled public donate dog or cat food to homeless pet owners. Nearly everyone in the homeless sample had received pet food from domiciled citizens. As Buzz explained: "I could be sitting here in the park, minding my business, reading a book. Someone will walk up. 'You're homeless? Here. Can I give you this?' They'd bring me wet food. Dry food. Dog treats. And I'm like, 'All right!' Well, I'm not going to say no. I've never had a problem feeding my dog. Ever."

Most of the homeless pet owners had similar experiences. A young Traveler said, "A lot of people just come up to me and say, 'Hey, do you want some dog food? Here, have some dog food.'" Ruthie, a middle-aged Straddler who had lived on the Sacramento streets on and off for five years, echoed these reports: "People say, 'Hey, do you need some food for him?' 'Hey, I got this.' You know, people are just like that. They're just very giving." Cory, a Traveler, recalled, "I've really only had to buy him dog food once. Like actually *had* to. 'Cause people see you with a dog, see you sitting on the sidewalk, and they just presume that you need help." I heard a similar account from Dee in Berkeley. "Because I live in People's Park," she said, "I'm really fortunate, because people come by and they just donate food all the time, you know what I mean? And there is a drop-in clinic on Monday night for youth that gives out dog food, and I get dog food from them." Consistent with this, Ronnie explained, "I've always been able to feed him. I've never run out of food. Once I get low on food, something comes by. Something happens."

"So you get donations?" I asked.

"Most of the time, when I'm running low on food, I save the money I spange and buy him food myself, but if I buy him food because I'm low, I end up getting like a twenty-pound bag [donated] the next day and I'm like, 'Oh, man. Why'd I buy the food?' I've actually taken back dog food that I've spent my own money on, 'cause later on in the day, somebody would buy me a better brand of dog food. And I'd be like, 'I don't need this,' and I take it back and get my money back almost every time."

In addition to donations from the public, homeless people obtain pet food from other sources. VET SOS, PALS, and the Mercer Clinic provide dog and cat food to their homeless clients. In addition, animal control services and humane societies in many cities will often provide free pet food. One Settled Outsider described how it works in Boulder. He typically hangs out in a particular area in a city park with other homeless dog owners. He said, "I've watched Animal Control pull up in their van and hop out with five or six twenty-pound bags of dog food, and be like, 'Yo! You need dog food here?'" He laughed and said, "These dogs are fed better than we are." I talked with animal control officers in Boulder, who confirmed that they do this regularly, especially during the summer months, when the city's transient and homeless populations run high. Many soup kitchens and drop-in centers also provide pet food. As a young Traveler said, "Dog food's pretty much free. I mean you can get it pretty easy at any drop-in center or dog place [meaning pet food store]. That's pretty much covered." In addition, those who receive SSI or other disbursements include pet food in their monthly expenses. Stan did this for Roxy's food, for example. Candy, a Settled Outsider whom we will meet in Chapter 5, looked at me as though I were a bit slow when I asked her how she fed her fifteen cats. She shrugged and explained, "I buy at the beginning of the month, you know," referring to when she gets her SSI check. She added, "They're very well cared for," and I could easily see that all her cats ate well.

In this sample, none of the pets of the homeless went hungry. Similarly, when Oswin Baker (2001) surveyed homeless pet owners in the United Kingdom, they reported that they easily obtained food for their animals. Although two geographically limited studies do not indicate a trend, this nevertheless indicates the change that has taken place over the past decade. When Aline Kidd and Robert Kidd (1994) surveyed homeless pet owners around San Francisco, more than half had difficulty feeding their animals and obtaining affordable veterinary care. Now, however, VET SOS reaches many homeless pet owners in the area. Pet owners in many other cities have similar support.

Because of these services and the generosity of ordinary citizens, the homeless people I interviewed had ample supplies of pet food among their belongings. This allowed them to feed their animals and engage in redefining ownership during confrontations about their ability to care for pets.

In sum, donations of food from some of the domiciled enabled the homeless to resist stigmatizing assaults from others. Such donations allowed homeless pet owners to assert that their dogs ate first and ate well, and thus reject accusations about their inability to care for their animals. Through this "enabled resistance," they could affirm a positive sense of identity despite consistent status affronts.

Pet Ownership and Moral Identities

This chapter contributes to the discussion begun by Snow and Anderson about how the homeless "salvage the self" when cast into stigmatizing social identities. Whereas Snow and Anderson focused on the forms of identity talk known as *distancing* and *embracement,* I have introduced *redefining* as another form that helps to minimize stigmatizing affronts. Although some homeless pet owners responded to affronts with open or contained defiance, the majority redefined pet ownership so that the meanings ascribed to it reflected the realities of their relationships with their animals. They asserted their ability to feed their animals, even at personal sacrifice, and to offer enhanced quality of life through constant companionship and freedom. They claimed that they could provide what other dogs lacked, and that their way of caring for an animal surpassed the typical standards, which require a house. Redefining differs from distancing, which would involve disassociating oneself from the roles of pet owner or homeless person. It also differs from embracement, which would entail the avowal of the negative social identity of irresponsible pet owner. If homeless pet owners simply agreed with the accusation that they could not provide for their companion animals, then they would accept the social identities imputed to them, which cast them as incapable of caring for themselves and therefore unworthy of animal companionship. Instead, redefining challenges the basis of the affront. By redefining pet ownership, the homeless pet owner can assert that *homelessness* does not imply *helplessness* (see Osborne 2002). Thus, the personal identity that emerges from pet ownership constitutes a *moral* identity. I use the term "moral identity" in Sherryl Kleinman's sense, to refer to "an identity that testifies to a person's good character" (1996:5; see also Katz 1975). The task of establishing a positive personal identity is as essential for homeless people as it is for the domiciled. Accomplishing it is far more difficult for the homeless, and for some, caring for an animal is part of the process. Together, redefining and enabled resistance allow homeless pet owners to assert personal identities characterized by responsibility and even self-sacrifice.

Earlier in this chapter, I referred to companion animals as "props." I did so cautiously because, in truth, they are much more than props. They require care, and the person who accepts the companionship of an animal consequently accepts responsibility for that care. For many of the people I interviewed, providing care became a way to mitigate the negative consequences of stigmatization brought on not solely because of homelessness, but also because of the *combination* of homelessness and pet ownership. By redefining pet ownership and emphasizing care, homeless pet owners could establish moral, personal identities that helped to manage the negative impact of stigma. Thus, the same conditions that produced the stigma provided the means by which to deflect it.

For homeless pet owners, the stigma management strategy of redefining becomes possible largely through what I have called "enabled resistance." The pet owners I interviewed could resist insults from some of the domiciled because of the goodwill of others. More specifically, donated food allows them to keep their dogs healthy. Indeed, a contented, well-fed dog is crucial for their ability to redefine pet ownership. Their claims about the advantages of freedom and constant companionship would have meant little if their animals went hungry. Their ability to contest stigmatization and redefine its basis arose because others empowered them to do so. This brings to mind what Stephen Lankenau observed in a study of status-enhancing acts by panhandlers. He described how the "regulars" who frequently donate money "serve as protectors in the midst of daily harassment." Panhandlers "endure the degrading aspects of panhandling by developing supportive relationships with certain passersby who provide both material resources, such as money or clothing, and an enhanced view of self" (311, 289). Regulars not only donate spare change, but also treat panhandlers as persons rather than pariahs. The relationships between the homeless people in this study and their benefactors both fit and depart from this description. In a few cases, donations of food came through established relationships with veterinary clinics or other service providers. In these instances, the interactions result not only in provision of pet food and services, but also in conveying a social identity for the homeless person. Over time, the veterinarian and staff learn the names of their clients and their animals, and talk to the clients as equals. But more often, the food donations come from strangers, some of whom simply drop off a bag of dog food without exchanging any words. These onetime encounters do not constitute the "supportive relationships" that Lankenau found; nevertheless, they provide the resources that enable resistance to stigmatization in other encounters. Through both confrontations *and* donations, homeless pet owners assert a positive moral identity, "salvaging the self," to use Snow and Anderson's phrase, from reminders of their stigmatized status.

* * *

In the chapters that follow, I develop the connections between identity and pet ownership more fully. The concept of moral identity appears throughout the discussion, but I shift the focus to examine the personal narratives pet owners tell about their relationships with their animals. The meanings that tellers assign to companion animals depend on the narrative logics and frames provided by the individual and social dynamics in each teller's life (see Frank 2010; Maynes, Pierce, and Laslett 2008). These stories reveal both the ways that selves are embedded in social and historical context and the importance of animals in human subjectivity.

Notes

An earlier version of this chapter, coauthored with Kristina Kahl and Jesse Smith, appeared in *Sociological Quarterly* (53:25–43) as "Confrontations and Donations: Encounters Between Homeless Pet Owners and the Public."

1. Teresa Gowan discusses the problems of the vehicularly housed (2010:227–228). In particular, she writes, "People living in vehicles get relatively little attention in the literature on homelessness, but they make up a significant proportion of the American population outside conventional housing. One national survey has suggested that this less visible fraction could even constitute the majority of the literally homeless" (2010:253; see also Link et al. 1995).

2. See James Scott's *Domination and the Arts of Resistance* (1990) for one of the best examinations of contained defiance.

3. Snow and Anderson also found a third pattern of identity talk not applicable to this analysis, which they refer to as "fictive storytelling."

4. Although *Down on Their Luck* does not incorporate animals, a related article notes that some of the homeless have pets to encourage social interaction (Anderson, Snow, and Cress 1994:133).

5. For an image of a dog gauge, see http://doglawreporter.blogspot.com /2011/01/forepaw-mutilation-in-medieval-england.html, accessed June 15, 2011.

6. In the only other extant study to survey the public on this issue, Heidi Taylor, Pauline Williams, and David Gray (2004) found that 74 percent of those polled in Cambridge, England (compared to 51 percent in my study), believed the homeless "should be allowed pets if they want them."

7. A voluminous literature examines the role of animals in social interaction with other people. The first study to explore this outside the clinical setting took place in East Yorkshire, England, and involved randomly giving retirees between the ages of seventy-five and eighty-one either a caged parakeet or a begonia (Mugford and M'Comisky 1975). The researchers administered questionnaires that captured the recipients' interest in and attitudes toward other people and their own psychological health. Those who received the birds reported favorable changes overall. They had more friends, more visitors, and more involvement in their community, compared with those who received plants. Although the authors note that parakeets do not solve all the problems of old age, the study opened the door for further research into the role of animals in human interaction.

Subsequent research confirmed that dogs, in particular, regularly serve as social catalysts. One highly cited Swedish study found that a majority of participants made statements such as, "My dog gives me the opportunity of talking with other people" (83 percent) and "The dog makes friends for me" (79 percent; Adell-Bath et al. 1979). A study in Great Britain revealed that people walking through a public park engaged in significantly greater numbers of conversations with strangers when accompanied by their dogs than when they walked the same route alone (Messent 1983). Conversations also lasted longer when the dog was present. Other species, such as turtles and rabbits, also encourage conversation (e.g., Hunt, Hart, and Gomulkiewicz 1992). Yet the mechanisms behind the socializing effect, as well as its potential benefits, remain unclear (see Hart 1995 and Wells 2004 for reviews).

4 Friend and Family

"I've been homeless on and off for, like, fifteen years. I can't seem to settle down anywhere," the woman told me. She had arrived well in advance of the start of the VET SOS clinic, and while the volunteers set up, she agreed to pass the time talking with me. She had a warm and friendly way about her. After she signed the consent form for the interview, she tapped the pen on my clipboard by the signature line and said, "Only my parents call me that. You can call me Ree. Everybody does." Then she introduced me to Sam, a young, energetic Rottweiler mix, and Rascal, whom she called a "Jack-huahua," a cross between a Jack Russell terrier and a Chihuahua. The three of them made quite a picture. Ree is short and stocky with light brown hair in dreadlocks. In body type, she and Sam looked well matched, but their bulk accentuated Rascal's tininess by contrast. "They're my best friends," she said without prompting. "They're my children, too."

After introducing her two dogs, Ree showed me how she had transformed the inside of her old Chevy van to accommodate the three of them. She had put makeshift curtains in the windows and taken out the backseats. She had filled the cargo area with a futon mattress, a refrigerator, a DVD player, several duffle bags, a pile of clothes, and numerous water bottles. In the mix, I saw beds, bowls, toys, and bags of food for Sam and Rascal. The scent of bodies, both human and canine, filled the small space. Ree had a third dog with her at the time, a mixed-breed with poor manners and strong signs of German shepherd in his bloodlines. The dog belonged to a friend who had gone to do an errand before the clinic began. He had taken too long, Ree said, and she had put the dog inside the van with Sam for company. She held Rascal while we sat on the van's bumper to talk. Sam stuck his head out of the passenger-side window to keep track of everything around him. His alert brown eyes did not miss a thing. As the starting time for the clinic approached, people and dogs of all shapes and sizes gathered nearby. Sam began to whine and yip, yearning to get out and play. "That's probably his favorite thing on earth," Ree said, "playing with other dogs. I want to make sure he can do that." She had brought him to the clinic to have him neutered so that she could more easily allow him to interact with a mix of dogs.

While Sam kept lookout, I asked Ree to tell me more about her dogs and about her situation in general. She was in her early thirties and had grown up on the Northern Plains. She'd had no pets while growing up, because her parents had not wanted animals in the

Photograph by Mark Rodgers, courtesy of San Francisco Community Clinic Consortium's VET SOS project.

"My dog is my family."

house. "They didn't want pet hair," she said, "and they didn't think I'd take care of pets." They did allow her to have goldfish, and she bragged that one had lived for two years. But everything changed just a few months before she turned eighteen, when she moved in with her boyfriend, who had a dog. "I've had animals ever since. Mostly dogs, but cats, too." In the fifteen years that have passed since then, Ree had taken to the road many times, always with animals. She told me about a cat who had traveled with her to forty-six states. "I had to travel with a litter box and a lid. It was a pain in the butt, but I wasn't going anywhere without my cat," she said. The cat had run off when she stopped to pick up some hitchhikers, and after a long search she had to move on. Since then, she had opted for dogs, describing them as "more portable." She kissed Rascal on top of his head and said, "Always have to have my dogs."

Ree fits the description of what I call a "Straddler." But unlike some Straddlers, who make it off the streets but become homeless again because of hard luck, unemployment, addiction, eviction, or other circumstances, Ree claimed to enjoy episodic homelessness. To be sure, not knowing the range of options available to her at any one time made it difficult to assess her voluntaristic portrayal of her situation. But Ree's occasional rootedness made me think of her as a Straddler, rather than a Traveler. As she explained, "Sometimes I'll work for a while, and I'll have an apartment and everything. Then I'll get anxious and want to go travel, and I'll move into a vehicle. I love to travel and I love to live in a vehicle for a while, but then I always miss cable TV," she said, laughing. "Once I get a job, it's easy to get inside," she added, using the term I heard from many of the homeless. "And having a home is always nice, but after a while I just want to hit the road. Like I said, I can't seem to settle down anywhere."

Ree still had ties to home, albeit loose ones. Her mother periodically forwarded mail—on the rare occasions when Ree knew where she intended to go and how long she would stay. She planned to spend the summer in San Francisco and then head to the Midwest to visit her sister and see her infant niece for the first time. She thought she might stay with her sister for a while; then again, she didn't know. She named other places that called to her and places where she had friends who would welcome the dogs and her. She talked about some repairs the van would soon need, the registration that would eventually need renewal, and consequently the money she would have to earn. I asked her what kind of work she had done.

"All sorts of things," she told me. "Nothing to write home about. Waiting tables. Bartending. Landscaping. Demolition. You name it. I don't care what it is. If I need work, I can do whatever."

"Did you finish high school?" I asked.

"Barely," she said with a laugh, "but yeah, I managed to finish. Lot of good it did me, though. I still can't figure out what I want to be when I grow up. But I don't care, and my dogs don't care what kind of job I have. Or if I even have one. Doesn't matter what I do. I'll stay inside for a while and work at whatever and then if I'm not working a job I'll fly a sign."

"What does your sign say?"

"Just 'Need gas and food. Please help,'" she replied. I asked if she mentioned the dogs when panhandling, and her response was emphatic. "I don't exploit them," she said. "Never. I fly a sign, but I leave my dogs in the van when I go out and do it. I don't want to use my dogs." She explained that sometimes people would see her with the dogs, or see the dogs in the van, and ask if she needed food for them. But she seemed to want to distinguish herself from someone who would use dogs to arouse sympathy.

The clinic began, and Ree's early arrival paid off as they called her name first. As we said goodbye, she opened the door of the van to let Sam out. I wished her well. "We'll do all right," she said. "My dogs, they're always there. I might not know where I'm going, but I'm not going anywhere without my dogs. They're my best buds, my kids."

Stories of Animals as Friends and Family Members

Many people I interviewed described their animals as friends. Others considered them family members—never a sibling or a parent, but often a child or even a baby, with all the dependency that those terms imply. The narratives frequently suffused the identities of friend and family (Spencer and Pahl 2006). Ree had done this in calling Sam and Rascal both her "best buds" and her "kids." Stories that cast animals as friend or family respond to certain circumstances of homelessness, to uncertainty, liminality, and contingency in particular. In addition, friend and family stories reveal the ongoing construction of what I call the "promissory self."

The narrative of the animal as friend or family has this story line: "I once had a home and a different kind of life. I no longer have those things. I don't know what the future holds, but this animal will be with me." For example, when I talked with Gordon, whom we met in Chapter 3, we discussed what his dog, Radar, meant to him. He said, "We don't got a lot in life, you know? Like me, I had a lot. I had a house. I had all that. Now I don't have anything but I still have him." When Gordon "spoke for" Radar, he referred to himself as "Dad." "I call him my son all the time," he told me, adding that he often teased his biological son by calling Radar his "*good* son."

Overall, Gordon's personal narrative conveyed the tensions in his life, of having and losing, with his dog as a steady presence and source of consistency amid unpredictability. Similarly, in an interview at the Homeless Youth Alliance clinic, Katie also voiced these tensions. She described her dog, Luna, as "the one stable factor in my life." She described spending most of the previous year couch surfing with friends or sleeping in her boyfriend's van as they moved around, sometimes getting jobs for a while. "People are never stable," she said. "They come and they go. Cities—I'm always bouncing back and forth, and they come and they go. But I always have my dog." When Katie described her relationship with Luna as "like having a kid," I followed up with, "So, she's your family?" She answered, "Absolutely," but quickly added, "*and* my best friend."

Although several people suffused the identities of friend and family in their stories, as Katie and Ree had done, the analysis revealed subtle differences between the two. In general, personal narratives that characterize the relationship primarily as friendship emphasize the companionship the animal provides. They also emphasize the constancy of the animal's presence as a comfort. For example, I often heard phrases such as the following:

> "You know, it's just company. It's someone that is with you all the time. You know, we're just there for each other. It's company."
> "He provides companionship, comfort, the sense of not being alone."
> "My cat is my best friend. He's pretty much my only friend. It's very hard for me to meet people and make friends, so he's basically my best friend. He makes being lonely not so lonely."
> "I know that I've always got him, no matter what. He's always there for me and I'm going to be there for him, too."

In contrast, the narratives that depict the relationship in terms of family emphasize the depth and intensity of the relationship, especially as compared with human relationships. For example, Pete said, "I'm just incredibly attached to these dogs. I love these dogs more than I do most humans. They're my family. They really are." Another man, a Boulder Straddler, said of his dog, "She's my family. She keeps me happy. It's like having a child. I love her as much as people love their children." A young Straddler in Berkeley described his dog as "the only person that'll never turn their back on you. It's the only family that I've got. I have a couple other people that, I guess, would be considered family, but they don't do anything family-like. I talk to 'em on the phone, but that's about it." A young woman in Berkeley, another Straddler, echoed his sentiment: "Your dog is the only family you have when you're on the street," she said.

Animal-as-family narratives also emphasize responsibility and caregiving, again in comparison to a human relationship of parent and child. For example, Sherri found herself homeless with her dog after coming out as a lesbian to her parents. She said, "I want to say it's like having a kid. Can't say it's a kid exactly. It might be harder with a kid. But they definitely give you a sense of, 'Okay. You gotta get the ball rolling because we can't be like this.'" Katie described how being homeless meant that Luna had to go everywhere with her. "It's kind of like having a kid," she said. "You can't just take off and do whatever you want to do." In many cases, the language of parent and child intersects with that of friendship. When Ree had said of her dogs, "They're my best friends," and added, "They're my children, too," I asked her to explain, and her response combined companionship and responsibility.

"I don't have any children," she said, "but they're always there. They keep me from being alone. They are a big responsibility. When I get upset or depressed, I don't have to think about that. It gives me something to do. 'You gotta take care of your dogs,' I tell myself. 'Go play fetch with Sam. He needs exercise. Quit feeling sorry for yourself. You have things to do. You have animals to take care of.'"

When I listened to Whit, an African American man in Miami who frequently acquired canine companions as he wandered the streets, he offered another way of distinguishing friends from family. Whit had a long history of heavy drinking and drug use, but he was clean and sober when we met. He had a gentle terrier mix he called Jack, but he recalled having had as many as five dogs hanging around him at one time. He talked about some dogs as friends and described others as family. I asked him about the difference. He thought for a few minutes and gave me an example: "Sometimes you just walk down the street and you see this dog, and you start petting it, start feeding it, and next thing you know, he just follows you, and you got a friend. Then, another comes by, then another, and then I got five dogs following me. So for a while, you got dogs all over you. You got all those friends. Sometimes they'd be off on their own after a while. When they stayed with me, and slept with me, and kept me company, then they was my family. They *wanted* to stay near me."

The scholarship on friendship often points out one critical difference between friends and family: we choose our friends, but not our family. Whit had another way of looking at it. For Whit, the dogs' choice to stay or to wander factored into whether he considered them friends or family.

"On the street, did they sleep with you?" I asked.

"Oh, yeah," he replied. "They slept near me and wouldn't let nobody come near me. When I got to drinking or something, the cops couldn't come and wake me up, because [the dogs] wouldn't let 'em come to me. And next thing I know, I woke up and had a ticket said, 'There's your dogs. Go down to 72nd and wherever and get 'em.'"

Wanting to understand, I asked, "So they would take your dogs to the pound?"

He nodded and said, "Yeah. And I'd say, 'But I ain't got no car and I can't get 'em on the bus!' They told me that after so long, they going to put the dogs to sleep. I couldn't go get 'em back. I never got to see 'em no more. They took my family away! To me, that was my family. That was who I stayed with and slept with every night."

Tears had come to Whit's eyes, and we both kept silent for a few moments. After he had cleared his throat and wiped his eyes, I asked, "What did you do when that happened?"

"I felt so lost without 'em," he said. "They was all I had. In those days, I'd just drink a little bit more. The pain would go away, and I'd say to myself, 'Okay. You're all right now.'"

It might be tempting to attribute higher value to my descriptions of the "depth" and "intensity" associated with narratives of family than to the "companionship" and "comfort" of friendship, but I do not intend to give any greater status to one relationship or the other. In the context of relationships in general, some people might rank friendship higher than family relationships because of its chosen and autonomous qualities and the potential strains within families. At the same time, some might rank family higher than friendship, in line with the old saying that "blood is thicker than water." I acknowledge that these hierarchies exist, but I have no intention to place either family or friend at the top, nor do I have evidence that the narrators intended to do so either.

Responding to the Problems of the Recently Dislocated and Straddlers

I heard stories of friend and family most often from the Recently Dislocated and the Straddlers, or among those who were newly or episodically homeless. I heard the designation of friend more often than that of family. Overall, twenty-two people—eleven in each category—described their animals as friends. An additional sixteen described them as family members, with the Recently Dislocated slightly more likely than Straddlers to do so. To be sure, people in other categories of homelessness referred to their animals in these ways, too, but to lesser extents. Only a few Travelers, for example, described their animals as friends, and as Chapter 6 shows, they tended to assign their animals roles as protectors. Overall, the newly or episodically homeless showed a greater affinity for friend-and-family narratives than did those in other categories of homelessness. Men and women used the designation of friend equally. Men tended to define their animals as family members more often than women did, but both sexes used the construction of child in nearly equal numbers. One could speculate that the construction of the animal as child might reflect, and perhaps represent attempts to repair, the traumatic childhoods that many homeless people have in their histories, but the data do not allow me to draw that conclusion definitively.

    At first glance, the narratives of friend and family simply represent culturally recognized vocabularies for talking about animals. Homeless or otherwise, people often depict their companion animals as best friends or members of the family (Cain 1983, 1985; Hickrod and Schmitt 1982; Sanders 2003; Voith 1983). Is it any wonder that homeless people, too, draw on these vocabularies? Perhaps not, but this easy answer misses the opportunity to understand what these animal identities accomplish within the narratively constructed worlds of the homeless. This, in turn, requires knowing something about the unique circumstances faced by the Recently Dislocated and the Straddlers. The experiences differ slightly for each type of homelessness.

Uncertainty and the Recently Dislocated

The Recently Dislocated face the primary issue of uncertainty in their new situation. Every detail of life, whether finding shelter, parking, or the next meal, requires effort. More than one person used the term "skill set" when referring to becoming homeless. As Emily, a long-term Straddler whom we'll hear more from later in this chapter, told me, the newly homeless "are not prepared for scrambling just to survive every day." This uncertainty generates at least three responses, the first of which entails acquiring survival skills. In David Snow and Leon Anderson's 1993 study *Down on Their Luck,* the Recently Dislocated often turned to social service agencies that could provide food and shelter. Many worked at the Salvation Army in exchange for a meal and a bed.[1] Homeless pet owners do not have this option and must devise other survival strategies. For example, Max, a Recently Dislocated woman in San Francisco whom I interviewed, rented a room in a house with her husband and her dog. The place was a "squat," an unoccupied residence, but Max and her husband paid rent to the man who had found it and designated himself as the landlord. They preferred paying for an illegal squat to sleeping in Max's truck. As she explained, "Finding a place to sleep is the hardest thing. But if my dog's not welcome, hey, you know what? I only go where my dog's welcome. I didn't bring her into this situation just to dump her off in the street, or to put her in a kennel somewhere. It's a lifelong commitment. We're family." Max's account reveals how the narrative of friend and family serves as a form of what C. Wright Mills (1940) called "motive talk," a way of explaining questionable acts and problematic situations. In answer to my questions about housing, she and other Recently Dislocated tellers described their arrangements in terms of their commitment to animals. Doing so helps to construct a moral identity, a topic I return to later in this chapter.

Along with acquiring survival skills, the Recently Dislocated cope with uncertainty by learning whom to trust. Snow and Anderson found that because of fear, distrust, and a belief that one will soon get off the streets, those recently dislocated tend to avoid socializing with other homeless people (1993:47, 178–179). This can backfire, however, because those with experience on the street have survival skills to share. But for some of the people I interviewed, having a dog facilitated contact with what they saw as the "right kind" of homeless people, those who knew the ropes and shared their knowledge. For example, Kim and her partner became homeless after losing first their jobs and then their apartment in Sacramento. Both in their fifties, they moved to San Francisco to find work, and planned to sleep in their car with their dog, Maggie, for "a few nights, at most a week or two." That turned into four months, which Kim describes as "the craziest times I've ever lived through." She recalled:

> The hardest thing is to find out how and where to get help. We went to a couple of different programs, and each one, they all have their little piece of the pie, and not knowing that, I'd go through the door, and they're like, "Well, do you have this? Do you have that? Do you have G.A.?" Well, what's G.A.? I didn't know. I had no idea that you can't get anything until you do that. So I was in perpetual meltdown. We were always trying to find a good place to park. Then the car broke down, and we had to stay right where we were. This old drunk guy who used to sleep near where we parked, he just died last week, but he liked Maggie and he said he liked the way we were a little family. He was the one who told us how to do that [apply for General Assistance]. Because we had Maggie, she attracted the right kind of person. We wouldn't have known who to trust without that.

As Kim explained, getting any help at all requires knowing how to get help. A person would not know where to start unless she or he had needed help before. The man who admired Kim and her partner's relationship with Maggie turned out to be a wealth of information. When the car broke down, Kim and her partner did not know how to get Maggie on the bus. The same man told them how to do that, too. Maggie helped them overcome their initial wariness of him. As a social facilitator, Maggie bridged the worlds of the newly homeless and the street person. When I met Kim, she had gained some survival skills that allowed her to navigate the social service bureaucracy. Her living situation had become more stable. She and her partner and Maggie had found a weekly rental in a single-room occupancy hotel and had made it onto a list for permanent housing. She stroked Maggie's satiny black fur as she added, "There's no way we would know the people we know, or be as comfortable in the circumstances we're in, were it not for her."

Another response to uncertainty involves trying to eliminate it by attempting to get off the street. The newly homeless often divide their energies between learning how to navigate a new and perplexing situation and trying to return to the domiciled life. In the role of friends and family, animals help in both aspects. For example, Maggie played an important role as a guide to material resources, but she also gave Kim and her partner a sense of emotional normalcy. As Kim said, "Maggie reminds us of what life can be like. She really is the whole thing. She's my friend and family. She gives me that little piece of 'I'm still here.'" Although many of the domiciled describe their animals as friends and family, too, few of us rely on them for this degree of existential certainty. For those who are newly homeless, having an animal in the role of friend or family member serves as a reminder of what life can be like.

Animals can also provide an incentive to get off the streets. At a VET SOS clinic, I met Isaac, an African American man in his twenties, and his dog, Raja, a tan pit bull. We sat under a tree and talked while Isaac waited for Dr. Strubel to examine Raja. Isaac explained that he was a cocaine and heroin addict. He had stayed clean for many years, but relapsed and "ended up on the streets." Just within the month before we met, he had entered a treatment program. Raja, whom he called his "best friend in all the world," had provided comfort but also motivated Isaac to get into treatment. "We were on the streets," he said, "sometimes in motels. Always moving around. It was hard. I had to hide him 'cause a lot of motels didn't allow dogs so I had to sneak him in. I got kicked out of a bunch of motels because when they came in and cleaned they seen him, and said, 'You got to go. Got to leave.' There's only been like two nights that we actually slept on the street all night, me and him."

"What was that like?" I asked.

"Oh, it was . . . it was pretty bad," he said. Then he shook his head and corrected himself. "It was terrible, actually, but I felt a little better because I had him with me. We had a blanket, so it was okay, but it was still rough. I didn't want to stay rough like that, so that's why I came into treatment, so we could have a better life. I got tired of living the way I was living. But me having him, I realized I didn't want to live like this. I didn't want to make the dog suffer, my best friend, living like this, homeless. I need to get myself together. I can have me a better life, and he can have a better life. That's how I looked at it."

Isaac decided to go into treatment and, after some difficulty, found a program that would allow Raja to accompany him. "The program people seen how much love I have for this dog," he said, "and they allowed him to come with me. He brightens my day every day. He keeps me going. He's a big part of my life. I really love him."

For the Recently Dislocated, such as Isaac and Kim, the narrative of animals as best friends and family responds to and mitigates the problems that face the newly homeless. The emotional ties help the Recently Dislocated cope with the uncertainty of street life. They provide a reminder of life off the street, as well as an incentive to work toward the goal of getting back to that life, or even to a better version of it.

Straddlers and Liminality

The issues differ for Straddlers, who have experienced street life before. As Snow and Anderson (1993) point out, Straddlers must cope with status ambiguity, or liminality (Turner 1967; Van Gennep 1961). The word "liminality" has its origins in the Latin term for "threshold," and Straddlers indeed exist within this ambiguity, positioned "betwixt and between" the domiciled world and life on the streets (Turner 1967:93; see also Snow and Anderson 1993:52). Austin's experience exemplifies the liminality of the Straddler status. He had found himself homeless multiple times. "I don't know how to count them anymore," he said. "Sometimes I think I have a home and then I find out I don't, and I'm on the street again." When we met, Austin was couch surfing in the homes of friends, but he sometimes had to sleep outdoors when friends could not accommodate him. He described his dog—the "super-cute" poodle mix we met in Chapter 3—as his family. He looked at me over the top of his glasses and said, by way of explanation, "I'm from Texas, and I never thought I'd say that about a little 'foo-foo' dog like this, but having him makes a world of difference because it keeps me going. It makes me feel like I belong."

Emily, another Straddler, depicted the liminal status well. For over a decade, she had bounced on and off the streets with her dog, Hobo, whom she called her best friend. Now in middle age, Emily recounted how her homelessness began:

> The first time I became homeless, what started this all out is, I was in an automobile accident, and I was in a coma for about two and a half months. And when I came to—see, I had been renting, and

my apartment was gone. I had been evicted while I was in the hospital in a coma. Everyone thought I was dead, except for my best friend. He said, "She's still somewhere." So he had put Hobo and my other dog in a kennel and was paying that bill. My friends put my car and things in storage. So when I got out of the hospital, I realized I was going to be homeless. I sold my car and bought a little truck with a trailer and we lived in the trailer. I thought it'd be just for a little bit. It was four years, because I couldn't find a place to rent with an eviction and the dog, no matter what. [Referring to Hobo. She found a home for her other dog.] So I'd gone downtown to cash my check, and I got mugged coming out of the check-cashing place. I went to the hospital because some of my teeth were knocked out. I was really a mess. Got out of the hospital. And when I'm coming down the street—I've got blood on me and my face is swollen—and I ran into someone from the old life, from when I was working and part of society, and they wanted to know what happened to me, and I told them in a nutshell, and two days later, they came back and said, "We don't have a house for you, but we have a place that can get you off the street with the dog." And they let me move into a junkyard. And I lived there for four years.

Pali Boucher, introduced in Chapter 2, came to visit Emily and heard gunfire from automatic weapons in the area. Pali posted a "Can you help my friend?" ad on Craigslist. The ad generated a living situation in a very rural area, where Emily could do some work in exchange for rent. She lived there another four years. But then she developed serious health problems, and in the course of treating them, doctors diagnosed her as HIV-positive. She moved back to San Francisco for treatment. "You need to be where it's cutting-edge," she said. "If you're going to take care of yourself, you need to be where they know what they're doing." She was living in another junkyard when we met. Hobo was now advanced in age, and she said, "What time we have left, I just want it to be quality. He is the most important thing to me. I'll live in that junkyard until he's gone. When the time comes that I lose him, I'll lose him. But not before."

"What then?" I asked her.

She had modest hopes, saying that she would want to get out of the junkyard and into a single room occupancy.

Emily's personal narrative manifests numerous liminal experiences, including a coma and encounters that contrast homelessness with her "old life" as "part of society." But if one lives on the streets long enough or often enough, even liminality can become routine and predictable. Over time, Straddlers usually make a number of friends on the street, or at the very least become tolerant and unafraid of other homeless people. In addition, they find sources of food and places to stay. Thus, Straddlers do not face the same unfamiliar and often frightening world that confronts the Recently Dislocated.

Precisely because most Straddlers become adapted to homelessness, they usually spend a considerable amount of time waiting within the context of their routines (see also Snow and Anderson 1993). They may have found out where to eat, such as a soup kitchen, but they must wait for serving time and, if they have a pet, must also wait for a friend to arrive to watch that pet, since animals are typically not allowed in facilities that feed the homeless. They may have found out how to get SSI benefits or food stamps, but only by waiting for appointments, waiting for the bus to get to the Social Security office, and waiting for notification of eligibility. They wait for checks to arrive and housing to become available. For those with pets, they also wait at veterinary clinics, which is what gave me the chance to interview them and predisposed them to talk. In the world of the domiciled, most of us would become infuriated at having to wait longer than twenty minutes or so in a veterinarian's office. Those familiar with life on the streets, however, take it in stride. For homeless pet owners, the companionship of an animal helps them cope with what I call "the tyranny of waiting." For example, Austin explained that having a dog occupied the time between when he woke up (when he was outdoors, he was often rousted early from his sleep by police) and when the city became active and he could find somewhere to hang out legitimately. He said: "It's lonely when you have to find somewhere to be at six in the morning until like, nine, ten, when things are open, and if you have a dog companion with you it gives you something to do, somewhere to go. You can come out to the park here and sit out here longer than you could do if you were by yourself. If I didn't feel the way I do about him, I wouldn't have him, because it's a lot of hassle sometimes. But he's family, and so he's with me all the time and that helps."

Austin's account points out how homelessness involves not only waiting for specific things such as appointments to happen, but also just waiting for time to pass. In Elliot Liebow's ethnography of a homeless shelter in Washington, D.C., he found that "killing time" ranked "high on most women's lists of hardships" (1993:29). When the women left this shelter each morning, the reality of their homelessness hit them, as they had to decide how to spend their day. But, as Liebow explained, when one is homeless, "You can't decide what to do because it doesn't matter what you do. You're not needed anywhere, not wanted anywhere, and not expected anywhere. Nobody cares what you do" (1993:30). He noted that when the women had tasks to accomplish, they often spread them out rather than trying to accomplish them quickly, and would structure an entire day around a single appointment. What might look to most of us like laziness or procrastination in fact provided a way to "distribute structure and meaning" in an otherwise uneventful stretch of time (1993:31–32). Similarly, Jason Wasserman and Jeffrey Clair noted in their study that "for those on the street, passing time becomes something of an art" (2010:125).

When I interviewed Mike, a white Straddler in his late twenties whom I met at the Mercer Veterinary Clinic in Sacramento, he described the blurred distinction between waiting for things to happen and waiting for time to pass. Mike's history included addiction and jail time. We talked as he waited for his dog, Ziggy, to be examined in preparation for neutering. I had seen Mike ride up on his bicycle long before the clinic was scheduled to start. His bike had a trailer attached, and in it he carried not only his few possessions but Ziggy, too. Mike had recently acquired Ziggy and the two had been camping in a tent, moving from park to park, evading rangers and the police. He described a typical day:

> We wake up. [Ziggy] wanders around a little bit, peeing and whatnot. I break camp and walk over here [Loaves and Fishes]. Get my lunch ticket. Go out to the street. Sit on Ahearn [Street] right there, because he's not allowed in the kennel yet [until neutered]. And we wait for lunch. I'll take a shower every two days, every three if it's cool out. I've got only two people that I let watch him. I go over to the Mission after that. I get dinner over there. I can't eat dinner in there because I can't bring the dog in, but they'll bring some food outside. . . . He occupies a lot of my time. A lot of it, and I love it.

Once neutered, Mike would be able to board Ziggy free of charge in the kennels at the Loaves and Fishes facility during the day. (Pet owners must walk their dogs twice each day and clean the kennel at day's end.) He would then be able to eat and shower without first finding someone trustworthy to watch his dog.

In addition to waiting as a part of each day, Mike waited in a "bigger picture" sense, for a future that held a different kind of life.

At the time I interviewed him, he was soon to learn his SSI status, and he would be getting off parole in ten days. Ziggy figured heavily in his plans. I asked him what would change when his parole ended. "I'm not going to do nothing to go back! [to jail] I'm just not going to do anything to go back. I'm not going to do stupid stuff. And now, I've got Ziggy. The responsibility of just having a dog is a step in the right direction, you know? I finally feel like I know what I'm doing."

For Straddlers, such as Mike, the friend-and-family narrative can provide a structure for daily life. For the Recently Dislocated, the narrative provides an anodyne for the uncertainty that accompanies their new status. In both cases, the animal represents hope. Consequently, possibility and promise characterize the stories of the self that emerge from these narratives.

The Promissory Self

Whether Recently Dislocated or Straddler, the teller of the friend-and-family narrative portrays him- or herself in hopeful, if tentative, terms. Ree's story illustrated this when she assured me that she would be okay. Kim, Mike, and others had plans for getting off the street. Those plans, however, depended on a chain of events largely out of their control.

As discussed, Straddlers must cope primarily with liminality, and for the Recently Dislocated, the main issue is uncertainty. For both groups, life remains very much up in the air. A better future, and perhaps even a life off the streets, is possible, but by no means certain. That future depends on a sequence of conditions falling into place. For example, I asked Kim how long she and her partner expected to have to wait for housing, and she said, "If all goes well, we think about a year." They simply did not know, and would not know, until it happened. Similarly, Austin said, "I thought I was getting [an apartment], but that was then, and I was stonewalled. I know that I will be getting one, I just have no idea when." Mike was counting on qualifying for SSI and getting off parole. Emily was looking forward to moving out of the junkyard, although she did not want to think about Hobo's demise. But none of them could influence the outcome beyond taking the essential steps along the way. In the meantime, much can happen to derail hopes and plans for getting off the streets (see also Snow and Anderson 1993:183–186). Time alone takes its toll. In Liebow's study, for example, he found that "the greatest threats to survival were discouragement and disappointment" (1993:178). To avoid these twin demons, the women he met kept their expectations low and developed a "one day at a time" philosophy. Although this staved off negativity, it also had its costs, including a failure to plan, even for the near future. Among the people I interviewed, I found that giving animals the identities of friend or family in one's narrative itself constitutes a form of planning. It helps dispel the contingent nature of daily life, this thinking that "I don't know what the future holds, but this animal will be there, and I will be there for him or her." Perhaps more accurately, the narrative *conceals* the contingency. Doing so, in turn, provides some of the normalcy enjoyed by the domiciled. Those of us with jobs and homes face contingency, too, but we can stave it off with schedules, insurance, savings, planning, diets, exercise programs—and denial. For the newly or episodically homeless, however, contingency has an "in your face" character.

The teller of the friend-and-family narrative gains elements of stability and predictability within an unstable, unpredictable lived experience. Ree, for example, contrasted her restlessness and her lack of interest in an occupation against her commitment to her dogs. Katie emphasized how people and places come and go, but how her dog was always there. Kim spoke of Maggie's role in learning how to get help and Austin told of how his dog helped him cope with the waiting. In these examples, as in others, the relationship with one's animal companion provides a refuge from uncertainty. Just having the animal to care for brings responsibility, reliability, and consistency to lives that have few conventional means of attaining these qualities. At the same time, the feeling of being needed that comes from the animal's dependence brings emotional benefits. For example, Ree found that the responsibilities of caring for her dogs lifted her spirits when she felt sorry for herself; the dogs reminded her that she had things to do.

As a self-story, the narrative of friend and family also conveys a sense of acceptance, an especially important element for selves that are *promissory:* neither what they once were nor what the tellers hope them to be. In the context of this tentativeness, the perceived unconditional love offered by an animal acts as a balm. The relationship with one's animal provides stability and certainty in the midst of uncertainty and contingency. Because it exists in a realm apart from the street, the relationship provides a point of permanence in a shifting terrain of the self. Much as a toddler exploring a room repeatedly returns to the parent before venturing off again, the relationship with the animal offers a way for uncertain selves to check in and then rest in security. Although the teller may not know where his or her next meal will come from, the animal provides important elements of predictability and permanence.

Granted, everyone has a promissory self to some extent. Sustaining a sense of self is never a fait accompli. None of us can know the future, and we all face existential questions along the road. The homeless do not have a monopoly on the act of imagining and anticipating how life could change if only one thing or another were to happen. But subjectivity is always embedded in social structure, and the personal narratives told by those who are newly or episodically homeless show how the story of the promissory self emerges from the narrative of animal as friend and family, in concert with certain conditions of homelessness. The emphasis on having a reliable friend or family member both reveals and responds to the promissory self.

The Power and Limitations of the Friend-and-Family Narrative

For the homeless tellers of this story, much of its power lies in its ability to bestow or restore a moral identity and a sense of self-worth, especially when resources for positive personal significance are in short supply. For those who are newly or episodically homeless, the promissory sense of self, with its hopes and goals for getting off the street, suggests that the person is directing him- or herself toward what one might generally call "the good." By drawing on the discourses of "friend" and "family," a homeless person connects this orientation toward the good with the self. The narrative suggests that the teller believes him- or herself to be a particular kind of person, one who is trustworthy and keeps his or her word.

Defining one's commitment in terms of friendship or family ties accomplishes what Jack Katz described as turning *acts* into *essences*. As Katz explained, an essence is "some inner quality of being, distinct from and additional to" conduct or activity (1975:1370). The examples of the new wife, widow, and lawyer illustrate how people can engage in actions without sensing that they "essentially possess those identities" associated with particular lines of conduct (1975:1370). In other words, one can act without seeing oneself as any certain kind of person. Yet the doing and the being, though distinct, are related. People tend to understand essences as providing the moral foundation for behavior. Consequently, people give moral significance to essences, believing them to capture and convey who a person really is.

In the case of animal companionship, the behaviors involved in providing care, taken alone, do not indicate any essence within the person enacting them. One could have a companion dog or cat without inherently sensing oneself to be any particular kind of person, moral or otherwise. The behaviors require a story in order to have meaning. As Katz explained, this meaning is created using nouns rather than verbs, but he referred "not to grammatical forms but to forms of understanding or meaning" (1975:1374, n. 4). For example, to say that someone drinks a lot is different from calling him or her an alcoholic. As a noun, the word "alcoholic" connotes an essence, and one with moral significance. Similarly, the designations of "friend" and "family" convey an essential morality. When a homeless person describes an animal companion as a friend or family member, the teller becomes a moral actor, someone worthy of friendship and family ties. For example, I heard the following from a young male Straddler: "Every day, all day long, I'm doing something for this dog that she can't do for herself. She is the closest thing that I think I'll ever have to a kid. This is my baby. And that makes me feel real good, real validated about me. She does not want to be apart from me, and that's really cool. It's unconditional love on both our parts, both sides of it." In this case, the speaker connects his acts as a guardian, indeed, as virtual parent, with a positive sense of self-worth. His account conveys a message about his essence: essentially good and caring, despite any feedback to the contrary he might receive from others or through self-judgments.

For tellers, this narrative has at least two limitations. First, although it bestows or restores moral agency and self-worth, it remains unclear—at least in my analysis—how far these benefits reach. The validation expressed by the Straddler just quoted, while valuable for his sense of self-worth, does not solve any of the material problems of life on the streets. Moreover, validation in one context might not carry over to other parts of one's sense of self. By connecting the telling of a friend-and-family narrative with a *moral* identity, I make no claims about the state of the tellers' lives and conduct outside of their relationships with their animals. I do not want to portray the narrators as angelic beings who never engage in any wrongdoing, nor do I want to romanticize homelessness or human-animal relationships. Rather, my claims about morality apply only to how the friend-and-family narrative supports a positive identity, especially within the context of the orientations of those who find themselves newly or episodically on the streets.

A second limitation of this narrative has to do with the imposition of the rhetoric of unconditional love and other experiences associated with friendship and family membership onto animals. This rhetoric appears in other narratives, too, but the closeness implied by friendship and family relationships made it especially common here. What we sense as "unconditional love" from an animal might have a better explanation, one that reflects the animal's reality more accurately. When we say that an animal loves us, we risk mischaracterizing the animal's ways of knowing, and we set human limits on its already complex social and emotional arrangements. As Arnold Arluke has put it:

> These views of perfect love from our pets persist, despite evidence to the contrary. The "one-person dog" is a myth. Animal behaviorists point out that the focused attention given to us by our pets is just the animal's pack behavior, orienting itself to the available human alpha male. Switch the owner and our pet's "loyalty" and "love" for us get switched to the next person. Cognitive ethologists add that while animals experience a range of emotions, we are on thin ice to assume that animals experience the same emotions felt by humans; even if they did, the intensity and meaning of these emotions would probably be different. Moreover, when owners are pressed to explain this perfect love, it is one-way because they put their own conditions on this idyllic relationship, imposing financial, physical, temporal, and emotional limitations on what their pets can expect of them. (2010:35)

Donna Haraway has called the imposition of "unconditional love" on dogs "pernicious." She claims that the emotions people feel for dogs "might be properly called love if that word were not so corrupted by our culture's infantilization of dogs and the refusal to honor difference" (2003:33, 39). She points out that we place a heavy burden on animals when we enlist them as friends and family members.

A person who claims to love his or her animal companion unconditionally today might face circumstances that set conditions on that commitment tomorrow. If I were to undertake a longitudinal study of homeless people and their pets, I would want to see how many "best friends" and "family members" remained with the same guardians over time. To be sure, the same commitment issues affect the domiciled, too, as evidenced by the numbers of animals surrendered to shelters annually (Irvine 2003). But the larger point here is one artfully made by Erving Goffman: what we know as the Thomas Theorem—that what we define or interpret as real will have real consequences—is "true as it reads but false as it is taken."[2] Goffman wrote that "defining situations as real certainly has consequences, but these may contribute very marginally to the events in progress" (1974:1). To put this in the context of the narrative of animal as friend and family, defining animals in this way does have consequences, but the hardships of the street, along with other challenges faced by those who must live there, constitute "events in progress" that four-legged friends and family members can neither change nor resolve.

* * *

At one of the VET SOS clinics, I talked with a woman who lived in her car with her cat. We discussed the various roles that animals can have in our lives. Our conversation turned to the stereotypical images in television commercials, in which the affable Golden Retriever plays with the children in the well-manicured yard or lounges with the family in the comfortably furnished living room, or the handsome cat curls up with the attractive couple on the couch. The woman said, "You know, when you have a home, your relationships with animals take place *at* home. But when you're homeless, they *are* your home." This image of *animals as home* struck me deeply. I listened carefully during other interviews, but no one else expressed it quite so well. Whatever the pitfalls in the language of "friend" and "family" may be, tellers do not use these terms to describe casual acquaintanceship. The narratives of animal as friend and family attest to a felt sense of emotional support, consistency, and predictability, qualities not easily found on the street. The narratives also serve as a reminder that we can only understand and meet the needs of the homeless if we take their relationships with their pets seriously.

Notes

1. Snow and Anderson point out that because the Salvation Army prohibits those who work there from socializing with other homeless people, at least at the time and in the location of their research, "the antipathy of the recently dislocated toward other homeless makes them prime candidates for jobs" at the organization (1993:181).

2. The Thomas Theorem claims: "If men define situations as real, they are real in their consequences" (Thomas and Thomas 1928:571–572).

5 The "Pack of Two"

While writing this book, I learned about Teresa Bush, a homeless woman in Durango, Colorado, and her six-year-old dog, Gyzmo.[1] One day in late September 2011, Gyzmo was waiting for Teresa while she used the bathroom in a popular downtown restaurant. In Teresa's absence, Gyzmo bit a passerby. The police arrived, ticketed Teresa with having a vicious dog and not displaying rabies tags, and impounded Gyzmo at the La Plata County Humane Society.[2] Gyzmo remained there until early November, when the case came before a judge. Just before the proceedings, Teresa reflected on the separation in an article in the *Durango Herald*. She said, "That dog is everything to me. She is me. I don't feel safe or whole without her." The paper quotes an acquaintance as saying, "I think she'll die without that dog."

The story ended happily. Teresa pleaded guilty to owning a vicious dog, and the judge ordered Gyzmo released to her. Gyzmo now had to wear a muzzle in public. The judge waived all fines except a five-dollar surcharge. The bite victim recovered.

Teresa Bush's depiction of her relationship with her dog as "everything to me," even her conviction that "she is me," struck a familiar chord. For the tellers of the stories in this chapter, animals make up so much of their lives that they cannot imagine living without them. That prospect becomes, if not impossible, then surely unthinkable. This kind of relationship came through in many narratives, and I begin with two examples. The first comes from Don, the resident of the San Francisco freeway encampment who appeared in Chapter 2. After that, Candy tells her story.

Don's Story

Fifty-one-year-old Don works as a "scrapper," which means he collects large metal items to sell to brokers. Many homeless people recycle for money.[3] The most visible are those who collect bottles, cans, and cardboard, pushing overladen carts or hauling bulky plastic bags to recycling centers. As Teresa Gowan explains, recycling keeps many of the homeless from relying on welfare; one of her informants said it kept him from having to deal with "poverty pimps" to get money. It also helps them avoid "the humiliation and anomie of panhandling" (2010:154). Recyclers occupy a distinct ecological niche in cities, and scrappers like Don occupy a niche within the recycling trade. Scrappers focus mostly on ferrous metals, or iron and steel. They will also collect nonferrous scrap metal, including aluminum sheeting, insulated wire, engine parts, and other items. They keep track of the varying prices of brass, lead, zinc, nickel, and various grades of copper, and they know how much the different buyers will pay. Moreover, Don and his friend Steve have created a specialty within scrapping. When they helped someone clean out a storage yard some time ago, they found a small boat with an outboard motor. The motor did not run and the yard owner did not want to have it repaired. He told Don and Steve that if they could haul it away, they could have it. Don put his mechanical skills to work, and the boat was soon seaworthy. He and Steve began using it to troll for metal lost in the water. "I don't have any real job skills," Don told me. "I know how to go to jail and that's about it. With this," he said, referring to scrapping, "I'm just doing the best I can."

Scrapping involves hard, physical labor in dirty, dangerous conditions. As we talked about the work, Don held his hands out to show me the rust stains and scars. He said that sometimes his hands become so sore and swollen from pulling metal out of the saltwater that he cannot make a fist. I asked about a tetanus shot, and he assured me that he had taken care of that.

Don had been out in the boat working when Dr. Strubel, Maya, and I arrived. We soon saw the boat enter the cove by the freeway, with Don at the wheel and a dog in the stern. As Don secured the boat at one of the piers, the dog, named Ace, hopped ashore to greet us. Another dog, Rowdy, joined us from the encampment. Don and Dr. Strubel talked for a few minutes. Don's other dog, Axel, was being treated for an injured paw, which Dr. Strubel had noticed on the visit I describe in Chapter 2. Scrapping poses risks for dogs, too;

the injury had occurred because some salvaged cable had rolled onto Axel's paw. A friend of Don's had agreed to allow Axel to recover in the comfort and safety of her RV. Once Dr. Strubel had the information she needed, Don and I sat down to talk. Ace and Rowdy played and wrestled with Maya, who has a soft spot for pit bulls.

Ace came over, leaned against Don's leg, and looked up at him with the big "smile" that pit bulls often have when they pant. As Don told me about scrapping, Ace reminded me why I was there. Ace squinted into the bright morning sun as Don rubbed him behind his right ear. To get things started, I asked Don to help me keep track of the seemingly endless stream of dogs in the encampment. It turned out that there were only four of them, all black pit bulls and all related. The story of how they came to live together began with a situation few of the domiciled would ever face. As Don explained:

> I had a dog named Hemi. You had to kind of keep your eye on Hemi because he was very protective of me. And I was staying—it was during a period of time when I wasn't staying down here. I was staying up at another place that was state property, like this, and the state police came up there, and Hemi wasn't on his leash, and he encountered the police in the path, and there was a confrontation, and the police pointed their guns at me, and my dog went after the police and they shot and killed him.

Although some time had passed since the shooting, Don was still upset by this. He started to choke up, but he continued his story: "And my friend Steve's dog had just had a litter, and he heard about it, and he came out and he said, 'Bro, my heart goes out to you but if you want another dog, Rowdy just had a litter, you got the pick. Come out and get one.'" Steve was the same man who now worked with Don. A year later, Don acquired a second dog, Axel, from the same mother. Now Steve, Don, and their four dogs lived and worked together. "I've always loved dogs," Don said. "I've always had a dog. I can't remember a time when I haven't. People don't recognize me if I'm not walking down the street with a dog, you know? They're going, 'Oh, that *is* you! You didn't have your dog with you.' I take my dogs everywhere with me."

"I can see you love them," I said. "Tell me what they mean to you."

"The world," he said, without missing a beat. "They're my rock. My everything." He paused for a moment. Tears welled up in his eyes, and when he spoke again, his voice quavered. He cleared his throat and continued:

How can I put it? You know, it's like sometimes you go out, and things aren't working out for you. Your pockets are empty and you come home and you got no food, you got no nothing. And people get disappointed at that, that you don't have anything, you know, that you haven't come home with something. I'm out here because of that. I limit myself to my friends because I continuously find myself disappointed. Disappointed at the way people are, you know? So I'm down here because I just don't want to be around people. And frankly, I don't know if it's a conscious effort to make it like this, you know, to dump all the garbage around here, but it keeps people away. It's like a comfort zone that way. A bubble. I'm just basically trying to stay out of the way.

When Don and I made small talk before the interview began, I learned that he and I were the same age. We had "high-fived" about being born the same year, 1958. During this research, when I met other homeless people who were my age, it humbled me to reflect on the different courses our lives had taken during the same span of time. Listening to Don talk about his disappointment made me wonder how I would get the discussion back to the dogs, but after we sat in silence for a moment, he gestured toward them and said, "And it's a selfish thing, but they help me more than I help them. They do!"

"How do they do that?" I asked.

"Because they're there. And they're happy to see me. And they love me. And it's unconditional. There's nothing, there's no conditions or expectations put on that. That's what's so great about dogs. It doesn't matter what's going on. They're just happy to see you."

He paused again. His lips trembled, and he pressed them tightly together for a few seconds. I felt a lump in my throat. I looked away and focused on the dogs frolicking nearby.

"Those cats right there," he said as he pointed to the dogs. We exchanged glances and both smiled at his word choice, and he said, "They don't care if you got a million dollars or you got nothing, or if you had the worst day in your life or the best day. They're just happy to see you."

Ace came up to us and plopped down on his side, asking for attention. Then he rolled over on his back, exposing his belly for a rub. Don took the cue, scratched him, and continued: "They don't lie to you," he said, "and they don't steal from you." He wiped his eye on the sleeve of his t-shirt and added, "And they'll take a bullet for you. They will. I've seen it."

Candy's Story

A second example also comes from San Francisco. When I accompanied Dr. Strubel on another "house call," we drove to where Candy lived, in a vehicle storage yard tucked within an industrial area. We parked and I helped unload some veterinary supplies. As we moved boxes and crates, Candy walked out from a narrow passage between a building and an abandoned vehicle. I guessed her age at about sixty. She was a stocky, transgendered woman with long, gray hair, large, pendulous breasts unencumbered by a bra, and three days' worth of gray stubble on her face. She wore black jeans, black shoes, and a black t-shirt, and she had a female tabby cat in a carrier. She set the carrier down while Dr. Strubel treated the cat for ear mites, and then asked about the others. Candy led us through the passage to her home: a "Type A" school bus, the short kind that accommodates ten to twenty passengers. The bus was painted black over the familiar yellow-orange. Even the windows were painted black. Candy invited me to look inside, and I saw that the seats had been removed to create one open space. Here, Candy, her lover, and their cats had made their home for five years. Candy had been homeless for ten years before moving into the bus. At the time I visited, she was caring for fifteen cats. They played, slept, groomed, and wound around our legs as Candy and I talked in the "kitchen," a tarp spread out near the entrance of the bus. Electric cords ran into one of the adjacent buildings where the owner of one of the businesses had agreed to provide power for an electric skillet and other appliances, such as the television in the bus.

All the cats had names and stories. Most had come to Candy with injuries or illnesses. Some had been dumped in the yard. Candy said, "When they get done with their animals, people just throw them in these lots and let them go." A few cats had arrived pregnant, and Candy found homes for the kittens, or at least for most of them; she always ended up keeping some. "All my cats are spayed or neutered, with the help of VET SOS, and all of them have their rabies shots and all that."

"I started collecting them about ten years ago," she told me. I found her choice of words interesting. "Collecting" is how authorities and counselors refer to "hoarding." But Candy seemed to have the care of the cats under control, thanks largely to VET SOS. She continued:

It was hard before we moved here because I had to keep 'em in a big carrier and push 'em around on my cart. And my first kitten—this one here—was given to me because her mother was attacked by rats while she was giving birth. The mother died, so [my friends] gave me her and her brother. And then ever since, people have been giving me kitties. The last one I got is Lucky. I found her in a garbage can. I was collecting cardboard to sell it, and she was in a cardboard box. That's Lucky, over there.

Candy pointed to a large cat lounging on her side in a sunbeam. Lucky indeed, I thought. She then pointed out two young cats wrestling nearby and said, "A building was being torn down, and I guess the mother was feral. My friends were able to rescue the kittens, but they couldn't catch mom, and they needed a surrogate, so I got to bottle feed 'em, which is something I enjoy doing. It keeps me busy. Now they're ready to go to new homes." People who knew that Candy would take them in had brought other cats to her. VET SOS was helping with the veterinary care, but Candy was providing the tender loving care. She was receiving an SSI check each month and budgeting money for cat food. VET SOS was providing donated food, too. She described how all the cats would come into the bus at night and wander the yard during the day, never straying too far from the open cans of cat food.

I asked if she ever found it just too much, taking care of so many cats. "Oh, no," she assured me. "Animals are a godsend, and if somebody else doesn't want 'em, I'll gladly take 'em. There's no limit on how many I could love."

"Do you see yourself, down the road, getting a real house or an apartment?" I asked.

"No," she answered emphatically.

"So you see this as permanent?" I asked.

"Oh, hopefully," she said. "I hope it's permanent. I've been here five years, and living here has been great. And besides, where would I go with all these cats?"

Narrative Themes

The personal narratives that deploy constructions of animals as "everything" do not follow a unitary plot, in the sense of an account of a succession of things happening. Unlike the narratives of friend and family, and those in the chapters that follow, the narratives of "everything" do not describe sequences of events. The notion of "everything," a signifier of extreme attachment, emerged in response to my asking people what their animals meant to them. As a statement of meaning, it represents an intense bond, which develops in different ways in different people's relationships with their animals. Two themes predominated in my analysis of the narratives. One has to do with a felt sense of emotional support, such as the "they'll take a bullet" bond Don feels with his dogs. A second involves rescue, especially when it comes to organizing one's life, as Candy's story suggests. To be sure, in lived experience and in narrative, the two often overlap. Candy and others who rescue animals can also claim to feel a close emotional bond with them. Nevertheless, I examine the characteristics of each theme separately before discussing their similar roles in the construction of the self and the maintenance of a sense of personal significance.

Emotional Support

The stories of how people sensed emotional support from their animals ranged from Don's poignant account to the straightforward and succinct version I heard from Stan, who said of Roxy, "She keeps me happy." Other stories, such as the one I heard from Gordon, fell somewhere in between. When we talked about what Radar meant to him, it took Gordon a few minutes to find words. At first, he said only, "He's my companion that I'll always be with." After a moment, he added, "Having a dog means a lot to us," nodding toward the other pet owners waiting at the Mercer Clinic. Then he seemed to hit his stride. He went on: "It's our whole life. It's something that we still get to treat good and that loves us no matter what. Doesn't care what we have. Doesn't care that we don't have a home. Doesn't care, you know? Something that will stay with us, and watch over us, and take care of us."

Gordon ran his hand along Radar's flank as the big dog lounged on his side in the sun. "He brings a lot of happiness," he said. "He brings a lot of love." Then he smiled and added, "He'll tell you himself." He glanced at some other men nearby, and they chuckled and nodded knowingly. One said, "You gotta see this." Gordon showed Radar a tennis ball and the dog sat up at full attention. Gordon then asked him, "Do you love Daddy?" Sure enough, in the garbled growling manner heard among many "talking" dogs on YouTube videos, Radar lifted his snout high and said, "Ri ruv raddy," which Gordon interpreted for me as "I love Daddy." People around us laughed, despite having seen the trick many times. Gordon tossed the ball to Radar. He caught it mid-air, and then lay down again and gnawed at the prize while holding it between his front paws.

Most stories of emotional support incorporated several aspects of hardship in the teller's life. For example, when I asked Paulette to elaborate on her statement that her little white dog, Chalkie, lifted her spirits, she began with an "acquisition story." Paulette is African American, in her mid-fifties, a native of San Francisco. She and her husband acquired Chalkie from a friend who moved and could not take the dog with him. When we met, they'd had Chalkie for a year. Paulette said, "When that guy gave him to us, he really did us a favor. He had no idea."

Paulette told me that she had lived with her husband and Chalkie in a van for three months since their landlord evicted them from their apartment. "The landlord and my husband got into an argument and he just put us out," she explained, without going into details about the disagreement. I asked her what it was like living in the van. She waved off any concerns I had and said, "Oh, we got a bed, a microwave, a TV, a refrigerator, all that in there, so we make it." She continued, explaining, "We stay on the same street all the time. We move from one side to the other for street sweeping." Both Paulette and her husband were receiving SSI payments, she said, and they could afford another apartment if they could find one that would accept Chalkie. "It's hard with a dog," she said, shaking her head. "We turned down two places 'cause they didn't accept no dogs. Some people might feel bad 'cause he's living like that," she said, referring to their van. "But it don't seem to faze him none. Long as he's with us, it don't matter to him."

She described what Chalkie meant to them. "We don't know what we'd do without him," she said. "When we're feeling bad, he makes us feel better. We wake up feeling bad, he wags his tail and licks you in the face. That makes my day. I'm good to go for the rest of the day." Then she said again, "I don't know what I'd do without him."

She and her husband had plenty of reasons to feel bad. They both had cancer, and Paulette was set to have surgery for a kidney tumor in a few weeks. "Tumors keep coming back," she said, shaking her head. "I been dealing with this for like five years. But I'm blessed because I love my dog."

Austin, too, said his dog comforted him in the face of illness. Since his HIV diagnosis, Austin had struggled with depression, but he added that, "waking up in the morning to this cute, adorable face, it's hard to be depressed." Just the presence of his dog lifted his spirits.

Many people said that their animals could sense their moods and respond with exactly what they needed. When I met Flora at the Mercer Clinic, she held her tan Chihuahua, Paco, closely and showered him with kisses between sentences. I said, "I can tell you have a special relationship with him." Flora said, "Oh, my god. I do. He's been my angel of my life." She started to tear up, and pressed Paco to her cheek. She described their living situation as "not good." "I can barely feed myself," she said. "I get donated food for him. People will say, 'Hey, here's a bag. Hey, I got extra this, extra that.' Every day. Always something. Someone always will ask, 'Do you need food for him?'"

Flora said she had escaped an abusive home and started living on the streets at age eleven. "I was tired of getting beat up," she said, "so I ran the streets, and my friends and their families supported me. They fed me and they clothed me. They took care of me."

She had married young and raised a family. But her children had grown and moved on, and her husband had died. When she talked about Paco, she described him as a person, as I had heard other homeless people do. "You know," she said, looking at Paco, "this is the longest that I've had a person in my life. I didn't have my husband this long. Or even my parents. My children are gone. They just went their own ways, so he's been my comfort. He's my angel."

Flora was suffering from panic attacks, which she attributed to "the life I have to live to survive." Paco stopped them, she claimed. "When I hold him and cuddle with him the panic goes away. I don't know. He's like my medicine."

"He is adorable," I said, and asked if I could hold him.

"Oh, yeah," she said. "He's a lovey dovey dog."

As Paco settled his warm little body into the crook of my arm, Flora looked on and said, "He's very attached to me. He knows when I'm sad. He knows when something's wrong."

"How does he know?" I asked. "What does he do?"

"He'll just give me those looks," she said. "I can't explain it to you, but he knows what I'm feeling. He knows. He lets me know everything is going to be all right, just by being here. He's just an angel. I've never in my life had such a bond with anything like I've had with this dog. Nobody or nothing."

Other people told me their animals "knew" when they felt sad. Isaac said of his dog, Raja, "It's like he knows when I'm feeling down. He comes over and he just nudges me with his nose and wants me to pet him. He just makes me feel better. Anytime I'm feeling depressed, he just knows, and he just wants to cuddle with me, play with me. He just calms me down and brings me out of my downward spiral. Brings me out of it."

Overall, I heard repeatedly that animals are "there for you." And not only dogs, but cats, too, were "there for" their homeless guardians. Indeed, although dogs more often served as social facilitators because of their public visibility, when it came to emotional support, cats pulled their weight. For example, Christine, her husband, and their son were staying in their car and with friends since losing their rental home when the owner went through foreclosure. We met as she was waiting at the Mercer Clinic. When I asked her what the cats meant to her, she said, "Everything. I mean, these guys have been my godsend. They're there for me every time I get depressed. This one, the one in the carrier, Beau, he's by my side constantly. If it wasn't for them, I wouldn't be able to make it through the day."

Rescue

The narrative theme of rescue refers to removing an animal from an abusive or neglectful situation, nursing an injured animal back to health, or some combination of these. To qualify as a narrative theme, a teller had to describe engaging in rescue activities regularly, often with single-minded dedication. Simply "rescuing" an animal from a shelter, as in adopting, although commendable, does not constitute rescuing as I use the term here. But Candy's story, for example, told of a life organized around saving cats. Likewise, other homeless people told me of their devotion to helping animals.

I met Bertie and five of her seven dogs at the Mercer Clinic. Bertie was in her mid-sixties, an Army veteran, with a long history of homelessness and pet ownership, and thus a similarly long history as a Mercer Clinic client. The veterinary student who acted as my gatekeeper at the clinic had said, "You really should start with Bertie." When I talked with Bertie, I learned that she and her dogs had arrived the night before to get a place at the front of the line. They had slept in her ancient station wagon, the dogs curled up around her, and all of them tucked under blankets. Now, Bertie sat on a lawn chair, and she had spread last night's blankets on the ground so that the dogs could enjoy the sun. Bertie and her dogs were the center of a cluster of homeless women and their animals, mostly dogs, but a few had cats in carriers, too. One woman in the group had just returned with a box of donuts, which they shared and offered to me. They lightheartedly teased the woman because she had gotten lost going to the donut shop a few blocks away. I said, "You mean the place on 16th Street?" They laughed again because even I knew the location after only a few hours in the area.

Bertie's two dogs, who needed no veterinary care at the time, had stayed home with her two cats. "Home" was a condemned building that still had electricity but no running water. Bertie told me she had saved each of the animals, and then told me each one's story. She found one dog wandering in traffic, limping on an injured leg, for which she arranged treatment. She intercepted another dog on his way to the city pound, where, because of his age, he would probably not have made it as an adoption candidate. One of the cats found his way to her building after a car had broken both front legs and his jaw. And on it went.

When I asked Bertie what her animals meant to her, she framed her efforts as part of her relationship to Jesus Christ, portraying her rescue activities as a way to gain access to the spiritual realm. She told me that Jesus had created animals, although her tone was one of reminding, rather than telling, as if I had known this and simply forgotten. Then she explained, "I'm doing my best to glorify His name by being responsible to His creations, and I hope He doesn't mind if I take care of them on his behalf. I always ask His forgiveness if I'm doing too much by rescuing these unwanted animals."

When I met Adele, elements of her story reminded me of those I heard from Candy and Bertie. She, too, lived in an abandoned building, this one in San Francisco's Mission District. She was around fifty years old, and had been homeless for four years after injuries left her unable to work and pay her rent. She called five cats who lived in the building her own, but she cared for others, "too many to count," she said, in her neighborhood. Her daily routine involved feeding and checking on numerous feral cats and stray dogs. She received donations of food from pet stores and, on the day we met, she had acquired a large bag of cat food from VET SOS. She described caring for animals as "just something I've done my whole life . . . as natural as breathing."

I heard many other stories like these, and some with dramatic twists. For example, Emily told me about seeing a dog chained up at a shop near the junkyard where she lived. One day, during football season, workers at the shop spray-painted the dog, a pit bull mix named Pinto, with the silver-and-black of the Oakland Raiders. "He was screaming," she said. "So I picked up a piece of rebar and backed the guys off. And then I realized he was chained and locked to a post, and I couldn't get him loose." She stayed with the dog until the workers left, and then went off and located some bolt cutters, cut the dog loose, and took him to her junkyard home. "He had never had toys," she said. "He had never had blankets. He had always been in that warehouse. That workplace. With nothing. And I gave him

Photograph by Mark Rodgers, courtesy of San Francisco Community Clinic Consortium's VET SOS project.

*After Emily rescued Pinto from being spray-painted,
he and Chester formed a "pack of two."*

blankets and rugs and toys." Pinto had lived ever since with a home-less couple Emily knew who lived in another junkyard. I talked to the man, named Chester, about this acquisition story, and he confirmed it, laughed, and said, "She stole him." He explained that Pinto's owner had found out where he was, acknowledged that the dog was being neglected, and agreed that they could keep him. "But, yeah," Chester said, laughing again. "She stole him."

   This account provides an opportunity to revisit a point I made in Chapter 2, and one that will remain salient throughout this book. The meaning embedded in personal narratives is more important to this study than the factual accuracy of the events they portray. Emily's story of this rescue may be true exactly as told, with her single-hand-edly taking on the men, or she and other tellers may have embel-lished on it as it circulated and became part of the folklore. Distinguishing fact from fiction, were it even possible to do, would make no difference for my purposes. The facts matter less than the meaning the personal narrative conveys. As I go on to discuss, in Emily's story, as in others recounted here, the inclusion of this event adds a moral component to the ongoing process of narrative self-con-struction. Without telling me, straight out, what kind of person she considers herself to be, and without my having to ask, Emily con-veyed her character through her personal narrative. Moreover, the narrative conveyed it in a positive light. Emily, Don, Candy, and other tellers un-self-consciously deployed narrative conventions embedded in "my animal is everything" to highlight positive versions of themselves. In the following section, I explore what made this possible.

Animals and Mattering

Stories of "my everything" reveal how animals can serve as symbolic resources for significance in the lives of their homeless guardians. When narrators describe their animals as making them feel loved and giving them a sense of purpose, they gain access to a construct that has profound significance for the self and social behavior: mattering. At its most elementary level, the term refers to the extent to which others notice us (Rosenberg and McCullough 1981; see also Schie-man and Taylor 2001; Elliott, Colangelo, and Gelles 2005). I espe-cially appreciate the definition of mattering as "the perception that, to some degree and in any of a variety of ways, we are a significant part of the world around us" (Elliott, Kao, and Grant 2004:339). To understand the importance of mattering, we need only to think about its absence. William James described this well when he wrote, "We have an innate propensity to get ourselves noticed . . . by our kind. No more fiendish punishment could be devised, were such a thing physically possible, than that one should be turned loose in society and remain absolutely unnoticed by all the members thereof" (1890:293–294).

Although James wrote of the importance of being noticed "by our kind," attention from animals counts, too. As the personal narratives in this chapter reveal, the nonjudgmental attention one receives from an animal can provide a welcome change from the everyday experiences of the homeless, for whom *not* mattering is a common plight. To sense another's delight in seeing you even though, as Don said, "your pockets are empty, you got no food, you got no nothing," is to matter. Those of us who have been greeted by a dog or cat at the end of a day—or even after a trip out to the mailbox—can understand this feeling. When Isaac said that Raja often nudged him at just the right time, or when Christine described Beau's constant companionship, they depicted mattering conveyed through the simple assurance that they exist. This proves especially precious to those who seldom matter to their own kind.

But the narratives suggest that relationships with animals do more than just satisfy the propensity to be noticed. Research on mattering incorporates two additional forms or dimensions, which are "anchored in specific others" (Rosenberg and McCullough 1981:165). In the first case, we sense our *importance* to another when that person shows concern for our well-being. In the second case, when another relies on us for their needs or wants, we perceive their *dependence* on us. In the narratives of "everything," animals symbolically allow tellers to experience both these forms of mattering. Whereas a focus on the theme of emotional support, as in the stories told by Don, Gordon, and others, brings a sense of importance into the narrative process of self-construction, stories that draw on the rescue theme, such as Candy's and Bertie's, express dependence. Because animal companionship typically involves both receiving and providing care, both feeling important to the animal and sensing the animal's dependence, the distinction between forms of mattering is mostly analytical. By describing an animal as "everything," narrators attest to social bonds and obligations.[4] This can provide a buffer against isolation and insignificance, and a contrast to claims that characterize the homeless as disaffiliated.

The two forms of mattering also shed potential light on a gender difference I noted in these narratives. Whereas more men than women emphasized emotional support in their narratives regarding their animals, more women reported engaging in rescue activities. Men thus incorporated a sense of importance into their narratives, while women included a sense that their animals depended on them. Other researchers have also found that men rely heavily on pets for emotional support. In their study of homeless pet owners in San Francisco East Bay areas, Aline Kidd and Robert Kidd found that "the pet was the only love in their lives for significantly more men than women" (1994:719).[5] Similarly, a man I interviewed said, "The best thing about having a dog is that it gives you something to care for, care about. I lost a lot of ties with my family, and he's all I have." To explore the potential reasons for this, I considered other sources of support, such as a relationship with a spouse or significant other. Although I do not have information on relationship status for every person I interviewed, the available data indicate that most of the women had partners or spouses, whereas the majority of the men were single. Research suggests that men tend to rely on their wives or partners where emotional matters are concerned, whereas women typically turn to close female friends and family members outside the relationship (Gerstel, Riessman, and Rosenfield 1985). Research also indicates that, for several reasons, homeless men receive little emotional support, if any, from either their families of origin or their ex-partners and children (Pippert 2007). Thus, it makes sense that the mostly single men I interviewed relied on their companion animals for the support that women may have found in other relationships. Dog ownership provides a socially acceptable way for men to express and receive affection. The element of importance gained from the perceived concern of their dogs provides an important source of self-worth, especially for men living on the margins.

As for why the women's narratives tended to focus on rescue activities and the satisfaction they consequently received, a voluminous literature finds that women demonstrate greater sensitivity toward animals.[6] Moreover, women consistently outnumber men in animal advocacy efforts. Explanations include evolutionary biology, empathy based on shared subordination, a closer connection with nature because of the ability to give birth, and socialization.[7] I did not gather data that might finally reveal the definitive explanation, but I can speculate that just as the conditions of homelessness deprived men of sources of importance, they deprived women of ways to respond to the dependence of others. It may be that the circumstances of street life limited women's ability to meet the needs of other people. Meeting the needs of animals through rescue provides a resource for lived and narrated experiences of mattering. This is not to portray animals as surrogates for people. Rescuing animals has its own rewards, and when presented with opportunities to engage in it, those who do so can benefit from the sense of mattering it brings.

Photograph by Mark Rodgers, courtesy of San Francisco Community Clinic Consortium's VET SOS project.

This homeless man and his dog are a "pack of two."

The Self-Story of the "Pack of Two"

The sense of self that emerges from the narratives of animals as "everything" continues the work begun by mattering. As I considered this particular self-concept, I recalled a passage from a book by the late Caroline Knapp, in which she wrote, "I'm thirty-eight and I'm single, and I'm having my most intense and gratifying relationship with my dog." She went on to say: "Before you get a dog, you can't quite imagine what living with one might be like; afterward, you can't imagine living any other way. Life without Lucille? Unfathomable, to contemplate how quiet and still my home would be, and how much less laughter there'd be, and how much less tenderness, and how unanchored I'd feel without her presence, the simple constancy of it" (1998:1–2, 6).

Knapp described her relationship with Lucille as a "pack of two," which is also the title of her book. This image nicely captures the sense of self I heard in the narratives recounted in this chapter. The term "pack," of course, suggests a wolf or dog pack, with pairs that are bonded for life at its core. The image connotes interdependence, exclusivity, loyalty, and other intense aspects of bonding. In borrowing the phrase, I aim to emphasize all of these qualities, but mostly the degree of influence the animal has in the guardian's construction of self. The members of a pack of two exist because of each other. When Teresa Bush, the homeless woman in Durango, said of her dog, "She is me," and when Emily said she and Hobo were "connected at the hip," they described a pack of two, as Don did when he said that people did not recognize him without a dog.

This image of existing in partnership with an animal casts a positive moral light on the narratively constructed self through two devices. First, through contemporary Western cultural constructions of animals as innocent, morally pure, good, and discerning, the image of a pack of two allows the teller to consider him- or herself good by association. In other words, the animal is good, and the animal appears to love me, so I must be all right, too. This is particularly the case where dogs are concerned, because culture has imbued them with an almost saintly character, deployed through the rhetoric of unconditional love and loyalty. And it is especially true for abandoned, injured, or neglected animals. Stories of caring for and building a relationship with them allow tellers to portray a sense of goodness achieved through compensating for, and even overcoming, an earlier betrayal the animal endured. In sum, because pets exist within a cultural framework of innocence and goodness, these notions also frame the self-definitions of the person for whom they constitute "everything." A positive moral identity emerges by association. This is not to say that anyone I interviewed described him- or herself in these morally positive terms. No one said, "By the way, this means I am a good person." Nor does the narrative suggest anything about the tellers' objective goodness or virtue. Rather, it highlights how the image of the pack of two helps in the narrative construction of a positive moral identity, regardless of the "reality" of anyone's character.

Second, in its emphasis on a connection with an animal, the image of the pack of two represents a gesture of moral solidarity. Defining oneself in coexistence with another species represents a form of borderland thinking. A "borderland" is a shared space, often a site of negotiation and struggle over who holds power within it.[8] The term refers to more than geographic space, extending to identities, language, and culture.[9] It also connotes the limitations of dualistic thinking, such as the divides between nature and culture, and human and animal (Wolch and Emel 1998). Dominant paradigms take the separation between these domains for granted, but alternative perspectives reveal them as ancient social constructions that came with the transition from hunting and gathering to farming. Nomadic humans made no effort to set themselves apart from or above nature (Ingold 1994). However, settled agriculture required the manipulation of soil, plants, and animals, and the designation of some creatures as "pests," all of which entailed "a radically different attitude to the natural world" (Serpell 1986:217). This new attitude defined nonhuman animals as not only "fundamentally different and ontologically separate" from humans, but also inferior to us (Wolch 1998:121; see also Thomas 1983; Tuan 1984). The human/animal and nature/culture dualisms are thus neither natural nor inevitable, but the product of the power humans exerted over other creatures and the natural world. Considering an animal as one's equal constitutes borderland thinking because it challenges human/animal dualism and acknowledges animals' influence on human identity.

In this light, a "pack of two" statement such as Teresa Bush's "she is me" constructs an animal as having significant social power. This does not mean that homeless pet owners consider themselves as engaging in political acts. But language such as "I don't know where I'd be without them" and "I would be lost without them" connotes a sense of the connections between two species, the way that Donna Haraway (2003) talks about "companion species." Her use of the concept goes beyond "companion animal" to acknowledge that humans coexist with, and indeed rely on, myriad other species, from dogs to honeybees to bacteria. Acknowledging this coexistence rather than taking domination for granted problematizes human exceptionalism, even if implicitly.

The Benefits and Pitfalls of the "Pack of Two"

For the tellers, the benefits of the personal narratives discussed in this chapter are twofold. The first lies in the sense of mattering, depicted through the language that conveys the bonds and obligations of pet ownership. Research since Emile Durkheim indicates that people who have social ties, and the accompanying sense of personal significance, enjoy better physical and mental health and live longer than their isolated counterparts. Stories in which animals provide a symbolic social bond may thus offer a protective factor against adversity. The second benefit comes through the positive moral identity gained by association with an animal, owing largely to the constructions of animals as morally pure and innocent. Tellers portray a nexus of caring about, in the sense of having concern for; caring for, in the sense of practices that stem from this concern; and feeling cared for, or the felt sense that the animal reciprocates emotionally. The sense of mattering and the moral identity that emerges from this nexus can benefit anyone, but especially those low on the ladder of social status. This does not imply that interviewees who described their animals as "everything" were happy-go-lucky, or that pet ownership offers a panacea for the problems of homelessness. Instead, the evidence of social integration and positive moral identity revealed in these personal narratives illustrates how, even in light of the deprivations of homelessness, people engage in "salvaging the self," to use Snow and Anderson's apt phrase once again. The narratives also point out how animals, as symbolic resources, contribute to these efforts. In light of the question of why a person who apparently cannot provide for him- or herself would have a pet, these narratives reveal the existential and social meaning that animals make available. As sources of mattering, animals "matter" for the self by providing relevance, and for society by strengthening the social bond.

One potential pitfall in this narrative comes in the form of a contrast between its emphasis on the emotional benefits of pet ownership and the research in that area. In light of the stressful life events that precipitate and accompany homelessness, the need for emotional support and loyal companionship comes as no surprise.[10] The emotional benefits portrayed in both the support and the rescue narratives would seem especially valuable. In other words, because animals are good for people, it is no wonder that the homeless would have pets. Yet, despite widely held popular beliefs that pets are good for people, empirical research has not confirmed that this is the case. Harold Herzog reviewed the studies conducted over the past three decades on what he calls "the pet effect" and concluded that it "remains an uncorroborated hypothesis rather than an established fact" (2011:237; see also Chur-Hansen, Stern, and Winefield 2010). For example, one study of senior citizens in Australia concluded that "owning a pet does not significantly increase one's perceived level of happiness or life satisfaction or significantly decrease one's level of depression" (Crowley-Robinson and Blackshaw 1998:170). A study in the United Kingdom examined loneliness before and after acquiring a companion animal. Subjects who had adopted pets reported feeling just as lonely afterward, and no happier than those who had not acquired a pet (Gilbey, McNicholas, and Collis 2007). Some research has even found that pet ownership has a negative impact on emotional well-being. One study found that pet owners suffered more from psychological problems such as anxiety, insomnia, and depression than those who did not own pets (Müllersdorf et al. 2010). Another found that senior citizens with pets "reported poorer mental and physical health and higher use of pain relief medication" than their non-pet-owning counterparts did (Parslow et al. 2005:47). The media seldom report these findings, focusing instead on studies with positive results that, as of yet, defy replication.

I describe the emphasis on emotional benefits as a *potential* pitfall in these narratives because it does not matter whether researchers declare the emotional benefits of pet ownership fact or fiction. Few people who claim to perceive an emotional bond with an animal would stop doing so after reading some of the studies that refute it. The stories and experiences of intense attachment would continue, highlighting the cultural potency and significance of the notion that animals promote emotional well-being. To restate what I have said before, the insights of these and other narratives in this book come not from their correspondence with any particular "truth" but from what they reveal about the symbolic means through which people experience their relationships with animals. The contrast between the research and the narratives illustrates this well. In the narratives, and in the subjectivity they express, cultural "truth," in the form of beliefs that animals are good for people, trumps empirical "truth," which questions those beliefs. The logic of cultural constructions structures experiencing and telling, regardless of what research says about the facts within those constructions. The strength of the narrative of animals as "everything" comes not through its objective truth, but through its insights about the need to feel significant and how narrative constructions of animals help to fulfill it.

Notes

1. I am grateful to Keri Brandt for bringing this story to my attention. Coverage appears here: www.durangoherald.com/apps/pbcs.dll/article?AID =/20111114/NEWS01/711149915/Is-this-dog-vicious-&template=printpicart and www.durangoherald.com/apps/pbcs.dll/article?AID=/20111116/NEWS 01/711159923/Gyzmo-walks&template=printpicart, both accessed March 26, 2012.

2. Colorado laws require a ten-day quarantine following a bite, to determine infection status. A dog owned by a domiciled person would be required to remain at home for the quarantine period. Because this is not possible for a homeless person, Gyzmo completed the quarantine at the Humane Society. After the ten days, the dog remained at the Humane Society awaiting the court date because of the charge of viciousness. Here, too, a dog owned by a domiciled person could have remained at home. Had Bush and Gyzmo had a home to go to, Gyzmo would not have spent so much time impounded.

3. See Teresa Gowan's (2010) ethnography of recyclers in San Francisco.

4. In this way, Emile Durkheim's (1951) studies of social integration and suicide emphasize the importance of mattering.

5. Men's reliance on their animals for emotional support does not mean that they are unable to have close relationships with people. In other work, I have debunked what I call the "deficiency argument," which "assumes that people who enjoy the company of animals lack the qualities or skills that would allow them to enjoy human company" (Irvine 2004a:19). If animal companionship appealed to and occurred primarily among loners, we would find rates of ownership to be highest for single people. Instead, the opposite is the case, with ownership highest in families and multimember households (AVMA 2007). Animal companionship simply offers unique pleasures, and people who have close relationships with other people can feel close to animals, too.

6. See Herzog 2007 and Herzog, Betchart, and Pittman 1991 for reviews. Herzog (2007) discusses some of the methodological pitfalls in studies of sex and gender differences, particularly the failure of many studies to report effect sizes and the direction and magnitude of the differences observed.

7. For reviews of these perspectives, see Donovan and Adams 2007 and Gaarder 2011.

8. Much of the research employing the concept of the borderlands examines the intersections of race and ethnicity. The seminal work on this is Gloria Anzaldúa's *Borderlands/La Frontera* (1987).

9. Jenny Vermilya (2012) uses the border concept to discuss the construction of species in veterinary medicine, examining how horses exist in a borderland between large and small animals.

10. The literature on homelessness and mental health is voluminous. I found the following particularly instructive: LaGory et al. 1989; LaGory, Ritchey, and Mullis 1990; Lee 1989; Ritchey et al. 1990; and Snow et al. 1986.

6 Protectors

The narrative of animal-as-protector, or more precisely, dog-as-protector, for I encountered no one with a cat in this role, occurred mostly among those who defined themselves as Travelers. With only two exceptions, all the Travelers I interviewed were between the ages of eighteen and twenty-four. Although every aspect of this research gave me insight into a world about which I previously knew little, the lives of the young Travelers took me into a truly foreign land.

I first entered this territory when I visited the Homeless Youth Alliance in San Francisco with VET SOS. The kids—more on this term in a moment—and their dogs streamed into the HYA as soon as the doors opened. The kids talked and ate—did they ever eat! The HYA keeps plenty of donated food on hand, for people and for dogs. Most of the kids headed straight for the kitchen area and poured out huge bowls of cereal or made stacks of peanut butter sandwiches. Others fixed grilled cheese sandwiches or bowls of ramen. I saw one young woman eating Nutella, the chocolate hazelnut spread, straight from the jar. The air in the roughly twenty-by-thirty-foot room quickly filled up with the scents of body odor, burnt toast, and dogs. The kids settled into the well-worn couches and chairs or sat on the scuffed wood floor, with their dogs close by. Those who wanted their dogs to sit told them to "kick it down." They tagged on "all the way" to send the dogs lying down. Dr. Strubel gave a short presentation on the benefits of vaccinations, licensing, and spaying and neutering, and then proceeded with the clinic. Although I wanted to understand the relationships the youth had with their dogs, I also received a crash course in street culture. The youth refer to themselves as "kids," although they are young adults, over eighteen. The Runaway and Homeless Youth Act defines "youth" as those under twenty-one years of age. However, San Francisco's Homeless *Youth* Alliance provides services to people between the ages of thirteen and twenty-nine, reflecting the flexibility in the definition of "youth" in homeless services (Ruddick 1996). In addition, there are "many different experiences of being young and homeless" (Gibson 2011:5; see also Ruddick 1996). The youth I met tended to use the term "street kids" for those who had left home, with or without parental consent, and "slept rough," on the street or in parks, or squatted in abandoned buildings. Street kids spend most of their waking hours in public, primarily urban spaces (Finkelstein 2005:3). Those who call themselves "Travelers" share these characteristics but "frequently move from city to city over a period of months and years" (Lankenau et al. 2008:66).

Travelers distinguish themselves from "gutter punks," who have punk hairstyles and extensive tattoos and piercings, and often use hard drugs. Travelers typically use alcohol and marijuana, which they call "weed," but they look down on "crackheads," "junkies" (heroin users), and "tweakers" or "meth heads" (methamphetamine users). I also learned about "crusties," the subset of street kids or Travelers who do not bathe or wash their clothes. Their hair becomes matted and their clothes stiffen, hence "crusty" with dirt. The kids told me about hopping freight trains, or "catching out," which I had thought went the way of Depression-era hobos and the few remaining tramps depicted in Douglas Harper's ethnography *Good Company* (2006). They compared notes about the various rail lines, the best cars to ride in, and the need for earplugs.

I made a second venture into this world through the veterinary clinic program run by People and Animals Living Safely, held at the YEAH Center in Berkeley. YEAH supports homeless "young adults" between the ages of eighteen and twenty-five. Between November and May, YEAH operates an overnight shelter, which also accommodates dogs. At the PALS clinic, the kids refined my understanding of the distinction between those who travel and those who consider themselves "homeless." As one young man explained to me, "When you're traveling, you're not homeless, because home is wherever you lay your head. You're not a humbum or homeless if you're only in town for a few weeks." Ronnie, whom we first met in Chapter 3, helped me understand that humbums "are the old people out there that have been out there for thirty years and haven't went anywhere. They've just been drinking or smoking crack on the streets for their whole life.

That's a humbum." Other kids told me that "homeless people" are those who are *trying* to get off the street, "unless they're crackheads or drunks," one added. In contrast, Travelers portray their status as one of choice. To be sure, their rhetoric of choice prevents understanding the options available to them. But, as mentioned in other places in this book, I take the position that if kids define themselves as Travelers rather than homeless, then Travelers is what they are.

Historicizing the Traveler

The image of wandering or hitchhiking youth constitutes an enduring figure in the history of the United States. It cuts across class boundaries, encompassing homeless kids hopping trains as well as college students taking a year off to backpack through foreign lands. Traveling in this manner, long known as "tramping," has Old World roots in skilled labor (Adler 1985). For centuries, nearly every skilled occupation required a period of travel on the way to mastering the trade; hence the "journeyman" designation, which could take a young person on the road for up to five years.[1] In Western Europe, tramping was formally organized by craft guilds and organizations, which arranged for accommodations and jobs with master artisans, or if none were available, provided funds to reach the next craft-society village. Around the time of the First World War, work became concentrated in cities, which had become connected by railroads that bypassed the towns and villages. People continued to wander in search of work, but their roaming was increasingly associated with laziness. As Adler wrote, "tramping ceased to be a typical feature of artisan life, and the status of the tramp declined. Once perfectly respectable, the tramp came to denote social marginality and vagrancy" (1985:341; see also DePastino 2003; Harper 2006).

The United States has no history of organized tramping as a part of trade obligations. Nor did "tramp" have a connotation of shiftlessness until after the Civil War.[2] In the depression that followed the war, scores of unemployed men hopped the newly abundant rail lines looking for work. The term "tramp" came to denote a person who traveled with "no visible means of support" (see DePastino 2003). In the years of westward expansion, adolescents often struck out on their own when illness or accidents took their parents. The nineteenth-century waves of immigration sent many poor young people into the streets and countryside in hopes of making a living. During the Great Depression, an estimated quarter million young people took to the road, escaping impoverished families or seeking work or adventure (Adler 1985; Minehan 1934; Uys 1999). Known equally as tramps and hobos by this time, some were running away, and others left with their parents' blessings. As the Depression wore on, their numbers, combined with the numbers of adult hobos, became a social problem that generated social scientific studies, public policy debates, and responses such as the Federal Transient Relief Service.[3]

Another wave of wandering young people came into public awareness during the 1960s and 1970s. They became known as "hip-

Photograph by Mark Rodgers, courtesy of San Francisco Community Clinic Consortium's VET SOS project.

Two Travelers pause with their dogs in Golden Gate Park.

pies," and they had reasons other than work for hitting the road. For them, "traveling was associated with music festivals, anti-war protests, sexual freedom, and drug experimentation" (Lankenau et al. 2008:66; see also Cohen 1973; Yablonsky 1968). Many hippies sought destinations such as the East Village in New York and Haight-Ashbury in San Francisco. Some who were too young to have traveled to Woodstock in 1969 began attending the annual Rainbow Gatherings held on national forest land each July since 1972. Around the same time, young adults began following the Grateful Dead, attempting to see as many of the band's shows as they could and becoming immersed in the "Deadhead" subcultures. Today's Travelers still flock to music festivals, and the Rainbow Gatherings remain a popular destination.

Although considerable research examines the factors that predispose youth to homelessness, the numerous risks they face on the street, and various topics related to education, little of this literature focuses specifically on Travelers (but see Lankenau et al. 2008). Moreover, although the literature on coping skills among homeless youth is vast, the research on how they understand the world, which is the source of their coping skills, is scarce (but see Kidd and Davidson 2007). Analyzing how Travelers narrate the role of dogs in their everyday lives contributes to both of these literatures. Their stories acknowledge the hazards of the streets, but focus on the narrative resources provided by animal companionship.

"The Dog Barked. I Was Safe."

One of the wonders of narrative lies in how we come to hear it as we do, particularly how we understand the temporal sequence.[4] Narratives tell us "first this happened, and then that happened." The second part of the sequence—the "and then"—explains the first, even though what happened in the first sentence occurred before the action in the second. If a teller changes the order, the meaning changes, too. Sociologist Harvey Sacks (1974) examined the link between description and action by considering two consecutive sentences in a story told by children: "The baby cried. The mommy picked it up." We understand that the crying explains the picking up. In interviews with young Travelers, I often heard a "Sacksian" story that essentially went like this: "The dog barked. I was safe." Story lines soon became more complex and took on more stages. The "and then" became "and then, and then, and then." The ensuing stories were full of accounts of why the dog barked. They incorporated the dog's discernment of threats as ranging from potential rapists to mountain lions, but the basic story line told of threat and safety, with the safety coming because the dog took action. The dog emerged as hero. The Traveler and his dog survived to face another day and another adventure.

Stories of animals as protectors unfold from a setting that places the main characters of the Traveler and the dog alone, often sleeping or attempting to do so. "One time, when we were setting up camp," Chris's story began. Another opened with, "We were in my truck, off in the woods. I had just fallen asleep." The story depicts the teller as either unable to see potential threats because of darkness or simply blind to what the dog can detect. For example, Buzz's story began, "Me and Jones, we were up in the mountains, and it was pitch black, but Jonesie, he was watching." Another male Traveler said, "She lets me know when something's coming around that I didn't know was there in the first place. It could be anything from a dog to another person." Protector stories usually credit the dog with a keen ability to discern an approaching person's intentions. As Buzz told me, "When people come around, when they're good, he's fine, how he is now. But if they're not, the hairs on the back of his neck will go up. His head will start to drop down. He'll watch 'em." Daniel observed similar powers of discernment in his dog, Biscuit: "She'll see things that I don't," he said, "and she'll point out things to me that I don't see, or that I don't know is happening, and she can pick up on feelings and senses that I won't. Like she'll see people come around, people that I talk to, and people in general that she doesn't like, and I'll see later on down the road, 'Okay, that's why she didn't like that person.' This person may have been doing bad things or had bad intentions. She can really tell. She knows when someone's here for the wrong reason."

I met Valerie and her dog, Mike, when they passed through Berkeley and stopped at the PALS clinic. The pair traveled together extensively, sometimes joined by a boyfriend when Valerie had one in her life. Twenty-two at the time, Valerie began traveling at fifteen. For a few months before we met, she had a van, but it had broken down, and she thought she might stay in the East Bay area for a while. When I asked where she and Mike slept, Valerie said matter-of-factly, "On the street." I followed up by asking, "What kinds of places do you find to sleep?" She looked at me as though I were a bit dense.

"Just actually on the street," she said. "On the sidewalk."

We both laughed at my slowness in grasping this, and she added, "It's not as bad as you might think, as long as I have him. I sleep on the street safe in my head," she told me, "because my dog is tied to my leg. No matter the size of the dog, it does always make people more wary about trying to fuck with you because they know that that dog is there to try to protect you." Likewise, a male Traveler who went by the name "Crash" summed up how his dog, Duffy, protected him by saying, "He's the perfect road dog. I can sleep anywhere, and if anybody tries to come up to me, he's on it."

With the characters established in the setting, and the role of the dog foreshadowed, the story unfolds. The plot begins to thicken with a "happening." Others have referred to this as a "complication" or a "complicating event" (Labov and Waletzky 1997). A real or imagined threat appears, something out of the ordinary, and usually in the form of an unknown person approaching. Travelers described frequent encounters with strangers, dangerous and otherwise. Several echoed Chris's explanation that "people like to go around and try to attack kids." Indeed, research on street kids points out that "living on the streets is fraught with danger, and homeless young people are often victims of physical assault, sexual abuse, and other forms of exploitation" (Bender et al. 2007:27).

Too often, the dogs detect actual threats. Valerie began a story about Mike as protector by describing the Oakland neighborhood where she stayed. "There are a lot of gangsters around that area, and being homeless, you're constantly surrounded by that. The other night, these guys just came up to where we were sleeping." Similarly, Chris continued the story that had begun with, "One time, when we were setting up camp," by adding, "this dude shows up."

As the protector narrative continues, it depicts the approach of a stranger, or just the vague sense of something wrong, as triggering the dog's response, which requires a subsequent response from the storyteller. For example, after establishing the setting, in this case a gangster-ridden area of Oakland, and the threat, the approaching men, Valerie continued: "I have Mike tied to my leg whenever I'm sleeping, and I felt him tense up. I can feel it when I'm half-awake. A second later, I woke up to his barking. The guys were just looking at us, and then they took off because Mike was just, he became a monster. And on several occasions, like that night, I most likely would've gotten robbed or raped or whatever if my dog wasn't there. After they left, I packed up and we took off as fast as we could."

Sometimes the threat comes in the form of an animal. Chris, for example, claimed a stray dog attacked him once as he slept and one of his dogs fought off the intruder. Travelers who camp in the woods also describe encounters with wildlife. Buzz typically spent weeks, even months, camping in remote areas with Jones. When I asked him about safety, he told me, "We can go way up in the mountains, and I ain't got to worry about bears and mountain lions and stuff like that. He'll let me know."

"What does he do?" I asked.

In a clear example of "speaking for" animals, Buzz explained, "He says, 'Dad, there's something over there in the bushes,' or 'Look here. Stop that. Go away.'" By putting words to Jones's purported thoughts, Buzz not only described the situation, but also constructed the intimacy of their relationship. I asked him how Jones would let him know about things. He was quiet for a moment, as if recalling. Then he said: "He'll sit up. Look around. And usually, just him getting up and moving would get me up, too. I'm like, 'Okay, my dog's moving. What's going on?' And then if it started getting too close he'd bark, you know, and be like, 'Yo, Dad. Something's not cool.' And I'd be like, 'Okay,' and I'd holler out, 'Leave us alone!' And the bear or whatever it was in the bushes would leave. Every time."

Chris had been camping with his dogs in various settings, from city parks to the woods to freight-train yards. "When I'm sleeping at night," he said, "if someone comes up on me that might be potential danger, [the dogs] hop up right away and make sure that it's a friend. And if not, they're growling and they scare away anybody, creatures, too, that might attack me."

The telling of the protector story continues, and the happening reaches a resolution. In most stories, the happenings did not result in harm or conflict. Instead, "The dog barked. I was safe." Valerie packed up her things and ran off with Mike. Buzz warned the bears, and they did as asked. Chris's dogs scared away the threat.

As the story ends, the teller evaluates it and sums up lessons learned from the happening. While not quite along the lines of "they all lived happily ever after," the narrators nevertheless return to a state of safety, having gained knowledge and experience that will help them next time. The event earned them additional "street smarts," such as "I know not to sleep in that part of Golden Gate" or "I don't go to Santa Cruz or Arcata anymore." The closing of the story also expresses the teller's stance toward the happening and its resolution, whether she or he considered it a genuinely frightening situation, a case of mistaken identity, a character-building experience, or something else. For young Travelers, the lesson often reinforces what they already knew: they can trust and rely on their dogs.

In many stories, the teller takes a moral stance, and one that they thought I should and would naturally share. For example, Valerie told me that Mike provided much better protection than a man could offer. Her last boyfriend had gone to jail several times, and she considered seeking protection from male friends at night instead of sleeping alone, but decided against it. She said, "I don't trust men as much as I trust my dog, and my dog is going to protect me." She paused, then looked at me with a smile and said, "*You* know what I mean," and not as a question. The emphasis she placed on "you," along with her declarative tone, implied my agreement, as though I too would naturally count dogs as more reliable than men.

Many stories ended with "but it's all worthwhile" justifications. The teller's stance at the story's end revealed either the wish to continue traveling or the fatigue that eventually comes with doing so. For example, although Chris has been on and off the road for eleven years—since the age of twelve—he was still looking forward to several decades of travel in his future. As we talked, I asked, "What would have to happen for you to live in a house again?" His response reminded me of Huck Finn's fear of having Aunt Sally "sivilize" him: "I'd probably have to be like forty-five!" he said. We both laughed, but I suspected for different reasons. Wanting greater clarity about his expectations, I followed up by asking, "So for the next twenty-some-odd years . . . ," and my voice trailed off.

"Yeah," he chimed in, nodding his head enthusiastically. "I'm cruisin'."

"Yeah?"

"Yeah," he said again.

"Even if you had the chance?"

"Oh, yeah. I'm not slaving myself for a box I don't want to be in," he said, laughing. "I don't like apartments. When I get in 'em, I start going nuts, because I'm like, 'Aargh! I don't like it here!'" He threw his head back, mimicking a fit. Then he settled himself and said, "I like to live out by nature." He nodded toward the dogs and said, "And whatever's out there, they've got my back."

But others had grown tired of constant motion. In this spirit, Ronnie closed his story with more than a suggestion of disillusionment. When we met, he had been traveling for three years. He became homeless after losing his job and then his apartment. He told me how after having lived on the streets for several months he had "met up with these hippie people." "I saw what they were doing, and I decided to travel, and therefore I wasn't homeless anymore. Not in *my* mind. I was *traveling*. It was my new thing I was doing. I stopped looking for a job and started traveling. And I made it here." This narrative conveys the conceptual device through which he became a Traveler instead of a homeless person. But after three years on the road, his outlook had changed: "I'm tired of traveling. It got old fast. Some people have been traveling for like twelve years. Riding freight trains and hitchhiking. Going all over. I don't know how I'd do it. I'm tired of it."

Dangers and Goodness on the Road

The dog-as-protector narrative has an obvious affinity for the Travelers' circumstances, which include significant elements of risk that warrant the need for protection. In addition to the physical dangers, which emphasize the dogs' powers of discernment, Travelers' personal narratives incorporate emotional hazards. Here, too, they describe the protection dogs offer (see also Rew 2000). Valerie explained, as she petted Mike, who was curled up beside her, "If it wasn't for that dog, I would've been raped and killed a long time ago. And a lot of other terrible things, too."

"Really?" I asked.

"Yeah. I'd be lonely. Suicidal. You know? Because, there have been times—I was just telling this the other night to Mike, when I was telling him I loved him so much before I went to bed—there've been times that we were hitchhiking by ourselves for weeks or months at a time, and the only person that was there to give me affection or to give affection to, was Mike. It's lonely as hell."

"I bet."

"Yeah," she said. "Lonely as hell. In the middle of nowhere, in some town where you don't know anybody, you know, or even here, where I know lots of people but it can be desolate sometimes. I don't know what I'd do without him."

Chris echoed Valerie's depiction of facing loneliness "in the middle of nowhere." He said of his two dogs, "If it weren't for them, I would have been really lonely when I was stuck in a boxcar out in the middle of nowhere. I don't know if I would have got through it so well, but they were very helpful with that. Every time I'd get kind of depressed, they'd come up and lick my face, tell me 'It's all right.'"

Although the Travelers' personal narratives portray a world full of potential dangers, they also incorporate the positive side of being on the road. The stories depict the dogs as helping Travelers to experience this, too. Because protector stories portray dogs as having keen discernment, some tellers describe themselves as acquiring this quality by association, and consequently enjoying more of the experiences of life on the road. For example, Valerie explained:

> Having a dog and being on the road has made me a better judge of people. Like if I was out here alone, I'd be more afraid, and I wouldn't have experienced half of what it's like. But because of him, I base [my judgments] on what people are doing with their life, rather than the way they look, because we all look ragged after a while out here. I've met a lot of people and had so many experiences because I'm out here. I'd say I have a very keen sense of awareness because of Mike. That's one attribute about me that's totally different than the way I was before. I'm very aware of my surroundings, and it has spread to every other part of my life, where I'm very focused about what's going on around me at all times. I just experience things more.

Expanding on the "social facilitation" component of animal companionship discussed in Chapter 3, Travelers often told me that their dogs brought good things their way, such as rides or food. For example, Matt described hitchhiking with his dog, Nala. "It's a little harder to travel with a dog," he admitted, "but on the other hand, I've had people pick me up and go, 'I never pick up hitchhikers. I don't give a damn about you, but your dog just looked so damn cute I had to give you a ride.'" Likewise, Malcolm said, "For every person who won't give me a ride 'cause I have a dog, there's another person who'll give me a ride because they're a dog lover."

The interview with Buzz was a case in point. As we talked, he sat in a Boulder park drinking beer with other Travelers. Several of them had dogs, which had given me reason for approaching the group. During the course of the interview, I asked Buzz, "What do you do for money?"

"I don't like money," he said, and then, for emphasis, said it again: "I really don't like money."

"Well, you need money for a few things once in a while," I responded.

"No, I don't," he said with a snort.

"No?"

He was adamant: "No."

I asked, "So you don't fly a sign or spange or anything?"

"I used to," he explained. "And I got tired of that. There's so much excess in this country, if you can't live, there's something wrong with you." He laughed, and several of his companions joined in. One added, "Seriously."

I moved the discussion on, but as we wrapped up the interview, I proved Buzz's precise point by handing him one of the gift cards I gave to every homeless person I interviewed. He accepted it while laughing loudly and waving it around for his friends to see.

"Once again, another way not to have to get money! This just happens. I don't need money." To Jones, who lounged between us, he said, "Jonesie Boy, you did it again."

"And I have dog food, too," I said. "I'll give you a bag of dog food."

"I have about a hundred pounds of dog food," he said, echoing what I had heard from many other homeless people. He opened one of his packs to show me. I also had socks to give out, a much-needed item among the homeless, but in this case I handed them over sheepishly, knowing that I had once again proved Buzz's point.

"I get given," he exclaimed. "People just give me stuff! This is the perfect example. Like, 'Here, I'll give you a gift card if you talk to me about Jones.' I'm not doing anything else today. I'm just sitting here, having a beer."

"It just comes to you," I said, shaking my head.

He nodded and explained, "Like I said, there's so much excess in this country, if you can't survive, there's something wrong with you. There's no reason you should not have what you need. All you gotta do is get up and go get it, and if you don't go get it, it'll walk up to you, like you just did."

"Because of Jones."

"Yup. Because of Jones," Buzz said, scratching the back of Jones's neck.

Travelers' narratives depict their dogs as attracting what they need and keeping hazards away, just what one needs in a world that holds both goodness and dangers.

The Self-Story of the Adventurer

The personal narratives of experiencing the world's goodness and dangers with only a dog as one's companion produce a self-story I call "the Adventurer." I observed two dimensions of this self, which I call the authentic dimension and the reflected dimension. Together, these tell of freedom and constraint, with the dog helping to resolve tensions between the two.

The Authentic Dimension

I use the term "authentic" here to denote *felt* authenticity, not to make any claims about the existence of a "real" self. In the interactionist formulation of the reciprocity between the person and society, the self is the product or offspring of the various statuses, roles, and relationships within which the person is situated (Mead 1934). A highly differentiated social context manifests itself in similarly differentiated selves, which encompass diverse identities. We reflexively view some aspects of the self as representing who we "really" are, while we consider others less authentic or even altogether false. As Ralph Turner puts it: "Some emanations I recognize as expressions of my real self; others seem foreign to the real me. I take little credit and assume little blame for the sensations and actions that are peripheral to my real self. Others are of great significance, because they embody my true self, good or bad" (1976:989; see also 1968).

In referring to an authentic dimension of the self among Travelers, I draw on this sense of "the real me." When Travelers talked about who they "really" were, they incorporated a Romanticist vocabulary into their personal narratives. By saying this, I do not mean that I found their lives romantic or glamorous in any way. On the contrary, their daily experiences often seemed banal and wholly unappealing. I use the term "Romanticist" only to connote a particular vocabulary of the self that "attributes to each person characteristics of personal depth: passion, soul, creativity, and moral fiber" (Gergen 1991:6; see also Baumeister 1986). In this view, life entails a struggle for the freedom to live by one's inner compass, "a unique and private source of meaning" (Gagnon 1992:225). Because society purportedly inhibits the expression of each person's basic human potential, the natural world, untainted by cold logic, becomes a place where the human self can unfold into its true destiny.

In the Travelers' narratives, I heard ample use of the Romanticist vocabulary of inner passions constrained by society. For instance, one Traveler philosophized, "The world's not going to make you happy. Number one life lesson: If you're not happy, stop. Find what makes you happy, and do it. Do whatever gives you goose bumps." What I heard from other Travelers, and what the research literature on homeless youth documents, indicates that some of them had good reason to adopt a negative view of society (see, e.g., Toro, Dworsky, and Fowler 2007 for a review).[5] A twenty-three-year-old woman at San Francisco's Homeless Youth Alliance said, "I guess society just kind of spit me out." Many constructed traveling as a preferable alternative to life circumstances and events. As one young woman said, "I was kicked out a lot, so I just kind of got used to it. Traveling was better than going home."

Kevin, a Chicago native who visited several east coast cities before arriving in San Francisco, portrayed the push and pull of desire and circumstances in describing his motivation for traveling: "I've wanted to travel for a while, and I had a little brush with the law, and I said, 'I'm out of here,' [and] got on the road. It took me a little bit of trouble to get me doing what I'm doing, but it's pretty cool. I like it. I wake up whenever I want to. I do pretty much whatever I want to do. Freedom, you know?"

Similarly, in contrasting constraint and freedom, Jason's narrative made full use of the Romanticist vocabulary:

> It makes me a lot happier, traveling. I have a lot more friends. I'm a lot more sociable. When I was younger and I had a place, when I would think what I'd be doing in like ten, twenty years out, my prospects for the future didn't look awesome. Just working at some job, slaving away until I'm sixty or fifty to have enough money to actually be able to live. Then by the time that I could actually be able to go do things, my health won't be there with me. I was a very grim fellow, and now I'm, for the most part, able to do what I want to do.

As mentioned earlier, many Travelers portray themselves as most comfortable in the natural world. This reflects the Romantic view that society, even in the form of an apartment, inhibits one's freedom. Chris said he hated the idea of working to live in "a box." Jason told me how his dog allowed him to stay outdoors by regularly warning him when the police entered their camp. He described the hassles of the "rude awakening" and having to pack up and move. Nevertheless, he said, "I like sleeping outside, though, and he makes it okay to do that. You know, we wake up with birds chirping, sunshine on my face. It's a lot nicer than being indoors." Nathan, too, deployed the image of the indoors as constraining. I had asked, "Do you see yourself settling down at some point in the future?"

"I don't know," he said. "Maybe. But man, I just love the outdoors! It was raining a couple days ago, and I went and stayed [in someone's apartment], and when I'm indoors, I feel cabin fever. I love having open sky. That's how we are out here. It's lovely."

Similarly, when I talked to a long-term Traveler in Boulder who regularly camped alongside the creek that runs through the city, he explained, "I have a problem with four walls. I sleep more comfortably outside. Even if I had a house, all I'd do is have one room for games, and be coming in and take showers and I'd be sleeping in the backyard. I prefer the sound of the air and stuff at night. I like to be able to look up through the trees and see the stars. Being in four walls, I just feel enclosed. And it feels really constricted to me at times."

Other studies of street kids have also found Romanticist vocabulary, without describing it in those terms. For example, according to one study, the kids "identified mainstream societal values as 'boring' when compared with their lifestyle, which involved freedom and interesting opportunities. Traditional societal structures were labeled as overly 'conforming, pointless, monotonous' while life on the streets was depicted as an opportunity to travel, to meet interesting people, and be independent of societal conventions and expectations" (Bender et al. 2007:34).

In the authentic dimension of the self, Travelers portray themselves as fulfilled when they resist social expectations. But their acts of resistance can often result in less-than-positive reflections from others.

The Reflected Dimension

Travelers encounter the verbal assaults so familiar to street people, and to some extent their youth makes them especially vulnerable to insults. Travelers see their lifestyle as offending the domiciled, who, they claim, assume they use drugs and routinely call out, "Get a job!" As Chris explained, "They say we're lazy and we don't work and all. Bullshit! I don't understand how we're lazy when we got eighty-pound packs on our backs and a guitar and dogs. I don't call that laziness." Other kids routinely suggested that the "yuppies" expressed such hostility because they envied the Traveler lifestyle.

The negative perceptions of the domiciled public came with verbal insults, but the perceptions of other audiences brought potentially serious consequences. For example, Travelers reported frequent confrontations with police, who purportedly see the kids as lazy drug users. Jesse expressed the sentiment I heard from many others when he told me, "The biggest hassle is that cops fuck with you. Hella cops just want to harass kids." In the youth parlance of northern California, "hella" means "a lot of," and Jesse claimed that police officers singled out Travelers for harassment.[6]

Although some Travelers might have an attitude toward the police, and others might have been engaged in activities that justifiably brought police attention, two developments suggest that their concerns had some basis in reality, at least in San Francisco. As I did this research, San Franciscans were preparing to vote on Proposition L, also called the "Sit/Lie Law" and the "Civil Sidewalks Law." The law, which took effect in December 2010, prohibits sitting or lying on a public sidewalk between 7 A.M. and 11 P.M.[7] In neighborhoods such as the Haight, Travelers and street kids—with their dogs—congregate on the sidewalk, often "spanging." To be sure, some drink and use drugs. In the months before the vote, proponents claimed Proposition L would prevent the obstruction of sidewalks and protect pedestrians from aggressive panhandlers. Opponents saw it as a business-funded attack against the poor and homeless, many of whom sit on sidewalks because they have nowhere else to go.[8] Travelers saw it as an effort to remove them from the Haight, where they had access to the Homeless Youth Alliance and felt safe, compared to other areas such as the Tenderloin. Around the time that I conducted this research, several reports had appeared in the media depicting the Haight as dangerous, largely because of street youth.[9] Although the proposition would not come to a vote for several months, many Travelers felt that the tensions behind it led to some "early enforcement."

In addition to the Sit/Lie Law, Travelers in San Francisco saw another reason why police might target them. In 2005, the city enacted a law requiring the sterilization of pit bull–type dogs over eight weeks of age. A first violation results in a fine of five hundred dollars. Many Travelers had pit bulls or dogs similar enough to fall under the law. Several had incurred fines and those who wanted to avoid the penalty had their dogs neutered through VET SOS. Many thought the law targeted Travelers. For example, Kevin believed that he had received a "Fix It Ticket" not just because he had a pit bull, but also because he was a Traveler: "I did get a ticket for not having her licensed," he said, "and after a whole bunch of back and forth, different offices, I still couldn't get her licensed because I didn't have her fixed and she's a pit bull. It's just this whole big tangled web of, if you got a pit bull and you got a pack on your back, cops are going to come after you. If Joe Local takes his unfixed pit bull on the street, the cops aren't going to look twice. But you know, if I get hassled a little bit because of it, it's worth it because she brings more good to me than she does bad."

Kevin displayed considerable initiative and compliance, but he believed the police were enforcing the law unevenly. "Here, in San Francisco, the way that the police see people like me, street kids, traveling kids, or whatever, with packs on their back, that's a tool that they use against you," he explained. "If they tell me to wake up and move, it's a minor inconvenience. But if they're telling me they're going to take my dog away, now you got my attention. So that makes it tough in this town, because the cops know that they can use our dogs as an upper-hand bargaining chip."

But not all Travelers will agree to have their dogs sterilized. Some believe it is cruel and unnatural. Some want to breed their dogs so that they can sell the puppies. Some see their dogs' bloodlines as worth reproducing. One of Chris's dogs had pit bull–type bloodlines, and he did not want to neuter him. He had not yet received a ticket, but he repeated an urban legend that portrayed the law as an attack against people like him. "I guess there's police officers going around right here now that are trying to look undercover," he told me, "and then they come up and they're taking people's dogs that are on the streets," he said.

"How are they doing that?" I asked him.

"They're just throwing 'em in the back of cop cars and then leaving with them."

"How are they getting away with that?"

"Because they have a thing against people that are on the streets," he said, echoing what I had heard from Kevin and other Travelers.

Stories about police officers shooting dogs circulated among the kids, emphasizing the use of fear tactics by the police. (Recall that a state trooper had shot Don's dog, Hemi.) For example, Dana, who was ending a long spell of traveling, described the power dynamic in such a situation:

> I was talking to a girl yesterday who said that the father of the dog that she had got shot by a cop. And I've heard different stories about that happening. The cops'll be, like, "Restrain your dog!" And you're restraining your dog and they'll shoot it anyway. But I think as far as police go, I think that it's a fear tactic that they can use against people, to be like, "You know, I could shoot your dog and there's nothing you can do about it." And it's true. There's nothing you can do about it if they shoot your dog. I mean, there are legal steps you could take, but they know that no street kid's going to get involved in that kind of thing.

Jesse reported having had a similar experience while he and his dog sat in a park with other Travelers, having a picnic of food they had collected: "The cops came down, and he was tied to my pack. The cop pulled a gun on him, you know. He was like, 'Get your dog on a leash!' And I'm like, 'My dog's been on a leash the whole time. You came up hella quick to my backpack. My dog's doing his job protecting my stuff.' The whole time, I grabbed my dog and moved him, the cop was holding his gun on him. It was ridiculous. I just got out of there. Forget this!"

As with other narratives in this book, I cannot verify these events. Regardless of whether they are fact or fiction, they narratively construct the constraints posed by society and portray the tellers as innocent. In doing so, these personal narratives help to build a moral identity around the relationship with the dog.

The Dog as Significant Other

In self-assessments, people do not value everyone's perceptions equally (Rosenberg 1973). We are selective about whose opinions we value. Travelers are cautious even about one another (see also Kidd 2003). Although relationships on the road can develop quickly, many are careful about whom they count as "family." As Jesse explained: "You just gotta be careful who you trust. You gotta learn. It's kind of hard to tell sometimes. Some people are just trying to hustle you, and you learn not to waste your time with them. And other people actually would share a forty with you [referring to a forty-ounce bottle of malt liquor, which is cheap and has a high alcohol content], or actually share food with you. Take care of those people. And be careful who's telling you who family is."

I asked Jesse, "How do you know whom you can trust?" Without a moment's hesitation, he said, "My dog is the best judge of character."

In the case of the Adventurer self-story, the narrative role of the dog becomes complex. Although dogs often *cause* negative appraisals, Travelers emphasize how they *shield against them*. As Jesse's statement indicates, dogs can serve as respected significant others: in other words, so goes the narrative, "If my dog likes you, I like you. If my dog doesn't trust you, I don't trust you, either." In this formulation, Travelers can rebuff negative appraisals using the dog as justification, even if the dog's presence brought on the negative appraisal in the first place, as in encounters with police. In addition, dogs shield against negative appraisals by providing what the Travelers see as unconditional love. As in other narratives, the Traveler consequently becomes deserving of that love, adding a positive moral dimension to the self. A street kid quoted in a study by Kimberly Bender and colleagues aptly summed this up by saying, "unlike supposed friends that you make out here that turn their back on you—a dog's not going to do that—if a dog knows how to behave, it's not going to like run off on you—he's gonna be there no matter what" (2007:33). Regardless of what passersby and police officers might say, the dog provides consistently positive feedback about the Traveler's self.

Dogs also shield against negative appraisals by serving as symbolic resources for narratively constructing a positive self-image. In many narratives, Travelers say that having a dog provides a sense of responsibility that influences their behavior for the better. Although some reported encounters with the police, most said that having an animal kept them on the straight and narrow. For example, Dana said that traveling with a dog "gives you some responsibility, so it gives you a purpose. I know a lot of people on the street feel pretty useless. I know I've felt that way, and I've talked to my friends when they're depressed, and it's kind of rough on the streets." In the study by Bender and colleagues, many of the kids they interviewed also brought this up. As the authors noted: "Caring for their animals provided the young people with a sense of pride and accomplishment. They were proud of how they treated their animals and how well behaved they were. The responsibility of caring for a pet provided meaning in the lives of pet owners, increased their sense of well-being, and motivated them to continue trying to meet basic needs and survive on the street" (2007:33).

For the most part, Travelers claimed that they avoided engaging in activities that might cause them to have their dogs taken away from them. They also wanted to avoid going to jail because of the separation from their animals. As Bender and colleagues pointed out, "Pets motivated them to be responsible and avoid situations that were likely to lead to separation from or harm to their pets" (2007:38; see also Rew 2000). For example, Ronnie admitted to me that he "sells a little weed" occasionally, but added, as he petted his dog, "I try not to do anything to get arrested because of him."

Several Travelers became emotional while talking about the possibility of separation from their dogs. Some said they would become violent in that case. For example, Malcolm said: "If I was going to jail and she was going to the dog pound, I'm pretty much sure I'd end up getting myself stuck in jail for longer."

His voice rose and began to waver slightly. He cleared his throat and continued: "Because you don't want to take my dog. No. Especially since I do nothing. Yeah, I might smoke some weed here and there, or drink some beer here and there, but I don't run around breaking crap or annoying people or anything like that. If I'm spanging with my sign, all I'm doing is just sitting there. I'm hurting nobody."

"So you'd be pretty upset if anything happened to her," I said, stating the obvious.

He said, "Yeah. If anything were to . . . ," his voice trailed off, and then he paused while tears gathered in his eyes. He wiped them away and looked at me, and I felt ashamed for having brought this on. "I don't even want to think about that," he said. "It wouldn't be very good."

When Dana told me about the police shooting Travelers' dogs, I asked how she would react if that happened. She confirmed Malcolm's position that she would only make the situation worse. "I know most homeless people would kill for their dogs," she said. "And I think if anybody were to ever hurt my dog, I could probably go to that level, and I'm not a violent person. I'm not crazy or anything. But if somebody hurt my dog purposefully, I don't think I'd be able to control myself. I'd need to be restrained. And I think a lot of people feel that way."

In describing the lengths they would go to for their dogs, Dana and Malcolm portray a potential reversal of roles in which the protector—the dog—becomes the protected. By envisioning this, they invoke both components of mattering: importance and dependence. They conse-quently add further support to the moral identities already built from constructions of unconditional love and innocence in their stories.

The Strengths and
Weaknesses of the Protector Narrative

Travelers' constructions of the discernment and judgment of their dogs allow them to experience the world's goodness and to take its dangers in stride. Although having a dog can bring on trouble, including negative feedback from others, Travelers' personal narra-

Photograph by Mark Rodgers, courtesy of San Francisco Community Clinic Consortium's VET SOS project.

*A Traveler's dog receives veterinary care
at a VET SOS clinic.*

tives also construct dogs as supportive significant others, providing positive self-reflections. Whether the stories of the heroism of dogs at campsites and on the street are factual or exaggerated, their main strength appears through their ability to provide a source of self-worth and a positive attitude. At least one study of street kids found this "essential in continuing to meet the day-to-day challenges of life on the streets" (Bender et al. 2007:33).

The positive attitude among the youth made a strong impression on me as I did this research. To be sure, I did not conduct a systematic study of Travelers, nor did I compare Travelers who had dogs with those who did not. Consequently, I cannot say definitively that dogs provided the necessary condition for the generally bright outlook I saw. But after interviewing a number of uncynical and optimistic Travelers, I got to thinking. While doing this research, I found myself in the situation of teaching upper-division undergraduates on Thursdays and interviewing Travelers on Fridays and Saturdays. Having these sequential experiences, I could not help making comparisons. Although my students and these Travelers were similar in age, and although many in both groups had dogs, they could not have differed more in outlook. My students had endless complaints about their lives. They grumbled about the amount of reading they had to do and the number of long papers they had to write. They protested that the faculty were apparently contriving to give all exams during the same week. They requested extensions on assignments and gave excuses for lateness based on the most trivial of events. None of the Travelers I met had graduated from college. Yet they seemed to see a better world, one that held more promise for them, than the world my students saw. The Travelers claimed to be living just as they wanted to live. Although one cannot know how much of this claim simply justified their limited options as a "choice," they had nevertheless adopted an impressive attitude toward their circumstances.

I checked myself for rose-colored glasses regularly. I know that I could have encountered people who were especially good at spinning identities. But speaking anecdotally, I saw less cynicism and even less fear among those who had taken to the road rather than taking the SAT. Although I saw fatigue, hunger, and dirt—a lot of dirt—among the Travelers, I also saw cheerfulness and a sense of competence that I have seldom seen on university campuses. In focus groups with homeless youth, Bender and colleagues found a similar perspective. They wrote: "Youth spoke of avoiding 'drama' and maintaining a 'no worries' attitude to prevent them from becoming overly stressed and pessimistic. . . . In addition to maintaining a positive attitude, participants discussed the benefits of living on the streets. It appeared that focusing on the positive aspects of street culture helped them maintain optimism about their lives" (2007:33–34; see also Kidd 2003; Rew 2000).

Despite the optimism and sense of self-worth it conveys, the protector narrative has two pitfalls. First, its appeal among youth can lead them to acquire dogs they cannot care for. Many strive to emulate the iconic image of the Traveler and his or her dog without having adequate resources for responsible pet ownership. Of course, all the kids I interviewed described *themselves* as responsible pet guardians, while *others* had acquired dogs for the wrong reasons, did not train them properly, or bred them irresponsibly. But the reality is that Travelers and homeless kids cannot afford veterinary care and many hold naive views that animals raised "naturally" will not need it. Many breed their dogs without considering what can go wrong for a female dog and her pups during whelping. At festivals and Rainbow Gatherings, many dogs contract communicable diseases, including the potentially fatal parvovirus. Because I conducted interviews at veterinary clinics, I talked only with kids who complied with vaccination requirements and, in many cases, with sterilization laws. In San Francisco and Berkeley, VET SOS and PALS provide invaluable services to young pet owners, but affordable veterinary care is simply out of the reach of thousands of others across the country.

A second, and related, limitation of the dog-as-protector narrative has to do with the burdens it places on dogs. Not every dog is built for the hardships of nonstop travel, for walking long distances and tolerating all kinds of weather. Not every dog can live up to expectations to love unconditionally. And not every dog can provide the kind of protection that Travelers need. Moreover, a fine line exists between a good protector and an aggressive dog. The need for the former could potentially lead to a tolerance or even cultivation of the latter. The context of this study did not allow me to learn the fate of dogs over time, especially for those who failed to meet the expectations placed on them. Nor did it allow me to learn the fate of their guardians. I wish them all well.

Notes

1. Meanwhile, a different system of travel had existed for the bourgeoisie. Youth of wealth and means had long enjoyed the rite of passage

known as the "Grand Tour," the circuit of cities and attractions of (primarily) Western Europe, which provided sightseeing and adventure as education. Thus, wealthy youth could travel openly for pleasure, but others did so under the cover of work: the "commoner's Grand Tour" (Adler 1985:341).

2. In the United States, "to tramp" referred to the march to battle. Use of the word "tramp" to refer to a "loose" woman did not start until the 1920s.

3. The Federal Transient Relief Service developed over 200 camps across the United States to house and feed migrants. Minehan argued that the camps fueled the problem they were designed to resolve. He wrote: "In 1934 alone it was possible for any male over 16 to travel from Maine to Florida, stopping off en route at transient camps where the food was fair and the conditions often excellent. You could enter and stay two or three days without doing a bit of work, perhaps inveigle the director into giving you some new clothes, and then leave. You did not have to travel any more than a day before you would reach another camp where you could rest for a while" (1936:138). This generated a polite but heated debate with George Outland, supervisor of boys' welfare for the Transient Relief Service in California in 1933 and 1934, and later a US congressman. Outland argued that the service "provided food, shelter and clothing, and in many cases friendly advice and counsel to thousands of boys who otherwise might have come into contact with crime, or have been beggars" (1937:278).

4. For more on temporal sequencing, see Labov and Waletzky 1997 and Frank 2010.

5. By agreement with the Homeless Youth Alliance, I did not ask directly what had led to a Traveler's homelessness. This protected the youth from potentially talking about illegal activities or upsetting experiences. However, if someone brought up one of these issues, I listened without asking probing questions.

6. Thanks to California native Amanda Shigihara for enlightening me about the meaning of "hella."

7. A first offense results in a verbal warning. After a second offense, a citation is issued and a conviction could bring a fine of fifty to one hundred dollars. Penalties increase for additional violations, with exceptions for medical emergencies, parades, protests, and other situations. San Francisco enacted a similar law, aimed at the hippies in Haight-Ashbury, in 1968. It was declared unconstitutional in 1979 after police used it in 1974 to target gay men (Harvey Milk's "Castro Fourteen").

8. For a discussion of how laws about public space criminalize homelessness, see Mitchell 1997.

9. See, for example, James 2011. Other cities have witnessed similar waves of complaints about youth in particular neighborhoods. New Yorkers compared homeless youth in the West Village to an "army of occupation" (Gibson 2011:3).

7 Lifechangers and Lifesavers

In Chapter 2, I introduced Pali Boucher, who helped establish VET SOS after more than twenty years of homelessness. Pali found joy in caring for other creatures also living on the streets, such as stray dogs, feral cats, and injured pigeons. Pali explained, "Being able to take care of animals and heal whatever was wrong was the only feeling I ever had in my life that was a good, whole feeling."[1] Along the way, she befriended a dog she called Charlie. But during Pali's frequent trips to jail for "stupid things, like trespassing," Charlie would end up impounded in the San Francisco Animal Care and Control facility. "One time," Pali recalled, "when they brought Charlie in, she had bitten somebody, and they put her to sleep. It was the first time in my life I realized that I wasn't just affecting myself by going out and being loaded, that I was directly responsible for the pain of somebody else." Pali began visiting the San Francisco Society for the Prevention of Cruelty to Animals. She had no intentions of adopting a dog, but she fell in love with Leadbelly, a constantly baying coonhound scheduled for euthanasia. "Somehow, I got the money, faked an address and adopted him," she said. They lived on the streets together, and as she recalled, "Every second of every day I was trying to keep that dog safe." She worried about how her drug use and drinking would cause her to lose Leadbelly as she had lost Charlie. "I was in and out of jail all the time," she said. "I narrowly dodged the bullet of losing my dog so many times that it just stressed me out too much, man. I had to make some changes."

Pali had missed some court dates and consequently had a warrant out for her arrest. A friend agreed to take Leadbelly if she were arrested—a prescient arrangement, as it turned out, for Pali soon spent six months in jail. Upon her release, she checked into a detox center, and visited Leadbelly on the weekends. He was "my life and my joy," she said. "I couldn't lose him because of old habits." Clean and sober after a year in rehab, she found subsidized housing that allowed dogs.

Pali had to say goodbye to Leadbelly in 2001, but she stayed sober because "he helped me learn how to take care of myself by taking care of him." She began Rocket Dog Rescue in his honor. "Leadbelly was a gift sent to me," she claimed, "and every step of the way it was my responsibility to follow through. Now, I want to devote my life to animals."

* * *

In this chapter, I examine narratives that construct animals as redemptive figures who keep people alive or turn their lives around. In general, redemption stories take the following plotline: "My life took the wrong course. I almost lost hope, but things turned out for the best." They depict a moral arc with redemption entering somewhere between losing hope and having things turn out for the best. Redemption can enter stories in various forms and combinations of forms. It can enter through religion, in the path from sin to salvation. It can enter through serious illness or injury, and it can enter because of separation through divorce or death. In the stories analyzed in this chapter, redemption takes animal form.

The theme of redemption exemplifies how historically and culturally specific models of stories combine with subjective experience in personal narratives. The concept of redemption has roots in the Hebrew Bible and related social and legal customs, but it found its fullest expression in Christian theology, through the atoning crucifixion and resurrection of Jesus Christ. Scholars point out that the redemption theme resonates with uniquely American ideals (McAdams 2006b; see also Bellah et al. 1985). For example, the Puritans viewed their "city on a hill" as a model community that would redeem the religious persecution they had endured (see Erikson 1966; Wills 1990). Later, the popular (and to some, laughable) Horatio Alger stories took variations on the redemptive plotline of hard work, crisis, struggle, and eventual success. Stories of redemption from adversity often appear in popular culture. For example, Dan McAdams found the theme of redemption in over half of the feature stories in *People* magazine over an eight-month period (2006b:20–22). Redemption also constitutes a significant element in self-help discourse. Groups based on the "twelve step" rhetoric of Alcoholics Anonymous offer a particular formula for redemption stories whereby personal growth comes out of addiction and "dysfunctional" relationships, thereby redeeming the hardship and abuse (Irvine 1999).

Before I offer examples of how animals fill the redemptive role, I want to point out that, with one exception, the tellers of these stories had made it off the street when I met them. In the preceding chapters, I have emphasized how the circumstances of homelessness shaped particular forms of narrative. Here, I include the stories of formerly homeless people for the same reason; getting off the street—or even the promise of doing so—creates an opening for redemption stories. Circumstances allowed these interviewees to tell a particular kind of story that I did not hear from those who were still on the street. I will let the examples make my point.

Constructing Animals as Lifechangers

Donna's Story

I met Donna in San Francisco at an event called Project Homeless Connect (PHC), which provides "one-stop shopping" for homeless people in over 200 US cities. By collaborating with businesses, non-profits, and government organizations, PHC offers everything from haircuts and dental work to legal assistance and veterinary care. The events feature music and food, and even "parking areas" for the shopping carts that often hold the life possessions of many homeless people. VET SOS regularly holds clinics at PHC events. In late spring of 2010, I interviewed pet owners at the event in Bayview Park, in the southeastern corner of the city. A 2011 article in the *New Yorker* described the predominantly African American Bayview–Hunter's Point area as "the poorest and most violent neighborhood in San Francisco" (Tough 2011:25), but a festival atmosphere filled Bayview Park that day. When we arrived well before the official start of the event, clients had already begun to line up with their animals.

Dr. Strubel had pointed Donna out and told me that I really needed to hear her story. Donna did not have an animal with her that day. Nevertheless, she waited in line to sign up for a veterinary examination. She then walked out of the crowd and I lost sight of her. When she returned to check on the progress of the list, I introduced myself. She explained that she had brought her friend Emily, the rescuer of the spray-painted dog whom I introduced in Chapter 5. Emily's dog, Hobo, needed a checkup, and because Donna had a car, she had provided transportation. Hobo did not like other dogs, so the three of them sat away from the crowd, across the street from the park. Emily stayed with Hobo while Donna periodically checked on Hobo's position on the examination list. Meanwhile, I talked with Emily about her relationship with Hobo. As our interview ended, she told me, "You know, you really should interview Donna." Clearly, I had to hear this story.

After Hobo's examination, Donna and I sat on the sidewalk leaning against a brick building with our legs stretched out in the sun. At fifty-three, Donna was petite and almost elfin-looking, with long, light brown hair and deep-set brown eyes that held my gaze intently. Her weatherworn skin and missing teeth spoke to a life of hardship. She explained that she was now living upstairs in her mother's Bernal Heights home, but had lived on the streets for nearly forty years. At age fifteen, she had begun drinking and using heroin. She said she had set out not only to follow her older sister's lead, but also to surpass her by becoming "a bigger dope fiend." Donna left home so that her mother would not have to see her hooked on heroin. She soon added crack to her repertoire, and supported her habit through prostitution. I asked what she felt the first time she sold her body. "I was scared," she recalled. "But I had to have that drug. I didn't care."

After leaving home, Donna's life consisted of homelessness, prostitution, drug addiction, and abusive relationships. She hitchhiked across the country numerous times, buying drugs and turning tricks at truck stops from Illinois to Washington. She recounted the time a john pushed her out of a moving tractor-trailer cab after refusing to pay for her services, and recalled, somewhat proudly, that she had "tucked and rolled" when she hit the ground. Eventually, she "got the virus," meaning HIV, from either "the sex or the needles." Her son, who was twenty-one at the time of this interview, fortunately "came out negative" when she gave birth to him. "I would never, ever shove a needle in my arm anymore," she told me. I asked her how she quit. She paused while tears sprang up in her eyes. She said softly, "Athena." She paused again, then looked at me and said, "She was the love of my life."

Athena, a German Shepherd/Labrador Retriever mix, was Donna's companion for ten years. I asked if she had a picture of her dog on the phone she held in her hand. She did not, but it mattered very little, because she gave me a detailed description that reminded me of J. R. Ackerley's portrayal of his beloved German Shepherd, Tulip.[2] After describing Tulip's often troublesome temperament, Ackerley wrote, "It is necessary to add that she is beautiful" (1965:8). He continued:

> Her ears are tall and pointed, like the ears of Anubis. How she manages to hold them constantly erect, as though starched, I do not know, for with their fine covering mouse-gray fur they are soft and flimsy; when she stands with her back to the sun it shines through the delicate tissue, so that they glow shell-pink as though incandescent . . . dark markings symmetrically divide up her face into zones of pale pastel colors, like a mosaic, or a stained-glass window . . . her sable tunic is of the texture of satin . . . no tailor could have shaped it more elegantly. (1965:8–9)

Reading this, I felt as though I had never really seen a dog, such was Ackerley's focus and admiration. Likewise, Donna described Athena's thick black-and-sable coat, her amber eyes rimmed in black, with the dark brows over them that make the dogs so marked especially expressive. In his book *Merle's Door,* Ted Kerasote reports, "The Hidatsa, a Native American tribe of the northern Great Plains, believe that these sorts of dogs, whom they call 'Four Eyes,' are especially gentle and have magical powers" (2007:3). This certainly seems to fit Athena, at least in Donna's description of her.

Athena and Donna came together through Pali, long a common denominator between homeless people and homeless animals in San Francisco. About a decade ago, Donna lived with an abusive boyfriend in a garbage-strewn underpass encampment. Worn out from addiction and hard living, the pair pitched a tent in her mother's backyard. Pali and Donna had known each other on the street, and, as Donna recalled, "Pali said, 'You need a dog in your life.'" Pali had rescued three-year-old Athena from death row in a shelter. Although it might not seem that a homeless drug addict in an abusive relationship would make the best guardian for a dog, the match saved two lives. As Donna explained, "Athena did everything for me. She got me out of an abusive relationship. It was either the dog, or him, and I chose the dog. He used to take my money. My shoes. Everything. The guy used to beat me up and Pali told me it was either the man or the dog, so I chose Athena. I got the dog. Got rid of the man."

With the boyfriend out of the picture, Donna moved from the yard into her mother's house, to her own space in what she called "the upstairs." But Pali had said, "You have to be clean to have the dog." Donna's mother agreed, so she faced a decision. "I realized Athena meant everything to me," she told me. "I said to myself, 'My dog comes first in my life. Would I rather use drugs, or feed my dog?' And I fell in love with Athena, so I gave up the needle. Gave up the pipe. I gave up liquor. Everything."

This intrigued me greatly, to say the least. I had heard and read horrendous accounts of alcohol withdrawal. I knew that similar misery accompanied withdrawal from heroin. I had heard about the cramping, nausea, and the feeling of "itchy blood." I could not imagine adding crack cocaine into the mix and withdrawing from all three at once. I wanted to know how Donna had done it. She said, matter-of-factly, "Cold turkey."

"You went cold turkey?" I repeated, just to make sure I had heard right.

"Cold turkey," she said again.

"By yourself?" I asked. "You went through withdrawal?"

"Yup. I went through withdrawal, and from there, I went to the methadone clinic. Got on methadone. Athena went with me, and everybody loved her, too. Athena was everything. Okay? Athena was everything. Everywhere I went, Athena followed. She knew the pet stores. She sat down at the coffee shop. Everything."

Donna also credited Athena with improving her HIV status. Once clean, Donna began taking care of herself, and she felt better. She went for a blood test and the results gave her proof. "She helped get my HIV level down. Yeah. Having Athena got my T-cells going up. When Athena came into my life, everything was beautiful."

Donna has never worked at any job other than being a prostitute, and her HIV, combined with dyslexia uncovered in middle age, prevents her from working now. Considered fully disabled, she receives monthly SSI checks. Athena had died over a year prior to the interview, from cancer, at age thirteen. A local pet supply store had held a memorial service for her. VET SOS arranged for cremation, and Donna has kept the ashes because she wants them mixed and distributed with hers when she dies. "We made it so that when I die, I'm going to be with her," she said, explaining how, having journeyed together in this world, they would meet again at the final destination.

Donna says she is in no hurry to reach that destination, however. Pali found her another dog, and a cat, too. She showed me the pictures of both on her cell phone. "I hope I don't die," she told me. "I got to take care of Buddy, my new dog. I will start AIDS medication Tuesday because I want to live for my dog." As if to make sure we both heard clearly, she repeated herself, saying again, "I'm going to take the HIV medicine because it's going to make me live for my dog." Donna quickly added that she loves the cat, too. "They mean everything in my life," she said. But she considers the dog special because she believes Athena chose him. As she explained, "After Athena died a year ago, Pali asked me to help another dog. So Athena sent Buddy. They have the same temperament. Everything Athena had, Buddy has. They're afraid of the same things. They like the same things." Donna had to stay in the hospital recently and she thought only of getting home to her dog and cat. "It killed me," she said. "Every day, I asked the doctor, 'When can I go home so I can be with my pets?' Just to have them in my life means everything."

Tommy's Story

I met Tommy at the Mercer Clinic in Sacramento. He had brought his young black-and-tan dog, Monty, for a checkup and nail trim. Tommy sat in a folding chair and I sat cross-legged on the ground next to him. The sun shone brightly and warmed us after what had started as a chilly morning. Tommy and I speculated about Monty's bloodlines, and we decided on a mix of Rottweiler and some kind of terrier. It really was anyone's guess. Monty weighed about thirty pounds. Monty let me pet him and he took the treat I offered, but he was much more interested in checking out all the other dogs passing by than in getting to know me. He wagged his tail, sniffed the air, and ventured out to the end of his leash before returning to check in with Tommy. He panted and did a little dance with his front paws. Then he repeated the routine all over again. As we watched Monty, I asked Tommy about his ten years of homelessness. At first, he shrugged and said he had been "down on his luck." As David Snow and Leon Anderson point out, this explanation both "exempts the homeless from responsibility for their plight, and it leaves open the possibility of a better future" (1993:204). After all, bad luck can happen to anyone and thus, as a causal account of homelessness, it salvages one's sense of self-worth. But as Tommy continued his story, he clearly saw less random forces at work. "I was a bad kid for many years," he told me. "I stole and I did drugs. Fighting. Stabbings. Shootings. Years of abuse." He had done time in jail.

When we met, Tommy had been living in his van outside of Sacramento for several months. The van did not run, but friends allowed him to park it on their property. Someone had abandoned Monty as a puppy at the church Tommy was attending. After no one came for Monty, the church staff suggested that he would make a good companion for Tommy. "I took him home," he said, using the language of the houseless but not homeless to describe his van, "and he's been the best thing for me." I asked him to tell me more. Tommy explained that he was suffering from debilitating depression, and added, "Monty helps with that."

"How so?" I asked.

"He makes me come out and walk with other people. He gets me socializing with other people. And he's like my best friend because, being homeless, you don't really have friends unless you're drinking and doing drugs and all. You just walk the streets and just try to find what you can on the streets. He gives me energy because he can make me get out and walk. He's just adorable to other people. They just come up, and it makes me feel better because I have mental illness also, where I don't like to be around people. And he just, he's just a joy to be with. He's good when people come up to our camp or something. He'll bark and let me know that somebody's there."

In this brief statement, Tommy assigned Monty most of the roles outlined in the preceding chapters. He depicted Monty as his best friend, social facilitator, and protector. He credited him with providing emotional support and promoting physical health. As his story continued, however, Tommy invoked an account of dog-as-lifesaver that I came very close to missing.

Now approaching forty, Tommy had been working in the construction trades for many years until he witnessed a fatal accident on a construction site. He saw his boss and another man die when they both fell from a great height. "I haven't worked since then," he told me. "It really screwed me up." A few months before I met him, Tommy had started receiving SSI payments after a long struggle to qualify as disabled. As he explained, "Seven years, I was fighting for my SSI. It took seven years to get that."

"No kidding?"

"Till they finally figured out that I'm not mentally stable," Tommy said. "They wouldn't take me for the physical. Three times, I had to go before the judge."

Now, he and Monty were getting by on a modest monthly check. Tommy was on a waiting list for a low-income apartment. He said he was doing well now, thanks largely to Monty's companionship and what he called his "psych pills."

I had begun to think of the interview with Tommy as unremarkable, providing more of the same kind of information I already had. Then, as we wrapped up, Tommy mentioned that he would soon start treatment for hepatitis C, a consequence of years of drug abuse and drinking. I had almost turned off the recorder when he said, "Monty also got me off alcohol and got me off drugs. Now I'm sober and I'm healthy." Clearly, the story was not over yet. Doctors refer to these moments as "doorknob conversations." After an uneventful office visit, with a hand already on the doorknob, the patient says, "I forgot to mention this, but . . ." or "It's probably nothing, but . . ." I asked Tommy how Monty had helped him stop drinking and using drugs. He explained that he had gotten sober by necessity in jail. After his release, he started attending the church where Monty had turned up as a stray. Tommy felt he was beginning to get his life back on track, but Monty provided the motivation he needed: "When I got out of jail, I told myself that I would never drink again or smoke again, and I told that to Monty, and every time I want to go to get a drink, he just looks at me, almost shaking that head, saying, 'You know what you just went through the last thirty-five years!'"

* * *

In both of these stories, Donna and Tommy tell a narrative that constructs the dog as redeeming them from the clutches of addiction. For now, I will postpone the discussion of how this narrative works. First, I want to present narratives that, while of the same sort, delve even deeper into human frailty. Whereas Donna and Tommy credit their dogs with *changing* their lives, the following section examines stories that construct animals as *saving* people's lives.

Constructing Animals as Lifesavers

Trish's Story

I met Trish on a cold December day in Boulder. She stood on the median at the exit of a busy shopping center with her Jack Russell terrier bundled up in a dog bed beside her. She was "flying a sign" that read, "Sober. Doing the best I can. Please help." I had finished some shopping and noticed her with the dog on my way out. The flow of traffic prevented me from stopping, but I circled the block, returned, and parked nearby. I went into the nearby restaurant and bought a large cup of hot tea. I brought it over to Trish and introduced myself. She expressed interest in my project and was eager to talk. In fact, she said she would enjoy the company.

Trish told me that her dog, Pixel, came from a pet store where she had done the feeding and cleaning nearly a decade ago. As a puppy, Pixel had contracted parvovirus and Trish attributed his survival to her care. Although Pixel recovered, the store owner thought he could no longer sell him, and offered the dog to Trish. She could hardly afford to feed herself, much less a dog, she said, but she took him anyway and the two had been inseparable ever since. On the day we met, Trish had bundled Pixel up in two jackets and brought his bed along so that he would stay warm. She said she sometimes tried to leave him in the mobile home in which they now lived, the first "home" with four walls that they had ever shared. But she explained that, after being with her around the clock for years, curling up next to her in cars and under bridges, Pixel had separation anxiety without her. "It's funny," she said, "because we have a place now, and he won't stay. He won't. He would rather be out here, cold and with me, than being there by himself."

Trish told me that she had been homeless "off and on" for over ten years. For her, *not* being homeless meant sleeping in a car or in the back of the pet store. When she was much younger, she had left home to follow the Grateful Dead, and she eventually landed in Boulder. By then, she had a heroin habit. When she could not get high, she drank to dull the cravings. "I didn't really like to drink," she explained, "but if I was sick from not having opiates, I had to drink because I couldn't walk, you know, or eat or do anything." When I met Trish, she had been clean and sober for two years. She had found an addiction rehabilitation facility that covered the costs of her treatment through a well-timed state program. "It was awesome," she said. "I just happened to call when the government was doing this study. They were paying for people's treatment, and then they wanted to follow them for six months. So, I went there and got sober." She found a friend to care for Pixel, "someone with a house," while she went through what she described as a "severe detox." Trish explained that when she was released from rehab, "I wanted to get off the streets but I had to find a job and try to do all those things I couldn't do before because I was messed up, which was really, really weird. It had been so long since I had to have a schedule. I loved it, though. I was like, 'I can do this.'" She supported herself by working various jobs that paid under the table, mostly cleaning houses. "It took about six months," she said, "and I got us off the streets. We lived out of my car." That work, however, had recently dropped off. "As it got colder, I started losing jobs," she said, "not by anything that I was doing, but I don't know, maybe they're afraid of the economy, afraid of whatever and they're trying to hold on to their money. The holidays are coming, and this and that."

Trish had had to sell the car and, when we met in midwinter, she and Pixel were sleeping in an abandoned mobile home. Although it was condemned, the trailer-park manager nevertheless charged her a "lot fee" of three hundred dollars a month. Without a job, she had to come up with the rent. She calculated that she needed to earn forty dollars a day. "Earning" meant panhandling, for Trish could not easily get work because of a felony on her record for possession of heroin. "I had that charge fifteen years ago," she explained.

"It was a felony then. Now it's a misdemeanor, apparently. But back then, twenty dollars' worth of heroin was a felony, so I have that on my record. I am having a hard time getting a job even at Burger King or McDonald's. Everybody does background checks now, so if I don't want to be homeless again, here I am." She brandished the cardboard sign to illustrate her point. Through it all, Pixel had kept her going, she said, even during her darkest times. She added that Pixel even kept her alive.

"It was something to lose, you know? Yeah. I was [on the streets]. I hated it. I was totally at rock bottom. I just wanted to die. But I couldn't, because he needed me. I didn't want to be out here anymore. I couldn't see the light at all anymore. And I'd asked for help so many times and I couldn't get it, so at some point, I was just, like, 'I'm done. I can't do this anymore.' But I couldn't give up because I had something else to take care of besides myself. So he kept me alive."

I asked, "You mean you might have committed suicide if it weren't for him?"

"Yeah," she replied. "I don't know if I actually could have gone through with it. I just wanted it over. I just didn't want to be here anymore. I never really thought about, 'I'm going to get a gun, or a knife, or a razor blade,' but I was losing all motivation. But, you know, I still needed to feed him and keep him warm at night. I didn't care about myself, but I had to care about him, you know? He got me through a really tough spot. If I would've had to be without him out there before, I don't think I would have made it, at all."

In the two years since that "tough spot," Trish believes that Pixel has helped her stay sober. "He definitely helps keep me on the straight and narrow," she told me. She claims that Pixel "hates the smell of alcohol," and has kept her away from "bad elements, or groups of people, because of the alcohol, the drugs, and all that." She claims that the dog will nip the heels of people who approach smelling of alcohol. Using the construction of discernment familiar from protector narratives, Trish said, "He's an awesome judge of character. He just knows." She looked down at Pixel and added, "Right, buddy?" The little dog never took his eyes off her.

Rudy's Story

Like Trish, Rudy credits his dogs, a pair of Dachshunds, with keeping him alive. He had his eight-year-old male with him when we met at the Mercer Clinic. We sat in the shade on folding chairs while he waited for his dog's turn to have a routine examination and vaccinations. Rudy declined to talk to me at first, because he said he did not consider himself homeless. Nevertheless, he soon seemed to realize that talking with me would pass the time. Reticent even then, he repeatedly said that he did not have much to say. But what he did say revealed his image of a powerful bond he felt with his dogs.

Rudy prided himself on never having slept on the street, but he had slept in nearly every kind of habitation imaginable. Now in his sixties, he was staying in the homes of family members around Sacramento. Like Tommy, he had worked in construction for most of his life. He had lost a finger and part of his thumb along the way, but he kept working until cancer forced him to stop. He held up crossed fingers and smiled as he said, "But right now, it's in remission." He explained that his SSI check of almost nine hundred dollars a month more than covered his expenses because, "Unlike most of the people around here who get Social Security, I don't spend it on drugs." Perhaps because Rudy saw himself as resourceful enough to have avoided sleeping on the street, he seemed to want to distance himself from the "truly" homeless people all around us (see Snow and Anderson 1993).

I asked Rudy how he spent his time, and he smiled and pointed to the dog. "I take him out about twenty times a day," he said. "Walk, walk, walk. I take him to the park. I got a female, too, that's ball nuts. She could play ball all day long. I talk to them. Pet them. He sleeps in my bed. They both do. One's up by my head. Other one's down by my feet. Other than that, I don't do much else. I take good care of my dogs. If I didn't have my dogs, I'd be unhappy."

Rudy explained that he had come close to losing his dogs not long ago. He had shared an apartment with a roommate, whom he described as "someone I thought was my friend." But Rudy had gone to jail for sixty days on what he called a "trumped-up" drug charge. While in jail, Rudy's landlord evicted him and the roommate sold everything—except the dogs.

"Why not the dogs, too?" I asked.

"Couldn't find nobody to buy 'em, I guess," he said, and added, "It's a good thing, too, 'cause they're keeping me alive."

I asked, "How are they doing that?"

The man of few words struggled to answer. After a pause, he said. "I can't really say. Just their aura, I guess you would call it."

"Their what?" I asked.

He looked at his dog, smiled, and looked back at me, sheepishly. "Love," he said. "It's unconditional. It's like mine for them." I could tell he felt embarrassed speaking this way. Just to ease the awkwardness I said, "So they just care for you no matter what?"

"Yeah," he said softly, stroking his dog's smooth copper coat and avoiding my eyes. The dog looked up at him adoringly. "Just like I do with them. I just love 'em. Just like they was real people."

Denise's Story

Lest it seem that people construct only dogs as having the power to transform or even save lives, other stories placed cats in the lifesaver role. I met Denise and her cat, Ivy, at a VET SOS clinic in Dolores Park. White, middle-aged Denise defied the stereotype of the homeless person. Slender and nicely dressed, she had white teeth and clean, neatly styled hair. Ivy, a tiny, black-and-white cat, sat sphinx-like in a carrier, with her white paws tucked neatly underneath her. I put my finger near the carrier's door for her to sniff. She leaned forward to check it out and, proclaiming me safe but uninteresting, turned her head just enough to look past me into the middle distance, as if to say, "Ho hum." Denise and I sought some shade from the afternoon sun. We found it on a nearby cement staircase, where we sat down to talk.

I asked Denise how she became homeless, and she explained that she had been self-employed as a graphic artist, but severe depression caused her to miss deadlines. Major clients lost faith in her, and the accounts gradually dwindled away. She fell behind on rent, and her landlord evicted her. She tried to find a place to live before she had to move out of the apartment, but that did not happen. When time ran out, she put her belongings in storage. She and Ivy had lived in her car for over eight months when we met. "Half of the car is taken up by her stuff," Denise said, "because there's a big carrier, which she sleeps in, and then her litter box, and her bowls, so she essentially has the whole back seat and then I'm in the front seat." Denise said she felt like she was living in a "glass display case." She was parking in her former neighborhood because it was safe. But because living in a car was illegal, she was trying to avoid trouble by obeying the area's parking laws. "My time is taken up just moving the car," she told me. "I have to keep moving it. I can't park more than two hours." Even when she could find a place, the traffic and lights kept her awake. "I get very little sleep," she said. "So I'm very sleep deprived." She admitted to shutting herself in her storage locker just to rest in dark, quiet privacy for a while. Sometimes she would bring Ivy with her, but other times she would let the cat sunbathe in her favorite spot on the rear ledge of the backseat. Although Ivy enjoyed this, it was putting Denise at risk. Her quandary echoed the concerns about "humaniacs" voiced by Linda in Chapter 3. As Denise said, "I'm really afraid that somebody is going to come along and go, 'Oh, no! Animal cruelty. A cat's locked in the car,' and report my vehicle. So I don't want to do anything that draws attention to the car at all, which means I don't want people to see her."

At the time of the interview, a friend was allowing Denise to shower at his apartment twice a week while he was at work. She would take her cat with her and claimed that Ivy "seems to know that we're going someplace else where she can run around. So she chirps, and her tail's up, and she purrs, and it's incredible to me. And it helps lift my spirits."

The eviction had made it very difficult for Denise to find another apartment, as it had for other people. In addition, Denise's situation did not qualify her for most of the housing programs available to the homeless. She never imagined she would live in her car for over eight months. As she explained, "I have a caseworker working very aggressively to find me housing, but in my particular situation, I kind of slip through the cracks. I don't fit into the demographic profile of the different housing prospects that are available. I'm not the right age. I'm not the right ethnicity. I'm childless. If I had children, there would be some housing."

Having Ivy initially made finding housing even more difficult. When I asked if she had considered finding Ivy another home, she shook her head side-to-side emphatically. Denise had adopted Ivy as a kitten from the SPCA five years prior to the interview. Ivy had come from an abusive situation, she said. She went on to explain: "She was a bit distant when I first adopted her, and then she grew to know me, but she's very frightened still of any new people, new situations. So I've kept her pretty protected, and that's why, when I became homeless, I didn't want to give her up, even though I know I had a lot of housing opportunities if I didn't have my cat."

Although Denise felt that she was protecting Ivy and doing the best thing for her, she explained to me that people often told her she had no right to keep a cat in her circumstances. When I asked her how she responded, she said: "I have a history with depression up to suicide ideation, and Ivy, I refer to her as my suicide barrier. And I don't say that in any light way. I would say most days, she's the reason why I keep going, because I made a commitment to take care of her when I adopted her. So she needs me, and I need her. She is the only source of daily, steady affection and companionship that I have. The only one. I can't imagine being without her, wanting to go on at all, without her."

By portraying Ivy as a "suicide barrier," Denise's account gives the cat significant influence on her construction of self. Fortunately, she would not have to decide between keeping Ivy and finding housing. Her doctor had provided documentation certifying Ivy as her necessary companion. The document qualifies Ivy as a "reasonable accommodation" to a disability, and landlords cannot refuse to rent to Denise because of Ivy, even if they usually do not allow pets. Meanwhile, Denise takes solace from how Ivy has adapted to their situation:

> I don't know what I would have done if eight months ago I'd known that I was still going to be homeless, how I would have done it differently. Because I actually do live each day thinking, "This has got to be the last day. I know I'm going to get a break

tomorrow," and it hasn't come. So I actually have to sort of not really think about my situation too much because I become—go into a state of despair. And it amazes me how she endures this. She knows where all her stuff is. She's got her bed, she's got her little cushion to lounge on. She's got her little sun deck. She knows where the food is. This is her place. That helps me keep going.

Redemption in Personal Narratives

Psychologist Dan McAdams, who has studied narrative and identity for decades, has examined the role of redemption in life stories (2004, 2006a, 2006b, 2008). He identifies the typical teller of a redemption story as an adult in midlife, concerned with what Erik Erikson (1950) called "generativity." I cannot do justice here to the theory of human development in which Erikson defined the term, but I can summarize generativity as an interest in leaving a positive legacy and making the world a better place. Following Erikson, McAdams argues that "generativity is the central psychological and moral challenge adults face, especially in their 30s, 40s, and 50s" (2006b:11). To understand generativity, it can help to place it against what Erikson posed as the contrasting potential outcome of the same life stage: stagnation, the feeling of being stuck or making no contribution.

In his research, McAdams most often hears redemption stories from American adults who score highly on psychological measures of generativity. Redemption stories resonate with midlife beliefs, values, and goals, but their roots extend back to childhood, reflecting a particular set of circumstances and experiences. McAdams found that generative adults often began life with some advantage or privilege. This could take the form of economic privilege, but it could also manifest itself as a talent or skill, a special destiny, or even the sense of being deeply loved. Whatever the case, such children gain a sense of being special. In addition, while growing up, the suffering of others makes an impression on them, and they consequently develop a robust sense of empathy. By adolescence, they have a strong commitment to religious, political, or ethical beliefs, which motivates them to want to take action, to help, and to make things better. In adulthood, generativity manifests itself as a desire to produce good things and see them grow and continue. This includes the family; generative adults make warm, involved, albeit disciplined parents. Their sense of commitment extends outside the family to the community and beyond. Generative adults engage in prosocial activities, such as volunteering or civic leadership. Overall, their experiences give them the skills and resources to engage in struggle and to triumph over the adversity that comes their way. The stories they tell of their lives essentially say, "I bear fruit; I give back; I offer a unique contribution. I will make a happy ending, even in a threatening world" (McAdams 2008:20).

According to McAdams, generative adults tend to tell redemption stories because of the combination of early advantage and moral commitment. The teller feels endowed with an essentially good self, guided by upstanding principles. This prompts him or her to see positive outcomes even from negative events. In this formulation, without the right predisposing factors in one's background, his or her orientation, and thus the stories, would take another tack. The redemption stories told by homeless pet owners challenge these assumptions because the tellers are *nongenerative* adults, not seemingly predisposed to tell redemption stories. Their backgrounds do not include privilege or a sense of a special purpose, but rather addiction, prostitution, violence, poverty, jail, disabling mental illness, and HIV. They did not grow up feeling secure and loved. While their generative peers-in-the-making developed moral commitments through religion or politics, these tellers focused on staying high, staying out of jail, or staying alive. Nevertheless, they envisioned brighter futures emerging out of their struggles. The construction of their stories around their pets highlights the symbolic power of animals.

Animals as Vehicles for Redemption Stories

As mentioned, redemption can enter a story in several ways, including the narrator's perseverance, the help of friends or benefactors, good fortune, or divine intervention. As an analytic tool, McAdams has outlined six "languages" of redemption, or "sets of images and ideas that people routinely draw upon when they try to make sense of the moves in their lives from negativity and suffering, on one hand, to positivity and enhancement, on the other" (2006b:41). These languages include *atonement* (or salvation), borrowed from religious sources, and *emancipation,* which yields a narrative of freedom from oppression. They also include the language of *upward mobility,* in the familiar form of the rags-to-riches story, and the language of *recovery,* which applies to stories of healing the mind or body. In addition, the list includes the language of *enlightenment,* in which knowledge brings the teller out of ignorance, and the language of *development,* which draws from sources in self-fulfillment and self-help discourses. People mix and match these languages in telling the stories that depict their lives as moving from suffering to a more positive outcome, if not to triumph.

In the stories recounted in this chapter, animals provide the medium for redemption. One of Donna's statements captures this well. She said, "When Athena came into my life, everything was beautiful." The other stories contain variations on this theme: "My life is better because this animal is in it." The redemptive power of animals works in the narratives in three related ways. First, animals' dependence draws on and encourages the guardian's sense of responsibility. In other chapters, I discussed the importance of caregiving and responsibility and their relationship to the moral identity. Here, I add that providing for an animal's needs can offer a direction or a structure for one's life. Rudy talked about his dog wanting to "walk, walk, walk." Donna said that she had to take care of her new dog, Buddy. In some narratives, the decision to provide care constitutes a turning point. Donna, for example, had to decide between her dog and her abusive boyfriend, with the drugs and other baggage that came with him. In other stories, caregiving and responsibility constitute a reason to keep going. Trish realized that Pixel gave her "something to lose." Denise described wanting to fulfill her obligations to Ivy by protecting her.

Second, the perceived unconditional love from animals also makes them especially well suited for incorporation into redemption stories by producing a sense of mattering—a reward for caring, in a sense. Donna, Trish, and Rudy described caring for their animals and consequently feeling cared for by them. Tommy, too, said Monty was both "the best thing" for him and "a joy to be with." Denise's story depicts the nexus of caring for and feeling cared for particularly well. Her commitment motivated her decision to live in her car rather than enter housing without Ivy. In turn, she described Ivy as providing "daily, steady affection."

To the best of my knowledge, only one other scholar acknowledges the construction of animals as a "suicide barrier," to use Denise's term. In Amy Fitzgerald's (2007) research on domestic violence, some of the battered women she interviewed described animals as their "lifeline." Although neither Denise nor any of those who mentioned suicide discussed having had this experience, Fitzgerald's research supports the argument about the importance of the nexus of caring and feeling cared for. She found two related ways that "pets kept [women] from 'leaving' the abusive situation through suicide." In some cases, women stayed alive to provide care for their animals. In others, animals "provided the women with the emotional and social support they needed to stay alive" (2007:372). In many cases, animals moderated suicidality in both ways. They gave women a sense of responsibility *and* they provided emotional support.

A third factor that makes animals appropriate for redemption stories involves our imagination of animals as simultaneously innocent and incorruptible. They embody ideal, hyper-positive identities to which the tellers can aspire. They stand as silent witnesses to human behavior, and the tellers, through the practice of "speaking for," make use of this capacity by casting animals as principled advisers. This appears strongly in the story told by Tommy and, to some extent, in that told by Trish. For example, Tommy described promising Monty that he would not drink or do drugs, and the dog "reminded" him to keep his promise. When he described Monty as looking up at him and saying, "You know what you just went through the last thirty-five years," Tommy "spoke for" his dog. In doing so, Tommy constructed Monty's identity for me. But more important, he also constructed the dog's identity for *himself*. He gave Monty the attributes of an older brother or a knowing uncle, someone wise to Tommy's ways, who pointed out that the past was not worth repeating. When Tommy "spoke for" Monty in this particular way, he added a twist to the concept. In most instances of "speaking for," the socially more competent party— in this case, the human caretaker—has the power to define the identity of the less competent actor, the dog. Guardians often create rather simple-minded, albeit lovable, identities for animals, especially for dogs (see Sanders 1993, 1999). In contrast, Tommy constructed a nearly heroic identity for Monty, which surpassed his own, in a moral sense, by always having Tommy's best interests in mind. Monty "reminded" Tommy that he must continue on the straight and narrow path by staying clean and sober. For Trish, Pixel's morally superior character comes through in his ability to read people and keep her away from bad "elements," thus helping her stay clean and sober. Both dogs allow for the telling of a redemption story by making sure the narrative's positive course does not take a negative turn. Constructed as silent witnesses, animals keep the tellers from lapsing into risky behavior. Their uprightness and discernment provide the equivalent of the moral compass that generative adults would have acquired growing up. These three factors allow animals to serve as both the mode of atonement and the medium of salvation in redemption stories. The animal's dependence offers immediate ways to express care, allowing for the manifestation of a "good" self. The fulfillment of the associated responsibilities requires a sacrifice, which, in these stories, involves giving up drugs and alcohol or deciding to live in a car. The perceived unconditional love the animal provides, and the accompanying sense of mattering, reward the sacrifice. And the construction of the animal as the provider of this love, while simultaneously innocent of the adversity in the teller's past and yet wise to it, adds an implicitly Christ-like element to the narrative. Moreover, animals' acceptance of their human companions, despite their histories, imparts additional Christ-likeness.

Animals and the Languages of Redemption

Narratives that construct animals as their redemptive hope draw on several existing languages of redemption. Some contain distinct elements of atonement and salvation, with the teller moving from sin to forgiveness. Narratives incorporating addiction and alcoholism show influences of the language of recovery, in which the teller moves from sickness to health.[3] The narratives recounted here also employ the redemptive language of development, suggesting personal growth and lessons learned in the struggle. More important, however, the stories depicted here suggest the need to expand the list of redemption languages. In particular, the narratives constructed around animals make sense of the tellers' moves from negative to positive, from instability to relative security, through fulfilling responsibilities to an "other." Consequently, I maintain that *commitment* belongs among the languages of redemption. Although a form of commitment appears in McAdams's work, it refers to a moral steadfastness across the life-span, associated once again with the precursors of generativity (2004; McAdams et al. 1997). In contrast, I use the term to denote commitment in the context of a relationship. It encompasses the virtues of friendship, love, and compassion to narrate a redemptive move from self-interest to interdependence, even selflessness.

The culture's imaginations of animals as innocents, knowing advisers, and providers of unconditional love give even nongenerative narrators access to redemption stories. The benefits these stories hold for these particular tellers represent a unique strength of the language of commitment. Redemption, in general, casts identity in a positive light, portraying the possessor as deserving forgiveness and salvation. In stories that emphasize commitment, however, accounts of the activities associated with caring for and about an "other" help to construct a distinctly *moral* identity. Stories of commitment thus bestow a sense of self-worth—essential for everyone, but especially difficult to accomplish when resources for establishing personal significance are scarce. For homeless people and others on the margins of society, the language of commitment can "salvage the self" from reminders of a stigmatized status.

The Power and Limitations of Redemption Stories

The main power of redemption stories comes through the sense of hope they convey. The tellers talk optimistically, if cautiously, about their futures. Because they have overcome significant obstacles, they express confidence in their ability to cope with the difficulties that come their way. This is not to say that they envision the future as entirely one of sweetness and light. Rather, these tellers have specific or focused goals. Tommy wants to stay clean. Donna wants to stay alive to care for her new dog and cat. Ivy helps Denise look forward to finding housing. In sum, they have reasons for optimism. Ample research documents the benefits of optimism for emotional and physical well-being (see Bennett 2011 and McAdams et al. 2001 for reviews). Overall, optimism offers a demonstrably healthier way to face the world than pessimism. In their roles as the vehicles for redemption, animals help provide this sense of hope.

Another strong point of the redemptive self involves what it reveals about relationships among the homeless. The commitment that provides the language for these redemption stories contrasts with claims about the supposed isolation and disaffiliation of the homeless, a topic I return to in the next chapter. At the broader societal level, the importance of commitment in these narratives also contrasts with enduring claims about American individualism. Redemption stories often employ a highly individualistic vocabulary, through which the person faces his or her struggles alone. In contrast, the language of commitment conveys a sense of interdependence, where the "real me" exists, and can even thrive, because of a desire to ensure a good life for the other. This counters some of the individualism that often characterizes stories of triumph over adversity.

As in the narratives discussed in previous chapters, the redemption story casts a positive moral light on the teller's sense of self. It portrays a self that merits redemption. But unlike the other narratives, redemption stories show how the skills involved in caring for animals can translate into those required for getting off the street. I do not argue that every drug-addicted or alcoholic homeless person should have a pet. But in some cases, at least, a commitment to an animal can turn things around.

One limitation of the redemptive self is that it is not available to everyone. The redemption story is a strategy for the construction of a particular kind of identity. In the perspective I have taken in this book, I have emphasized how positionality shapes one's narrative. Consequently, it is important to reiterate that, with the exception of Denise, the tellers of these redemption stories lived more or less stably. They had made it off the street, albeit some to a "houseless but not homeless" situation. They did not live in circumstances most of us would want to emulate, but they had nevertheless attained a certain quality of life they had not experienced before, or for a long time. Even Denise believed her worst days were behind her. The tellers have survived addiction, abuse, alcoholism, depression, thoughts of suicide, and the hardships of street life. Telling a story about rising above adversity comes more easily for them now than it would have years ago. Although anyone, in any circumstance, can construct a story in which things work out for the best, it is easiest to do so when the reality of one's situation supports this conclusion. Unfortunately, that is not the case for many of those I interviewed for this book.

Finally, constructing redemption stories around animals may lead the tellers to downplay their part in their own struggles. In other words, by crediting their animals with providing the catalyst for overcoming adversity, the tellers of redemption stories may inadvertently obscure the reality that they did the "heavy lifting" of going through withdrawal, staying sober, or staying alive. Moreover, my research did not delve into the impact of these animal-centered narratives over time, but I do wonder what will happen to the sense of hope and moral steadfastness of the narrators in the absence of their animal heroes. Donna's story of Athena suggests that animals' influence endures even after their death. If this holds true for others, then we can understand relationships with animals as a symbolic force of culture that shapes an enduring redemptive self.

Notes

An earlier version of this chapter appears in an issue of the *Journal of Contemporary Ethnography* as "Animals as Lifechangers and Lifesavers: Pets in the Redemption Narratives of Homeless People," http://jce.sagepub.com/content/early/2012/08/21/0891241612456550.

1. Quotes from Pali are from interviews by Lord Martine (2002) and Sally Stephens (2006).

2. Ackerley calls Tulip an "Alsatian," as was the custom in Britain. After World War I, German Shepherds were renamed Alsatians out of fear that anti-German sentiment would make the dogs unpopular. The Kennel Club of the United Kingdom maintained that designation until 1977, when dogs could be registered either as Alsatians or as German Shepherds. In 2010, the General Committee of the Kennel Club agreed that "Alsatian" would cease to be the Kennel Club's formal name for the breed.

3. Similarly, Teresa Gowan (2010) found frequent use of "sin" and "sickness" discourses among the homeless, although in accounts of the path *to* the street instead of *away* from it.

8 Implications for Research and Policy

In many ways, homeless pet owners have much in common with those who live in houses. Homeless people enjoy talking about their pets, and they will eagerly tell acquisition stories. They do their best to keep their animals safe and provide for them. They recognize that their animals have minds, emotions, and identities, and they appreciate the companionship that only animals can provide. But in other ways, homeless pet owners differ significantly from the domiciled. The circumstances of homelessness make them vulnerable to situations that domiciled owners will never encounter. Few of us need to worry about police officers shooting our dogs, nor do we have to fear that our animals will be confiscated. We do not have to sleep with our dogs tied to our legs. We do not have to field insults as we walk our dogs or bring our cats to the veterinarian. We face no accusations of being unworthy of animal companionship. And most of us will never have to think about whom to feed first, or voice this as evidence of our ability to care for our animals.

The issue of pet ownership among the homeless touches on questions about inequality, morality, and identity, among other topics. In bringing this book to a close, I want to summarize the major contributions that have emerged from this analysis.

Animals and the Self

I began this book with stories that raised the question of whether homeless people can take care of animals. As I explained, even I said no at one time. I had changed my mind long before I began this research, but writing this book forced me to think about what "taking care" means. However one chooses to define care, not every homeless person can or will provide it. But having money and a home does not guarantee that one can or will do so, either. To understand this, one only has to consider the twelve-hour trip Mitt Romney's dog, Seamus, took in a crate strapped to the roof of the family car in 1983. One could also consider the "care" given to dogs at 1915 Moonlight Road in Smithfield, Virginia. The fifteen-acre property behind the palatial white house owned by Michael Vick was the home of a dog-fighting operation called Bad Newz Kennels.[1] These high-profile examples notwithstanding, most domiciled people who neglect, ignore, or mistreat their animals have the benefit of privacy, thanks to a roof and four walls. The number of animal hoarders, or "collectors," who escape notice attests to the safety provided by a house. But the person who must pass time in public spaces, and whose physical appearance reveals his or her living situation, faces a different level of scrutiny. To many observers, homelessness constitutes evidence of failure. In particular, it suggests a *moral* failure, an inability to "take care" of oneself attributed to a lack of integrity, responsibility, work ethic, or some other characteristic presumably possessed by the domiciled. Through a reverse halo effect whereby a perceived negative characteristic colors impressions of the entire person, homeless people become morally unfit as pet owners. They cannot take care of pets because they obviously cannot take care of themselves.

Because of this presumption, one of the main issues that has emerged from this research concerns the construction of positive moral identities, adding to the discussion begun by Snow and Anderson about how the homeless try to "salvage the self," to employ their apt phrase a final time. I portrayed homeless people as engaging in a type of identity work that combines talk with a form of "props," although I used the concept cautiously because I applied it to animals. I argued that animals help people construct moral identities in several ways. For example, animals require care, and engaging in caregiving activities imparts a sense of mattering to the caregiver. In addition, pet owners can construct a moral identity when they see themselves as coexisting with animals. I argued that identifying as such represents a moral act with a political dimension because it implodes the socially constructed boundary between humans and animals. Although homeless people, or the domiciled, for that matter, do not use this jargon to talk about closeness with their animals, references to morality and politics nevertheless capture the implications of putting oneself on an equal footing with animals. To be sure, culture is rife with references to animals as best friends and family. But where animals are concerned, such references usually occur in real or virtual quotation marks (Hickrod and Schmitt 1982). We treat animals "as if" they were friends or family, but we reserve these statuses for other humans. Homeless people challenge the "as if" qualification because, for many of them, their animals truly *are* their sole sources of affection and close companionship.

Reflected Appraisals

Another concept that winds through the discussion in this book concerns the impact of feedback from others on the sense of self. In the symbolic interactionist depiction of the self, we form our self-concepts using the responses of others. This paradigm also applies to socialization more broadly, in which others and reference groups offer a "looking glass" that reflects how well we conform to expectations. Reflected appraisals also predominate in research on deviance, especially the work that takes the labeling perspective (Becker 1963; Goffman 1963b). The individual acquires a deviant identity, whether of the criminal or the mental patient, when she or he accepts the evaluations of others.

Other scholars have pointed out that the emphasis on reflected appraisals in the formation of the self-concept results in an image of a conformist, passive actor (Gecas and Schwalbe 1983). In contrast to this image, Snow and Anderson illustrated how homeless people actively embraced or disassociated themselves from the negative assessments of others. The personal narratives of homeless pet owners expand on this by challenging or at least providing qualifications to the reflected appraisals approach. For example, although Travelers were frequent targets of insults and negative feedback from others, they claimed to be highly selective of whose responses and evaluations mattered to them. Many described relying on the judgment of their dogs to inform them of whom to trust. Moreover, the affection—in their words, the unconditional love—they received from their dogs provided consistent, positive feedback for their sense of self-worth. The dog consequently becomes a supportive significant other. In sum, narratives in which animals act as significant other reveal an active, agentic self influenced but not determined by reflected appraisals.

Animal-facilitated Social Interactions and Mattering

The research literature on homelessness contains only occasional acknowledgments that homeless people have pets, pointing out their role as social facilitators, or catalysts for interaction with other people. The topic of animal-facilitated social interaction has received consistent attention in the research on human-animal relationships. This book suggests the need for cross-fertilization and a potential focus on the outcomes of animal-facilitated interaction. For example, the human-animal research has found mixed results when examining whether the appearance of the person or his or her dog influences interaction with others. The people I interviewed recalled instances of animal-facilitated social interaction that took place regardless of the appearance of the person or the dog. Darrell's massive pit bull Buddy initiated as much interaction for his scruffy owner as did Austin's tiny poodle mix. To be sure, my methods in this regard were unsystematic. But the consequences of animal-facilitated interaction may hold more promise than investigations of the occurrence of the interaction itself. Thus far, the literature suggests that increased interaction expands one's social networks. In turn, a broader network makes a greater number and variety of resources available to its members, which might therefore improve well-being. In most cases, however, the scope of the needs of homeless people makes it unlikely that their social networks can meet them. Jay Irwin and colleagues point out that social networks have limited ability "to improve individual's lives when those networks are resource poor" (2008:1941). In addition, the longer people are on the streets, the more likely they are to associate mainly with other homeless people, most of whom have few resources to share. To be sure, animal-facilitated interaction can provide social psychological benefits, especially through being noticed by "one's own kind," as William James put it. But it can just as easily result in confrontations, and research can reveal the dynamics at work in both outcomes.

The Benefits of Pet Ownership

In claiming that pets provide a sense of mattering and help people construct a moral identity, I do not want to portray pet ownership as a panacea for any condition, much less the considerable difficulties and challenges of homelessness. In any case, the jury is still out on the potential benefits of pet ownership. The media has cherry-picked the research, fueling the hold that the "pet effect" has on the popular imagination. As systematic reviews of this research reveal, some studies indeed document benefits, but attempts to replicate results seldom succeed in doing so. Moreover, some studies find negative results, in which pet owners seem worse off than their counterparts who do not have animal companions. Other studies show no differences. In sum, the claim that pets are good for people remains a hypothesis rather than a fact. Simply having an animal companion appears to have no clear connection to well-being. Although we define the attention of a dog or cat as signifying unconditional love and acceptance, this is our construction of their experience.

At the same time, I argue that the activities associated with caring for an animal do seem to benefit people by increasing the sense of mattering. Caring and feeling cared for seem to improve people's sense of self-worth. This idea could inform studies of how animals mediate certain benefits while not causing them directly. Because the topic of whether and how animals increase the sense of mattering has potentially weighty therapeutic implications, future studies could focus on parsing out the dynamics of the processes involved.

Strategies for Coping with Stigma

This research also reveals previously unarticulated strategies for coping with stigma. Pets make their homeless owners especially vulnerable to the verbal assaults routinely faced by homeless people in general. In addition to the shouts of "Get a job" commonly hurled at people on the street, homeless pet owners routinely hear that they do not deserve the companionship of an animal. I introduced the strategies of redefining and enabled resistance as ways to respond to confrontations with the domiciled.

Redefining

When faced with stigmatizing accusations, many homeless pet owners countered them by extolling the care they provided for their animals and "condemning the condemners." They emphasized constant companionship and contrasted it with leaving an animal alone all day, as most domiciled owners must do. They highlighted the freedom their animals enjoyed, again in contrast to the constraints faced by the pets of the domiciled. In short, they redefined "good" pet ownership to incorporate the realities of their daily existence. Overall, redefining indicates a rejection of the values behind the assaults on their ability to care for animals, rather than simply a defense against humiliation. In this way, the homeless make positive moral sense of their pet ownership.

The concept of redefining suggests future avenues for research on relationships between people and companion animals. Thus far, the research has focused mainly on relationships that occur within households. To some extent, this makes analytic sense; the majority of human-animal relationships exist in that setting. But the practice of redefining pet ownership in the context of homelessness suggests a way to explore how people construct other kinds of relationships with animals. One possibility concerns the debate about indoor and outdoor cats. People who advocate keeping cats indoors point out the dangers cats face from cars, potential abusers, and other animals, as well as the dangers cats pose to native birds and small wildlife. People who allow—or even keep—their cats outdoors point out the need for cats to hunt and enjoy the air and sunshine. People on both sides of the issue contend that they provide better care for their cats. Understanding how both parties in the debate construct their definitions of care can shed light on what is not only a style of pet ownership but also, in some areas, an issue of ecological concern.

The concept of redefining also holds promise for understanding stigmatization outside the realm of homelessness. To develop its theoretical implications, further investigations might seek out other instances of redefining to determine the conditions under which people adopt it. Moreover, if redefining also occurs in situations that do not involve stigma, it would help to understand what prompts it. Katherine Edin and Maria Kefalas's (2005) study of low-income, unwed mothers, mentioned in Chapter 3, suggests one possibility. The young women redefined the importance of marriage and motherhood to put the latter before the former. Redefining issues related to "career" in an era of high unemployment and economic recession suggests another example. The cohort known as "Generation Y," or the "Millennials," may be redefining adulthood as they remain in or return to their parents' homes. These examples involve the creation of a moral identity. This has relevance for everyone, not just the homeless, and understanding how people secure moral identities through redefining would add to the understanding of the general social process of identity construction. Potentially, redefining can generate social change as successive cohorts adopt and modify new definitions of social behavior. Research can show the conditions under which it becomes more than a personal strategy and evolves to have a broader social impact.

Enabled Resistance

The concept of enabled resistance also has potential applications beyond the realm of homelessness and pet ownership. I have shown how pet food donated by some members of the public allows homeless pet owners to challenge stigmatizing criticism from others. When confronted about one's ability to provide adequate care for one's animal, saying "I feed my animal first" confirms that one can meet this basic, practical aspect of caretaking. In addition, it helps present a moral identity by constructing the speaker as making sacrifices for his or her animal and putting the animal first. The homeless people I interviewed relied on enabled resistance for their redefinitions of pet ownership. When they portrayed themselves as first-rate caregivers, even surpassing the standards set by most pet owners, the donations of food they received helped substantiate their claims.

Enabled resistance is not restricted to homeless pet owners, and thus the concept could apply to numerous other areas of research. Enabled resistance can occur whenever one party deploys resources provided by a second party to counter assaults from a third. This could involve situations in which one group marshals money, volunteers, and other resources from another group to launch an action against a third group. In this sense, many political and social movements engage in enabled resistance. But I intended the concept to apply to a response to stigma. In this context, "resistance" suggests not just opposing forces, as in a social movement fighting a piece of legislation, for example. Rather, I intended to connote a refusal to accept a derogatory label when others have provided the basis for the refusal. Whenever any group challenges a stigmatizing assault with assistance from others, they engage in enabled resistance. Thus, it can apply to groups involved in combating stigma based on religion or sexual preference. For example, the student organizations called "gay-straight alliances" use enabled resistance. Straight peers become allies, advocating for lesbian, gay, bisexual, and transgender (LGBT) students facing discrimination and harassment. They help LGBT students resist stigmatizing assaults from homophobic others.

Calling the resistance "enabled" does not detract from the effort involved, nor does it deny ownership of either the fight or the victory. Instead, it emphasizes the coalitions and interdependence that are essential to any struggle.

Bringing Animals into Narrative Analysis

This book engages with several issues within the growing research that focuses on personal narratives, or life histories. By showing how certain life circumstances within the context of homelessness generate particular stories of animals and the self, I have entered two lively, ongoing conversations. In one, the discussion revolves around the cultural shaping of narrative. In the other, it examines the inclusion of deliberately silenced or marginalized voices. At the heart of both of these issues lie large and searching questions about how the individual is embedded in the social.

The Cultural Shaping of Narrative

This conversation assumes that although stories offer subjective accounts of human experience, their analysis highlights the influence of culture. The narratives examined in this book reveal culturally specific conventions about how Americans in the twenty-first century can talk about relationships with animals. Norms and beliefs about what animals can allegedly be and do for people make stories such as the friend-and-family narrative, as well as protector narrative, possible. Likewise, stories about receiving emotional support reveal the beliefs that prevail about the purported benefits of animals. The stories provide insight into the tellers' interior worlds. Sociologically speaking, however, the more interesting and analytically more valuable revelation lies not so much in the details of the interior world but in understanding how structures and forms beyond the individual shape that world. Although each story is unique to the subjective experience of the teller, the models and the logics for telling the story are not.

Narratives of relationships with animals add a focus on the interplay of selfhood, positionality or social location, and the role of the animal to the discussion about the cultural shaping of narrative. Scholars have used other approaches to examine the various roles we assign to animals and how selfhood manifests itself in both animals and human caregivers in interaction (e.g., Alger and Alger 1997, 2003; Irvine 2004a; Sanders 1999, 2003). But the nexus of selfhood, positionality, and role has not been examined in animal narratives up to now. As I hope to have shown, homeless pet owners make for especially appropriate narrators of this combination of relationships, experiences, and situations. Which leads to the second conversation.

Including Silenced or Marginalized Voices

Since the 1993 publication of David Snow and Leon Anderson's *Down on Their Luck,* a number of studies have incorporated the voices of homeless people into the research literature. Most recently, Jason Wasserman and Jeffrey Clair's *At Home on the Street* and Teresa Gowan's *Hobos, Hustlers, and Backsliders,* both published in 2010, take seriously the experiences of homeless people, told in their own words. Other works along the way have done so, too. Although the authors do not make explicit use of narrative analysis per se, they nevertheless rely on extensive interviewing that captures subjective experiences. By examining a hidden population among the homeless, I intend my study of pet owners to introduce another set of voices. As I interviewed people and heard them say, for example, "No one's ever asked me that before," I realized that this project represented an opportunity to expand the perspectives on homelessness. Although pet owners represent a small proportion of the overall homeless population, their voices bring new questions into discussions of topics about which they alone can provide insight. The matter of animal-friendly affordable housing offers just one example.

But the voices of homeless *people* are not the only ones introduced in this book. The animals have voices, too. Within the literature on homelessness, animals constitute an unacknowledged presence, seen only as "props" in the true sense of the word. They have received only passing reference in extant ethnographic studies. To be sure, hearing their voices requires that humans "speak for" them through the identity-constructing practice common to human-animal relationships. But animals' voices wind through the discussion, for example in the form of Flora's dog, Paco, telling her she would be fine, of Buzz's dog, Jones, alerting him to potential dangers in their camp, and of Tommy's dog, Monty, warning him to stay clean and sober. These interlocutions provide insight into how people construct the identities of animals and simultaneously construct identities for themselves.

The narratives of redemption analyzed in Chapter 7 represent an innovative way to introduce animals' voices. Even when the stories do not involve "speaking for" animals, their identities, intentions, and influence nevertheless come through. In short, animals provide an element of hope in the stories. Pali describes Leadbelly as a gift, sent to help her learn to take care of herself. Similarly, Donna credits Athena with getting her clean and sober, as well as improving her HIV status. Rudy, Trish, and Denise believe they owe their lives to their animals.

I argued that animals make particularly appropriate vehicles for redemption stories because our constructions of them make them well suited to the task of redeeming human lives. I pointed out that relationships with animals provide redemptive hope in three ways. First, their dependence on people for their care enhances the owner's sense of responsibility—often in scant supply among the homeless. Second, the perceived unconditional love from the animal reinforces responsible caregiving through mattering. Third, because of our constructions of animals as innocent, morally upright witnesses, they provide a sense of conscience, guarding against destructive behavior that could spiral out of control.

Other Insights

Two additional insights hold promise for other areas of narrative studies. One pertains to the tellers of redemption stories. As discussed, research suggests that such tellers are typically "generative" adults, people in midlife who grew up with some sense of privilege and acquired a reliable moral compass and thus a belief that they could triumph over adversity. However, I heard redemption stories from people, such as Pali, who grew up on the street and did several stints in jail, and Donna, who became a prostitute in her teens to support her drug habit. Animals provide the moral compass, special status, and other experiences that facilitate the telling of redemption stories among these nongenerative adults. Perhaps other groups of nongenerative adults also have the capacity to tell these stories, and if so, research could reveal what makes this possible. A focus on the social and cultural underpinnings of the tendency to tell redemption stories could bring the discussion out of the realm of psychological traits or dispositions. Granted, Dan McAdams (2006b) acknowledges the cultural origins of redemption stories, particularly emphasizing their distinctly American form. But the personal narratives of former addicts, alcoholics, and prostitutes raise questions about the emphasis on, indeed the requirement of, generativity.

The second insight pertains to the addition of commitment to the languages of redemption. By this, I refer to commitment to care for an animal, exemplified by many people's decision to live outside or in vehicles rather than part with their animals. Although a form of commitment appears in the research on redemption stories, it emphasizes solitary engagement with a struggle. The commitment described by homeless pet owners emphasizes interdependence and facing adversity with their animals. The language of commitment thus highlights the role of relationships in homeless people's lives, and I turn now to this topic.

Contributions to the Research on Homelessness

I came to this research without a background in homelessness. I faced a steep learning curve, and although I read a great deal, I still cannot claim to know this vast literature very well. Nevertheless, I can suggest two areas in which this research enhances the stock of knowledge.

Social Relationships

First, the narratives of relationships with animals shed new light on the types and benefits of social relationships among the homeless. As mentioned in Chapter 2, until approximately the 1980s, research depicted homelessness primarily as a condition of "disaffiliation," reinforced by stereotypes of skid row residents. Since then, however, scholars have disagreed on the extent and the role of disaffiliation in homelessness.[2] In *Down and Out in America,* Peter Rossi claimed it still constituted a major issue, writing that "both the old and new homeless are relatively isolated socially" (1989:43). Others have pointed out that "application of earlier disaffiliation explanations of skid row to contemporary homelessness is dubious. Clearly, the majority of homeless persons have confidants, friends, relatives, and acquaintances" (LaGory, Ritchey, and Fitzpatrick 1992:209). As Timothy Pippert's research on homeless men revealed, even those who defined themselves as "loners," preferring to sleep and travel by themselves, did not live in total isolation and were "found to take part in group activities and even travel with someone on occasion" (2007:6).

Not all the social ties homeless people have are dependable. For example, when I talked with Pete in Sacramento, he described some of the circumstances that led to his living in a tent with his dogs. He has a son, but as he explained, "I can't stay at his house, you know, because he can't have dogs, and anyway he lives in a little, tiny place. And so many of my friends are right on the borderline. They're barely caring for themselves. They can't take anybody else in." Others told of having severed some ties and simply worn others out. But many of the homeless not only *have* social ties, they *depend* on them. As Gwendolyn Dordick writes in her ethnography set in New York City, "The homeless I met survive through their personal relationships. . . . Homelessness encourages a process in which personal relationships are mobilized in the production of what the physical environment fails to provide: a safe and secure place to live" (1997:193). Similarly, Pippert's research (2007) reveals partnerships between "road dogs," or dyads of transient men who pair up, initially to share and exchange resources necessary for survival on the streets and while traveling. Pippert found that some "road dog" relationships evolve into a form of "fictive kinship" in which the men view each other as family members. Snow and Anderson point out that the instability of street life makes interactions easy but superficial, and often fraught with distrust; they use the term "tenuous ties" (1993:182–197). Indeed, friendships with other homeless people can even impede one's efforts to get off the streets. This becomes more so the longer one has been homeless (Snow and Anderson 1993).

In sum, research has documented a range of social relationships among the homeless, "ranging from casual acquaintances to street families" (Lee, Tyler, and Wright 2010:508; see also Molina 2000; Smith 2008; Snow and Anderson 1993). This book suggests the need to recognize the relationships that exist between homeless people and their companion animals. Animals matter for many homeless people, and if as much as a quarter of the homeless population in some areas have pets, service providers and policymakers need to acknowledge this. The homeless person with a pet is not alone; she or he constitutes what Erving Goffman called a "with" (1971:19), meaning that other people see the person and the animal as together, much in the same way that they perceive human couples as "with" each other.[3]

This holds especially true for people and their dogs. But Denise's story, and Candy's, too, point out that the image we need would also incorporate cats. Recognizing that many homeless people share bonds with their animals that they describe with the vocabularies of "friend," "family," and "my everything" would provide a more comprehensive understanding of the experiences of people on the streets.

Pet Ownership and Housing

The second area of research this book can inform concerns housing. Recognizing the bonds that homeless people share with their animals would greatly enhance both the research and the policy on housing, which as of yet do not acknowledge that most American households include companion animals. If there were one "magic wand" policy change I could make based on this research, I would ensure that responsible pet owners could keep their animals when they move into rental housing. Absent a magic wand, I recommend research on the beliefs, customs, and other issues that undergird no-pets policies and on what might reform them. Exploring the full range of issues involved would bring scholars of human-animal relationships into the ensuing conversations about homelessness, housing, and inequality.

Not surprisingly, when listening to homeless pet owners as they consider their most pressing problems, one quickly learns that housing counts as most salient. I talked with many people about what it would take to get them off the street. With some exceptions, such as Candy and her fifteen cats, and the Travelers who claimed to love life on the road or to find the idea of "living in a box" repugnant, most looked forward to living in a house or apartment again. Some had taken steps to qualify for and obtain affordable rental housing, but I have already mentioned the years-long wait that people face in cities such as San Francisco. People consistently said that they would not accept housing if it meant separation from their pets.

One does not need expertise in housing policy to know that the United States faces a serious shortage of affordable places to live. Moreover, studies by organizations such as the National Low-Income Housing Coalition find the rental housing shortage most severe at the lowest income levels. The occupation of many of the lowest-rent units by households belonging to higher-income categories exacerbates the shortage. At the same time, a growing list of other factors contributes to the housing crisis. The number of people living in poverty has increased. Large segments of the work force can find only jobs with low wages and little security. The combined burden of low income and high rent sends people to apply for housing assistance. Meanwhile, federal support for low-income housing has declined in value and become more difficult to obtain, as have other forms of public assistance.

At first glance, it may seem trivial, even frivolous, to suggest adding the issue of pet restrictions onto the list of factors that research and policy on housing need to address. But I propose two sociologically relevant reasons for doing so. First, the practice of prohibiting pets in rental housing disproportionately affects the poor. The application of differing standards to the pets of the poor has a long history, some of which I traced in Chapter 3. No-pets policies date back to the earliest public housing project, in late Victorian-era London (Jones 1971). Tenants were forbidden from keeping dogs because their owners were purportedly incapable of caring for them. As this book reveals, those who live on the margins still hear this criticism.

To be sure, some people, rich and poor, cannot provide proper care for animals. But the questions around the continuation of no-pets policies beg for systematic investigation. By this, I refer in particular to what justifies the policies, and how closely the reality fits the assumptions behind those justifications. Many landlords assume that dogs, in particular, will damage property, and invariably, some will. However, human tenants will often incur more damage and create more problems. During the course of this research, I came across the following statement from an astute landlord: "Dogs are welcome in this apartment. I never had a dog that smoked in bed and set fire to the building. I never had a dog who played music or the TV too loudly. I never had a dog get drunk and knock holes in the walls. So if your dog can vouch for you, you're welcome, too."[4]

The best approach, as I see it, is not to prohibit animals altogether, but to develop research-based ways to assess the real problems they might cause. The presence of animals can raise health and safety risks, but there are ways to minimize many of these. Property owners can require pet screening, for example, with pet owners providing documentation of vaccinations and any training the animal has had. Many workplaces now allow employees to bring pets with them, even into high-powered corporate settings. Perhaps they can offer insights at the levels of policy and practice that can apply to housing.

The issue of screening raises the question of owner responsibility, which leads to a second sociologically relevant reason to study pets and housing. Many of the homeless pet owners I interviewed believe they demonstrate responsibility, commitment, and unique survival skills. They also claim to avoid risky behaviors because of concerns about the consequential separation from their animals. My research indicates that, at least in cities where homeless pet owners have access to veterinary care, they comply with laws about vaccinating, spaying, neutering, and licensing. In short, the skills associated with pet ownership would seem to apply to escaping homelessness and remaining housed. In this light, resources aimed at re-housing would be well spent if they were aimed at pet owners. Well-designed research could assess whether pet owners have more success in staying housed than their non-pet-owning counterparts and, if so, what factors lead to their success. From a social psychological perspective, research could examine what values, attitudes, and beliefs undergird both responsible pet ownership and successful tenancy. It could also explore the social forces that influence these values, attitudes, and beliefs, and how people construct them in the context of pet ownership.

In sum, research on pet policies addresses issues that have disproportionate impact on the poor. It can contribute not only to the literature on housing and homelessness, but also to the research on inequalities more generally.

* * *

The discussion of housing leads me, in a roundabout way, to revisit the importance of veterinarians for this research. As I discussed, veterinarians provided access to a number and variety of homeless pet owners and took me into settings I would never have ventured into on my own. Their assistance constitutes a major strength of this book. But it also constitutes a limitation. Because I relied so heavily on veterinarians, this study took place in communities having existing support for the pets of the homeless. The people I interviewed had access to pet food and veterinary care for their animals. Thus, I cannot generalize these findings to homeless pet owners in other parts of the country.

Veterinarians are the unsung heroes of this research, and of homeless pet owners in general. Those who serve the homeless volunteer their time in free clinics and raise funds to provide vaccinations and supplies. They play tremendous roles in enabling resistance. They also play a valuable but largely unrecognized role in protecting public health by vaccinating animals against diseases that can spread to humans. Moreover, they refrain from judgment as they care for the companions of the poor. In the course of providing this care, they hear stories, and they have stories of their own to tell. Although I heard some of these, I did not collect them, for veterinarians were not the subject of this research. But the stories told by those who provide compassionate care to the pets of people who cannot pay for their services beg to be heard. They can shed additional light on the cultural constructions of animals, the consequences of inequality, and other topics that only research can reveal.

Veterinarians alone cannot solve the problem of homelessness among people who have pets. They cannot simply keep pets healthy so that those animals and their owners can continue to live on the streets. Although veterinary services for the pets of the homeless are essential, housing remains the major issue facing this hidden population.

Finally, in this book I have frequently noted and even praised the adaptability, creativity, and optimism of many of the homeless pet owners I met. In portraying them in these ways, I risk being seen as romanticizing homelessness, and that is not my intention. Failed housing policy in the United States has forced some people to adapt to horrendous living conditions. Having a pet might help them do so while remaining optimistic, but it does not make the circumstances acceptable.

Notes

1. In a fitting tribute, in spring 2011, the former Bad Newz Kennels became the home of Good Newz Dog Rehab Center for Chained and Penned dogs, run by the nonprofit Dogs Deserve Better, which purchased the property to fulfill its mission to end "the cruelty of chaining and penning dogs for life." See www.dogsdeservebetter.org, accessed March 29, 2012.

2. Timothy Pippert (2007) provides a comprehensive review and analysis of the challenges to the disaffiliation perspective.

3. Clinton Sanders (1999, see especially chap. 2) has undertaken extensive analyses of interactions between dogs and people in public, building on Goffman's notion of a "with." He points out that the epitome of a human-canine "with" is the person accompanied by a guide dog (1999:chap. 3; 2000). He also analyzes people's strategies for coping with the negative responses of others to dogs' misbehavior (1990).

4. See http://rhol.org/rental/pets.htm, accessed March 21, 2012.

References

Ackerley, J. R. 1965. *My Dog Tulip*. New York: New York Review Books.

Adell-Bath, M., A. Krook, G. Sandqvist, and K. Skantze. 1979. *Do We Need Dogs? A Study of Dogs' Social Significance to Man*. Gothenburg: University of Gothenburg Press.

Adler, Judith. 1985. "Youth on the Road: Reflections on the History of Tramping." *Annals of Tourism Research* 12:335–354.

Alger, Janet M., and Steven F. Alger. 1997. "Beyond Mead: Symbolic Interaction Between Humans and Felines." *Society & Animals* 5:65–81.

———. 2003. *Cat Culture: The Social World of a Cat Shelter*. Philadelphia: Temple University Press.

Anderson, Leon, and David A. Snow. 2001. "Inequality and the Self: Exploring Connections from an Interactionist Perspective." *Symbolic Interaction* 24:395–406.

Anderson, Leon, David A. Snow, and Daniel Cress. 1994. "Negotiating the Public Realm: Stigma Management and Collective Action Among the Homeless." *Research in Community Sociology* 1:121–143.

Anderson, Nels. 1923. *The Hobo: The Sociology of the Homeless Man*. Chicago: University of Chicago Press.

Anzaldúa, Gloria. 1987. *Borderlands/La Frontera: The New Mestiza*. San Francisco: Aunt Lute.

Arluke, Arnold. 2006. *Just a Dog: Understanding Animal Cruelty and Ourselves*. Philadelphia: Temple University Press.

———. 2010. "Our Animals Ourselves." *Contexts* 9:34–39.

Arluke, Arnold, and Clinton R. Sanders. 1996. *Regarding Animals*. Philadelphia: Temple University Press.

AVMA (American Veterinary Medical Association). 2007. *US Pet Ownership & Demographics Sourcebook*. Schaumburg, IL: Center for Information Management of the AVMA.

Bahr, Howard M. 1970. *Disaffiliated Man: Essays and Bibliography on Skid Row, Vagrancy, and Outsiders.* Toronto: University of Toronto Press.

———. 1973. *Skid Row: An Introduction to Disaffiliation.* New York: Oxford University Press.

Bahr, Howard M., and Theodore Caplow. 1974. *Old Men Drunk and Sober.* New York: New York University Press.

Baker, Oswin. 2001. *A Dog's Life: Homeless People and Their Pets.* Oxford: Blue Cross.

Barak, Gregg. 1991. *Gimme Shelter: A Social History of Homelessness in Contemporary America.* New York: Praeger.

Barthes, Roland, and Lionel Duisit. 1975. "An Introduction to the Structural Analysis of Narrative." *New Literary History* 6(2):237–272.

Baumeister, Roy F. 1986. *Identity: Cultural Change and the Struggle for Self.* New York: Oxford University Press.

Becker, Howard S. 1963. *Outsiders: Studies in the Sociology of Deviance.* New York: Free Press.

Bekoff, Marc. 2002. *Minding Animals: Awareness, Emotions, and Heart.* Oxford: Oxford University Press.

Bellah, Robert N., Richard Madsen, William M. Sullivan, Ann Swidler, and Steven M. Tipton. 1985. *Habits of the Heart.* New York: Harper and Row.

Bender, Kimberly, Sanna J. Thompson, Holly McManus, Janet Lantry, and Patrick M. Flynn. 2007. "Capacity for Survival: Exploring Strengths of Homeless Street Youth." *Child Youth Care Forum* 36:25–42.

Bennett, Oliver. 2011. "Cultures of Optimism." *Cultural Sociology* 5:301–320.

Berger, Ronald. J. 2008. "Agency, Structure, and the Transition to Disability: A Case Study with Implications for Life History Research." *Sociological Quarterly* 49(2):309–333.

Berger, Ronald J., and Richard Quinney, eds. 2005. *Storytelling Sociology: Narrative as Social Inquiry.* Boulder: Lynne Rienner.

Blau, Joel. 1992. *The Visible Poor: Homelessness in the United States.* New York: Oxford University Press.

Blumberg, Leonard U., Thomas E. Shipley Jr., and Irving W. Shandler. 1973. *Skid Row and Its Alternatives.* Philadelphia: Temple University Press.

Bogard, Cynthia J. 2001. "Claimsmakers and Contexts in Early Constructions of Homelessness: A Comparison of New York City and Washington, D.C." *Symbolic Interaction* 24:425–454.

———. 2003. *Seasons Such as These: How Homelessness Took Shape in America.* Hawthorne, NY: Aldine de Gruyter.

Bogdan, Robert, and Steven Taylor. 1989. "Relationships with Severely Disabled People: The Social Construction of Humanness." *Social Problems* 36:135–148.

Bogdan, Robert, Steven Taylor, Bernard DeGrandpre, and Sondra Haynes. 1974. "Let Them Eat Programs: Attendants' Perspectives and Programming on Wards in State Schools." *Journal of Health and Social Behavior* 15:142–151.

Bogue, Donald. 1963. *Skid Row in American Cities.* Chicago: University of Chicago Press.

Branaman, Ann. 2003. "Interaction and Hierarchy in Everyday Life: Goffman and Beyond." Pp. 86–126 in *Goffman's Legacy,* edited by A. J. Trevino. Lanham: Rowman and Littlefield.

Brazelton, T. Berry. 1984. "Four Stages in the Development of Mother-Infant Interaction." Pp. 19–34 in *The Growing Child in Family and Society,* edited by N. Kobayashi and T. B. Brazelton. Tokyo: University of Tokyo Press.

Bruner, Jerome. 1987. "Life as Narrative." *Social Research* 54:11–32.

———. 1994. "The 'Remembered' Self." Pp. 41–54 in *The Remembering Self: Construction and Accuracy in the Self-Narrative,* edited by U. Neisser and R. Fivush. Cambridge: Cambridge University Press.

Bryant, Clifton D. 1979. "The Zoological Connection: Animal-Related Human Behavior." *Social Forces* 58:399–421.

Burghardt, Gordon M. 1998. "The Evolutionary Origins of Play Revisited: Lessons from Turtles." Pp. 1–26 in *Animal Play: Evolutionary, Comparative, and Ecological Perspectives,* edited by M. Bekoff and J. Byers. Cambridge: Cambridge University Press.

Buseh, Aaron G., and Patricia E. Stevens. 2007. "Constrained but Not Determined by Stigma: Resistance by African American Women Living with HIV." *Women & Health* 44:1–18.

Cain, Ann. 1983. "A Study of Pets in the Family System." Pp. 71–81 in *New Perspectives on Our Lives with Companion Animals,* edited by A. Katcher and A. Beck. Philadelphia: University of Pennsylvania Press.

———. 1985. "Pets as Family Members." Pp. 5–10 in *Pets and the Family,* edited by M. Sussman. New York: Haworth.

Cartmill, Matt. 1997. "History of Ideas Surrounding Hunting." Pp. 197–199 in *Encyclopedia of Animal Rights and Animal Welfare,* edited by M. Bekoff. Westport: Greenwood.

Charmaz, Kathy. 1983. "The Grounded Theory Method: An Explication and Interpretation." Pp. 102–126 in *Contemporary Field Research: A Collection of Readings,* edited by R. M. Emerson. Boston: Little, Brown.

———. 1991. *Good Days, Bad Days: The Self in Chronic Illness and Time.* New Brunswick, NJ: Rutgers University Press.

———. 2000. "Grounded Theory Methodology: Objectivist and Constructivist Qualitative Methods." Pp. 509–535 in *Handbook of Qualitative Research,* 2nd ed., edited by N. K. Denzin and Y. Lincoln. Thousand Oaks, CA: Sage.

Chur-Hansen, Anna, Cindy Stern, and Helen Winefield. 2010. "Gaps in the Evidence About Companion Animals and Human Health: Some Suggestions for Progress." *International Journal of Evidence-Based Healthcare* 8:140–146.

Cohen, Erik. 1973. "Nomads from Affluence: Notes on the Phenomenon of Drifter-Tourism." *International Journal of Comparative Sociology* 14:89–103.

Cress, Daniel M., and David A. Snow. 1996. "The Outcomes of Homeless Mobilization: The Influence of Organization, Disruption, Political Mediation, and Framing." *American Journal of Sociology* 105:1063–1104.

Cronley, Courtney, Elizabeth B. Strand, David A. Patterson, and Sarah Gwaltney. 2009. "Homeless People Who Are Animal Caretakers: A Comparative Study." *Psychological Reports* 105:481–499.

Crowley-Robinson, Patricia, and Judith K. Blackshaw. 1998. "Pet Ownership and Health Status of Elderly in the Community." *Anthrozoös* 11:168–171.

Culhane, Dennis, and Randall Kuhn. 1998. "Applying Cluster Analysis to Test a Typology of Homelessness by Pattern of Shelter Utilization: Results from the Analysis of Administrative Data." *American Journal of Community Psychology* 26:207–232.

Department of Housing and Urban Development, Office of Community Planning and Development. 2010. *The 2009 Annual Homeless Assessment Report to Congress.* www.hudhre.info/documents/5th HomelessAssessmentReport.pdf. Accessed July 26, 2011.

DePastino, Todd. 2003. *Citizen Hobo: How a Century of Homelessness Shaped America.* Chicago: University of Chicago Press.

Derber, Charles. 1979. *The Pursuit of Attention: Power and Individualism in Everyday Life.* New York: Oxford University Press.

Derr, Mark. 1997. *Dog's Best Friend: Annals of the Dog-Human Relationship.* New York: Holt.

Donovan, Josephine, and Carol J. Adams. 2007. "Introduction." Pp. 1–20 in *The Feminist Care Tradition in Animal Ethics,* edited by J. Donovan and C. Adams. New York: Columbia University Press.

Dordick, Gwendolyn A. 1997. *Something Left to Lose: Personal Relations and Survival Among New York's Homeless.* Philadelphia: Temple University Press.

Durkheim, Emile. 1951. *Suicide.* New York: Free Press.

Edin, Katherine, and Maria Kefalas. 2005. *Promises I Can Keep: Why Poor Women Put Motherhood Before Marriage.* Berkeley: University of California Press.

Eighner, Lars. 1993. *Travels with Lizbeth.* New York: St. Martin's.

Elliott, Gregory C., Melissa F. Colangelo, and Richard J. Gelles. 2005. "Mattering and Suicide Ideation: Establishing and Elaborating a Relationship." *Social Psychology Quarterly* 68:223–238.

Elliott, Gregory C., Suzanne Kao, and Ann-Marie Grant. 2004. "Mattering: Empirical Validation of a Social-Psychological Concept." *Self and Identity* 3:339–354.

Erikson, Erik. 1950. *Childhood and Society.* New York: Norton.

Erikson, Kai. 1966. *Wayward Puritans: A Study in the Sociology of Deviance.* New York: Wiley.

Eskanazi, Joe. 2009. "Service with a Snarl." *SF Weekly,* June 17. www.sfweekly.com/2009-06-17/news/service-with-a-snarl. Accessed August 6, 2011.

Finkelstein, Marni. 2005. *With No Direction Home: Homeless Youth on the Road and in the Streets.* Belmont, CA: Thomson Wadsworth.

Fisher, Berenice, and Joan Tronto. 1990. "Toward a Feminist Theory of Caring." Pp. 35–62 in *Circles of Care: Work and Identity in Women's Lives,* edited by E. Abel and M. Nelson. Albany: State University of New York Press.

Fisher, John Andrew. 1991. "Disambiguating Anthropomorphism: An Interdisciplinary Review." Pp. 49–85 in *Perspectives in Ethology,* vol. 9, *Human Understanding and Animal Awareness,* edited by P. Bateson and P. Klopfer. New York: Plenum.

Fitzgerald, Amy J. 2007. "'They Gave Me a Reason to Live': The Protective Effects of Companion Animals on the Suicidality of Abused Women." *Humanity & Society* 31:355–378.

Frank, Arthur W. 1995. *The Wounded Storyteller: Body, Illness, and Ethics.* Chicago: University of Chicago Press.

———. 2010. *Letting Stories Breathe: A Socio-Narratology.* Chicago: University of Chicago Press.

Gaarder, Emily. 2011. *Women and the Animal Rights Movement.* New Brunswick, NJ: Rutgers University Press.

Gagnon, John H. 1992. "The Self, Its Voices, and Their Discord." Pp. 221–243 in *Investigating Subjectivity,* edited by C. Ellis and M. Flaherty. Newbury Park, CA: Sage.

Gardner, Carole. 1995. *Passing By: Gender and Public Harassment.* Berkeley: University of California Press.

Gecas, Viktor, and Peter J. Burke. 1995. "Self and Identity." Pp. 41–67 in *Sociological Perspectives on Social Psychology,* edited by K. S. Cook, G. A. Fine, and J. House. Boston: Allyn and Bacon.

Gecas, Viktor, and Michael L. Schwalbe. 1983. "Beyond the Looking-Glass Self: Social Structure and Efficacy-Based Self-Esteem." *Social Psychology Quarterly* 46:77–88.

Gergen, Kenneth. 1991. *The Saturated Self: Dilemmas of Identity in Contemporary Life.* New York: Basic.

Gerstel, Naomi, Catherine K. Riessman, and Sarah Rosenfield. 1985. "Explaining the Symptomatology of Separated and Divorced Women and Men: The Role of Material Conditions and Social Networks." *Social Forces* 64:84–101.

Gibson, Kristina E. 2011. *Street Kids: Homeless Youth, Outreach, and Policing New York's Streets.* New York: New York University Press.

Gilbey, Andrew, June McNicholas, and Glyn M. Collis. 2007. "A Longitudinal Test of the Belief That Companion Animal Ownership Can Help Reduce Loneliness." *Anthrozoös* 20:345–353.

Glaser, Barney G., and Anselm L. Strauss. 1967. *The Discovery of Grounded Theory.* Chicago: Aldine.

Goetting, Ann. 1995. "Fictions of the Self." Pp. 3–19 in *Individual Voices, Collective Visions: Fifty Years of Women in Sociology,* edited by A. Goetting and S. Fenstermaker. Philadelphia: Temple University Press.

Goffman, Erving. 1955. "On Face-Work: An Analysis of Ritual Elements in Social Interaction." *Psychiatry* 18:213–231.

———. 1961. *Asylums.* Garden City, NY: Anchor.

———. 1963a. *Behavior in Public Places: Notes on the Social Organizations of Gatherings.* New York: Free Press.

———. 1963b. *Stigma: Notes on the Management of Spoiled Identity.* Englewood Cliffs, NJ: Prentice Hall.

———. 1967. *Interaction Ritual: Essays on Face-to-Face Behavior.* New York: Doubleday Anchor.

———. 1971. *Relations in Public.* New York: Basic.

———. 1974. *Frame Analysis: An Essay on the Organization of Experience.* New York: Harper and Row.

Goode, David A. 1984. "Socially Produced Identities, Intimacy, and the Problem of Competence Among the Retarded." Pp. 228–248 in *Special Education and Social Interests,* edited by S. Tomlinson and L. Barton. London: Croom-Helm.

Gowan, Teresa. 2010. *Hobos, Hustlers, and Backsliders: Homeless in San Francisco.* Minneapolis: University of Minnesota Press.

Grigsby, Charles, Donald Baumann, Steven E. Gregorich, and Cynthia Roberts-Gray. 1990. "Disaffiliation to Entrenchment: A Model for Understanding Homelessness." *Journal of Social Issues* 46:141–156.

Gubrium, Jaber. 1986. "The Social Preservation of Mind: The Alzheimer's Disease Experience." *Symbolic Interaction* 6:37–51.

Gubrium, Jaber, and James A. Holstein. 1999. "At the Border of Narrative and Ethnography." *Journal of Contemporary Ethnography* 28 (5):61–73.

Haraway, Donna. 2003. *The Companion Species Manifesto: Dogs, People, and Significant Otherness.* Chicago: Prickly Paradigm.

Harper, Douglas. 2006. *Good Company: A Tramp Life.* Boulder: Paradigm.

Harrington, Michael. 1980. *Decade of Decision: A Crisis of the American System.* New York: Simon and Schuster.

Hart, Lynette A. 1995. "Dogs as Human Companions: A Review of the Relationship." Pp. 162–178 in *The Domestic Dog: Its Evolution, Behaviour, and Interactions with People,* edited by J. Serpell. Cambridge: Cambridge University Press.

Herda-Rapp, Ann, and Theresa L. Goedeke, eds. 2005. *Mad About Wildlife: Looking at Social Conflict over Wildlife.* Leiden: Brill.

Herman, Nancy J. 1993. "Return to Sender: Reintegrative Stigma-Management Strategies of Ex–Psychiatric Patients." *Journal of Contemporary Ethnography* 22:295–330.

Herzog, Harold. 2007. "Gender Differences in Human-Animal Interactions: A Review." *Anthrozoös* 20:7–21.

———. 2011. "The Impact of Pets on Human Health and Psychological Well-Being: Fact, Fiction, or Hypothesis?" *Current Directions in Psychological Science* 20:236–239.

Herzog, Harold A., Nancy S. Betchart, and Robert B. Pittman. 1991. "Gender, Sex Role Orientation, and Attitudes Toward Animals." *Anthrozoös* 4:184–191.

Hickrod, Lucy Jen Huang, and Raymond L. Schmitt. 1982. "A Naturalistic Study of Interaction and Frame: The Pet as Family Member." *Urban Life* 11:55–77.

Holstein, James A., and Jaber Gubrium. 2000. *The Self We Live By: Narrative Identity in a Postmodern World.* New York: Oxford University Press.

Hopper, Kim. 1991. "Homelessness Old and New: The Matter of Definition." *Housing Policy Debate* 2:757–813.

———. 2003. *Reckoning with Homelessness.* Ithaca: Cornell University Press.

Hunt, Susan J., Lynette A. Hart, and Richard Gomulkiewicz. 1992. "Role of Small Animals in Social Interactions Between Strangers." *Journal of Social Psychology* 132:245–256.

Huss, Rebecca J. 2005. "No Pets Allowed." *Animal Law Review* 11:69–129.

Ingold, Tim. 1994. "From Trust to Domination: An Alternative History of Human-Animal Relations." Pp. 1–22 in *Animals and Human Society*, edited by J. Serpell and A. Manning. London: Routledge.

Irvine, Leslie. 1999. *Codependent Forevermore: The Invention of Self in a Twelve Step Group*. Chicago: University of Chicago Press.

———. 2000. "Even Better Than the Real Thing: Narratives of the Self in Codependency." *Qualitative Sociology* 23:9–28.

———. 2003. "The Problem of Unwanted Pets: A Case Study in How Institutions 'Think' About Clients' Needs." *Social Problems* 50:550–566.

———. 2004a. *If You Tame Me: Understanding Our Connection with Animals*. Philadelphia: Temple University Press.

———. 2004b. "A Model of Animal Selfhood: Expanding Interactionist Possibilities." *Symbolic Interaction* 27:3–21.

———. 2009. *Filling the Ark: Animal Welfare in Disasters*. Philadelphia: Temple University Press.

Irwin, Jay, Mark LaGory, Ferris Ritchey, and Kevin Fitzpatrick. 2008. "Social Assets and Mental Distress Among the Homeless: Exploring the Roles of Social Support and Other Forms of Social Capital on Depression." *Social Science & Medicine* 67:1935–1943.

James, Scott. 2011. "The Haight Pays a Price for Sit/Lie News Coverage." *New York Times,* April 1. www.nytimes.com/2011/04/01/us/01bcjames.html?_r=1. Accessed September 1, 2012.

James, William. 1890. *The Principles of Psychology.* New York: Holt.

Jay, Timothy. 2000. *Why We Curse: A Neuro-Psycho-Social Theory of Speech*. Philadelphia: John Benjamins.

———. 2009. "The Utility and Ubiquity of Taboo Words." *Perspectives on Psychological Science* 4(2):153–161.

Jencks, Christopher. 1994. *The Homeless.* Cambridge: Harvard University Press.

Johnson, Timothy P., Thomas F. Garrity, and Lorann Stallones. 1992. "Psychometric Evaluation of the Lexington Attachment to Pets Scale." *Anthrozoös* 3:160–175.

Jones, Gareth Steadman. 1971. *Outcast London: A Study in the Relationship Between Classes in Victorian Society.* London: Oxford University Press.

Josselson, Ruthellen. 1996. *Ethics and Process.* Vol. 4 of *The Narrative Study of Lives.* Thousand Oaks, CA: Sage.

Josselson, Ruthellen, and Amia Lieblich. 1993. *The Narrative Study of Lives.* Vol. 1 of *The Narrative Study of Lives.* Thousand Oaks, CA: Sage.

————. 1995. *Interpreting Experience.* Vol. 3 of *The Narrative Study of Lives.* Thousand Oaks, CA: Sage.

Kalof, Linda, and Carl Taylor. 2007. "The Discourse of Dog Fighting." *Humanity & Society* 31:319–333.

Katz, Jack. 1975. "Essences as Moral Identities: Verifiability and Responsibility in Imputations of Deviance and Charisma." *American Journal of Sociology* 80:1369–1390.

Kaufman, Joanne M., and Kathryn Johnson. 2004. "Stigmatized Individuals and the Process of Identity." *Sociological Quarterly* 45:807–833.

Kerasote, Ted. 2007. *Merle's Door: Lessons from a Freethinking Dog.* New York: Harcourt.

Kete, Kathleen. 1994. *The Beast in the Boudoir: Petkeeping in Nineteenth-Century Paris.* Berkeley: University of California Press.

Kidd, Aline H., and Robert M. Kidd. 1994. "Benefits and Liabilities of Pets for the Homeless." *Psychological Reports* 74:715–722.

Kidd, Sean A. 2003. "Street Youth: Coping and Interventions." *Child and Adolescent Social Work Journal* 20:235–261.

Kidd, Sean A., and Larry Davidson. 2007. "'You Have to Adapt Because You Have No Other Choice': The Stories of Strength and Resilience of 208 Homeless Youth in New York City and Toronto." *Journal of Community Psychology* 35:219–238.

Kleinman, Sherryl. 1996. *Opposing Ambitions: Gender and Identity in an Alternative Organization.* Chicago: University of Chicago Press.

Knapp, Caroline. 1998. *Pack of Two: The Intricate Bond Between People and Dogs.* New York: Dial.

Kusmer, Kenneth. 2002. *Down and Out, On the Road: The Homeless in American History.* New York: Oxford University Press.

Labov, William, and Joshua Waletzky. 1997. "Narrative Analysis: Oral Versions of Personal Experience." *Journal of Narrative and Life History* 7:3–38.

Labreque, Jennifer, and Christine A. Walsh. 2011. "Homeless Women's Voices on Incorporating Companion Animals into Shelter Services." *Anthrozoös* 24:79–95.

LaGory, Mark, Kevin Fitzpatrick, and Ferris Ritchey. 2001. "Life Chances and Choices: Assessing Quality of Life Among the Homeless." *Sociological Quarterly* 42:632–651.

LaGory, Mark, Ferris Ritchey, and Kevin Fitzpatrick. 1992. "Homelessness and Affiliation." *Sociological Quarterly* 32:201–218.

LaGory, Mark, Ferris J. Ritchey, and Jeffrey Mullis. 1990. "Depression Among the Homeless." *Journal of Health and Social Behavior* 31:87–101.

LaGory, Mark, Ferris Ritchey, Timothy O'Donoghue, and Jeff Mullis. 1989. "The Homeless of Alabama: A Diversity of People and Experiences." Pp. 1–20 in *Homelessness in the United States,* vol. 1, *State Surveys,* edited by J. Momeni. Westport: Greenwood.

Lankenau, Stephen E. 1999. "Stronger Than Dirt: Public Humiliation and Status Enhancement Among Panhandlers." *Journal of Contemporary Ethnography* 28:288–318.

Lankenau, Stephen E., Bill Sanders, Jennifer Jackson Bloom, Dodi Hathazi, Erica Alarcon, Stephanie Tortu, and Michael C. Clatts. 2008. "Migration Patterns and Substance Use Among Young Homeless Travelers." Pp. 65–83 in *Geography and Drug Addiction,* edited by Y. F. Thomas, D. Richardson, and I. Cheung. Guilford: Springer.

Lee, Barrett A. 1989. "Homelessness in Tennessee." Pp. 181–203 in *Homelessness in the United States,* vol. 1, *State Surveys,* edited by J. Momeni. Westport: Greenwood.

Lee, Barrett A., Kimberly A. Tyler, and James D. Wright. 2010. "The New Homelessness Revisited." *Annual Review of Sociology* 36:501–521.

Leonard, Amanda. 2011. "The Plight of 'Big Black Dogs' in American Animal Shelters: Color-Based Canine Discrimination." *Kroeber Anthropological Society Papers* 99:168–183.

Liebow, Elliot. 1993. *Tell Them Who I Am: The Lives of Homeless Women.* New York: Free Press.

Link, Bruce, Jo Phelan, Michaeline Bresnahan, Ann Stueve, Robert Moore, and Ezra Susser. 1995. "Lifetime and Five-Year Prevalence of Homelessness in the United States: New Evidence in an Old Debate." *American Journal of Orthopsychiatry* 65:347–354.

Maines, David R. 1993. "Narrative's Moment and Sociology's Phenomena: Toward a Narrative Sociology." *Sociological Quarterly* 34:17–38.

"Market Report: Growth in US Pet Ownership Slows with Economy." 2011. www.petfoodindustry.com/Columns/Market_Report/Market _Report_Growth_in_US_pet_ownership_slows_with_economy.html. Accessed July 27, 2011.

Martine, Lord. 2002. "Saving Dogs Helped Her Save Herself." *San Francisco Chronicle,* November 29. www.sfgate.com/cgi-bin/article .cgi?f=/c/a/2002/11/29/WB241239.DTL. Accessed March 2, 2012.

Maynes, Mary Jo, Jennifer L. Pierce, and Barbara Laslett. 2008. *Telling Stories: The Use of Personal Narratives in the Social Sciences and History.* Ithaca: Cornell University Press.

McAdams, Dan P. 1993. *The Stories We Live By: Personal Myths and the Making of the Self.* New York: Guilford.

———. 2004. "The Redemptive Self: Narrative Identity in America Today." Pp. 95–115 in *The Self and Memory,* edited by D. Beike, J. Lampinen, and D. Behrend. New York: Psychology Press.

———. 2006a. "The Redemptive Self: Generativity and the Stories Americans Live By." *Research in Human Development* 3:81–100.

———. 2006b. *The Redemptive Self: Stories Americans Live By.* New York: Oxford University Press.

———. 2008. "American Identity: The Redemptive Self." *General Psychologist* 43:20–27.

———. 2011. "Narrative Identity." Pp. 99–115 in *Handbook of Identity Theory,* vol. 1, *Structures and Processes,* edited by S. Schwartz, K. Luyckx, and V. Vignoles. New York: Springer.

McAdams, Dan P., Ann Diamond, Ed de St. Aubin, and Elizabeth Mansfield. 1997. "Stories of Commitment: The Psychosocial Construction of Generative Lives." *Journal of Personality and Social Psychology* 72:678–694.

McAdams, Dan P., Jeffery Reynolds, Martha Lewis, Allison H. Patten, and Phillip H. Bowman. 2001. "When Bad Things Turn Good and Good Things Turn Bad: Sequences of Redemption and Contamination in Life Narrative and Their Relation to Psychosocial Adaptation in Midlife Adults and in Students." *Personality and Social Psychology Bulletin* 27:474–485.

McCall, George J., and J. L. Simmons. 1978. *Identities and Interactions.* New York: Free Press.

McNicholas, June, and Glyn M. Collis. 2000. "Dogs as Catalysts for Social Interactions: Robustness of the Effect." *British Journal of Psychology* 91:61–70.

Mead, George Herbert. 1934. *Mind, Self, and Society.* Chicago: University of Chicago Press.

Melson, Gail. 2001. *Why the Wild Things Are: Animals in the Lives of Children.* Cambridge: Harvard University Press.

Menache, Sophia. 2000. "Hunting and Attachment to Dogs in the Pre-Modern Period." Pp. 42–60 in *Companion Animals and Us: Exploring the Relationships Between People and Pets,* edited by A. L. Podberscek, E. S. Paul, and J. A. Serpell. Cambridge: Cambridge University Press.

Messent, Peter. 1983. "Social Facilitation of Contact with Other People by Pet Dogs." Pp. 37–46 in *New Perspectives on Our Lives with Companion Animals,* edited by A. Katcher and A. Beck. Philadelphia: University of Pennsylvania Press.

Mills, C. Wright. 1940. "Situated Actions and Vocabularies of Motive." *American Sociological Review* 5:904–913.

Minehan, Thomas. 1934. *Boy and Girl Tramps of America.* New York: Grosset and Dunlap.

———. 1936. "Boy and Girl Tramps of the Road: The Chronicler of Our Youthful Hoboes Discusses Their Schooling." *Clearing House* 11:136–139.

Mitchell, Don. 1997. "The Annihilation of Space by Law: The Roots and Implications of Anti-Homeless Laws in the United States." *Antipode* 29:303–335.

Mitchell, Robert W., Nicholas S. Thompson, and H. Lyn Miles, eds. 1997. *Anthropomorphism, Anecdotes, and Animals.* Albany: State University of New York Press.

Molina, Edna. 2000. "Informal Non-Kin Networks Among Homeless Latino and African American Men." *American Behavioral Scientist* 43:663–685.

Mowbray, Carol T., Deborah Bybee, and Evan Cohen. 1993. "Describing the Homeless Mentally Ill: Cluster Analysis Results." *American Journal of Community Psychology* 21:67–93.

Mugford, R. A., and J. G. M'Comisky. 1975. "Some Recent Work on the Psychotherapeutic Value of Cage Birds with Old People." Pp. 54–65 in *Pets, Animals, and Society,* edited by R. S. Anderson. London: Bailliere Tindall.

Müllersdorf, Maria, Fredrik Granström, Lotta Sahlqvist, and Per Tillgren. 2010. "Aspects of Health, Physical/Leisure Activities, Work, and Sociodemographics Associated with Pet Ownership in Sweden." *Scandinavian Journal of Public Health* 38:53–63.

Nack, Adina. 2008. *Damaged Goods? Women Living with Incurable Sexually Transmitted Diseases.* Philadelphia: Temple University Press.

Neisser, Ulric, and Robyn Fivush, eds. 1994. *The Remembering Self: Construction and Accuracy in the Self-Narrative.* Cambridge: Cambridge University Press.

Osborne, Randall E. 2002. "'I May Be Homeless, but I'm Not Helpless': The Costs and Benefits of Identifying with Homelessness." *Self and Identity* 1:43–52.

Outland, George E. 1937. "Boy Tramps of the Road: A Further Statement." *Clearing House* 11:277–279.

Parslow, Ruth A., Anthony F. Jorm, Helen Christensen, and Bryan Rodgers. 2005. "Pet Ownership and Health in Older Adults: Findings from a Survey of 2,551 Community-Based Australians Aged 60–64." *Gerontology* 51:40–47.

Pippert, Timothy D. 2007. *Road Dogs and Loners: Family Relationships Among Homeless Men.* Lanham: Lexington Books.

Plummer, Ken. 1983. *Documents of Life: An Introduction to the Problems and Literature of a Humanistic Method.* London: Allen and Unwin.

————. 1995. *Telling Sexual Stories: Power, Change, and Social Worlds*. London: Routledge.

Polkinghorne, Donald E. 1988. *Narrative Knowing and the Human Sciences*. Albany: State University of New York Press.

————. 1991. "Narrative and the Self-Concept." *Journal of Narrative and Life History* 1:135–153.

Pollner, Melvin, and Lynn McDonald-Wikler. 1985. "The Social Construction of Unreality: A Case Study of a Family's Attribution of Competence to a Severely Retarded Child." *Family Process* 24:241–254.

Poresky, Robert H., Charles Hendrix, Jacob E. Mosier, and Marvin L. Samuelson. 1987. "The Companion Animal Bonding Scales: Internal Reliability and Construct Validity." *Psychological Reports* 60: 743–746.

Pullen, Suzanne. 2006. "Jefferson Award: Ilana Strubel, Vet for Pets of Homeless." *San Francisco Chronicle,* January 7. www.sfgate.com /opinion/article/Jefferson-Award-Ilana-Strubel-vet-for-pets-of -2524102.php#ixzz24xhAIYAz. Accessed August 30, 2012.

Rew, Lynn. 2000. "Friends and Pets as Companions: Strategies for Coping with Loneliness Among Homeless Youth." *Journal of Child and Adolescent Psychiatric Nursing* 13:125–140.

Ritchey, Ferris J., Mark LaGory, Kevin M. Fitzpatrick, and Jeffrey Mullis. 1990. "A Comparison of Homeless, Community-Wide, and Selected Distressed Samples on the CES-Depression Scale." *American Journal of Public Health* 80:1384–1386.

Ritvo, Harriet. 1987. *The Animal Estate: The English and Other Creatures in the Victorian Age*. Cambridge: Harvard University Press.

Robins, Douglas M., Clinton R. Sanders, and Spencer E. Cahill. 1991. "Dogs and Their People: Pet-Facilitated Interaction in a Public Setting." *Journal of Contemporary Ethnography* 20:3–25.

Rosenberg, Morris. 1973. "Which Significant Others?" *American Behavioral Scientist* 16:829–860.

Rosenberg, Morris, and B. Claire McCullough. 1981. "Mattering: Inferred Significance and Mental Health Among Adolescents." *Research in Community and Mental Health* 2:163–182.

Rosenwald, George C., and Richard L. Ochberg, eds. 1992. *Storied Lives: The Cultural Politics of Self-Understanding*. New Haven: Yale University Press.

Rossi, Peter H., 1989. *Down and Out in America*. Chicago: University of Chicago Press.

————. 1990. "The Old Homeless and the New Homelessness in Historical Perspective." *American Psychologist* 45:954–959.

Ruddick, Susan. 1996. *Young and Homeless in Hollywood: Mapping Social Identities*. New York: Routledge.

Sacks, Harvey. 1974. "On the Analysability of Stories by Children." Pp. 216–232 in *Ethnomethodology,* edited by R. Turner. Middlesex: Penguin.

Sanders, Clinton R. 1990. "Excusing Tactics: Social Responses to the Public Misbehavior of Companion Animals." *Anthrozoös* 4:82–90.

———. 1993. "Understanding Dogs: Caretakers' Attributions of Mindedness in Canine-Human Relationships." *Journal of Contemporary Ethnography* 22:205–226.

———. 1999. *Understanding Dogs: Living and Working with Canine Companions.* Philadelphia: Temple University Press.

———. 2000. "The Impact of Guide Dogs on the Identity of People with Visual Impairments." *Anthrozoös* 13:131–139.

———. 2003. "Actions Speak Louder Than Words: Close Relationships Between Humans and Nonhuman Animals." *Symbolic Interaction* 26(3):405–426.

Schieman, Scott, and John Taylor. 2001. "Statuses, Roles, and the Sense of Mattering." *Sociological Perspectives* 44:469–484.

Scott, James. 1990. *Domination and the Arts of Resistance: Hidden Transcripts.* New Haven: Yale University Press.

Sermons, M. William, and Peter Witte. 2011. *State of Homelessness in America.* Washington, DC: National Alliance to End Homelessness.

Serpell, James. 1986. *In the Company of Animals.* Oxford: Blackwell.

———. 1988. "Pet-Keeping in Non-Western Societies: Some Popular Misconceptions." Pp. 34–52 in *Animals and People Sharing the World,* edited by A. N. Rowan. Hanover: University of New England Press.

Shapiro, Kenneth J. 1997. "A Phenomenological Approach to the Study of Nonhuman Animals." Pp. 277–295 in *Anthropomorphism, Anecdotes, and Animals,* edited by R. Mitchell, N. Thompson, and H. Miles. Albany: State University of New York Press.

Shlay, Anne B., and Peter H. Rossi. 1992. "Social Science Research and Contemporary Studies of Homelessness." *Annual Review of Sociology* 18:129–160.

Singer, Randall S., Lynette A. Hart, and R. Lee Zasloff. 1995. "Dilemmas Associated with Rehousing Homeless People Who Have Companion Animals." *Psychological Reports* 77:851–857.

Smith, Hilary. 2008. "Searching for Kin: The Creation of Street Families Among Homeless Youth." *American Behavioral Scientist* 51:756–771.

Smith-Harris, Tracey. 2004. "There's Not Enough Room to Swing a Dead Cat and There's No Use Flogging a Dead Horse." *ReVision* 27:12–15.

Snow, David A., and Leon Anderson. 1987. "Identity Work Among the Homeless: The Verbal Construction and Avowal of Personal Identities." *American Journal of Sociology* 92:1336–1371.

———. 1993. *Down on Their Luck: A Study of Homeless Street People.* Berkeley: University of California Press.

Snow, David, Susan G. Baker, Leon Anderson, and Michael Martin. 1986. "The Myth of Pervasive Mental Illness Among the Homeless." *Social Problems* 33:407–423.

Snow, David A., and Michael Mulcahy. 2001. "Space, Politics, and the Survival Strategies of the Homeless." *American Behavioral Scientist* 45:149–169.

Spencer, Liz, and Ray Pahl. 2006. *Rethinking Friendship: Hidden Solidarities Today.* Princeton: Princeton University Press.

Stephens, Sally. 2006. "For the Love of a Dog." *Woofer Times,* January. www.rocketdogrescue.org/pdfs/woofertimes06.pdf. Accessed March 2, 2012.

Stokes, Randall, and John P. Hewitt. 1976. "Aligning Actions." *American Sociological Review* 41:838–849.

Stone, Gregory P. 1962. "Appearance and the Self." Pp. 86–118 in *Human Behavior and Social Processes,* edited by A. M. Rose. Boston: Houghton Mifflin.

Strauss, Anselm. 1969. *Mirrors and Masks.* San Francisco: Sociology Press.

Sykes, Gresham, and David Matza. 1957. "Techniques of Neutralization." *American Sociological Review* 22:664–670.

Taylor, Heidi, Pauline Williams, and David Gray. 2004. "Homelessness and Dog Ownership: An Investigation into Animal Empathy, Attachment, Crime, Drug Use, Health, and Public Opinion." *Anthrozoös* 17:353–368.

Taylor, Steven J. 1987. "Observing Abuse: Professional Ethics and Personal Morality in Field Research." *Qualitative Sociology* 10:288–302.

Thomas, Keith. 1983. *Man and the Natural World: Changing Attitudes in England, 1500–1800.* London: Allen Lane.

Thomas, W. I., and Dorothy Swaine Thomas. 1928. *The Child in America: Behavior Problems and Programs.* New York: Knopf.

Toro, Paul A., Amy Dworsky, and Patrick J. Fowler. 2007. "Homeless Youth in the United States: Recent Research Findings and Intervention Approaches." Pp. 1–33 in *Toward Understanding Homelessness: The 2007 National Symposium on Homelessness Research,* edited by D. Dennis, G. Locke, and J. Khadduri. Washington, DC: US Department of Housing and Urban Development and US Department of Health and Human Services. http://aspe.hhs.gov/hsp/homelessness/symposium07. Accessed January 18, 2012.

Tough, Paul. 2011. "The Poverty Clinic." *New Yorker,* March 21.

Tuan, Yi-Fu. 1984. *Dominance and Affection: The Making of Pets.* New Haven: Yale University Press.

Turner, Ralph H. 1968. "The Self-Conception in Social Interaction." Pp. 93–106 in *The Self in Social Interaction,* edited by C. Gordon and K. J. Gergen. New York: Wiley.

———. 1976. "The Real Self: From Institution to Impulse." *American Journal of Sociology* 81:989–1016.

Turner, Victor. 1967. *The Forest of Symbols: Aspects of Ndembu Ritual.* Ithaca: Cornell University Press.

Uys, Errol Lincoln. 1999. *Riding the Rails: Teenagers on the Move During the Great Depression.* New York: Routledge.

Van Gennep, Arnold. 1961. *The Rites of Passage.* Chicago: University of Chicago Press.

Vermilya, Jenny R. 2012. "Contesting Horses: Borders and Shifting Social Meanings in Veterinary Medical Education." *Society & Animals* 20:123–137.

Voith, Victoria. 1983. "Animal Behavior Problems: An Overview." Pp. 181–186 in *New Perspectives on Our Lives with Companion Animals,* edited by A. Katcher and A. Beck. Philadelphia: University of Pennsylvania Press.

Wagner, David. 1993. *Checkerboard Square: Culture and Resistance in a Homeless Community.* Boulder: Westview.

Wasserman, Jason Adam, and Jeffrey Michael Clair. 2010. *At Home on the Street: People, Poverty, and a Hidden Culture of Homelessness.* Boulder: Lynne Rienner.

———. 2011. "Housing Patterns of Homeless People: The Ecology of the Street in the Era of Urban Renewal." *Journal of Contemporary Ethnography* 40:71–101.

Wells, Deborah L. 2004. "The Facilitation of Social Interactions by Domestic Dogs." *Anthrozoös* 17:340–352.

———. 2007. "Domestic Dogs and Human Health: An Overview." *British Journal of Health Psychology* 12:145–156.

———. 2009. "Associations Between Pet Ownership and Self-Reported Health Status in People Suffering from Chronic Fatigue Syndrome." *Journal of Alternative and Complementary Medicine* 15:407–413.

Wells, Deborah L., and Peter G. Hepper. 1992. "The Behaviour of Dogs in a Rescue Shelter." *Animal Welfare* 1:171–186.

Wills, Gary. 1990. *Under God: Religion and American Politics.* New York: Simon and Schuster.

Wolch, Jennifer. 1998. "Zoöpolis." Pp. 119–138 in *Animal Geographies: Place, Politics, and Identity in the Nature-Culture Borderlands,* edited by J. Wolch and J. Emel. London: Verso.

Wolch, Jennifer, and Jody Emel. 1998. *Animal Geographies: Place, Politics, and Identity in the Nature-Culture Borderlands.* London: Verso.

Wright, Talmadge. 1997. *Out of Place: Homeless Mobilizations, Subcities, and Contested Landscapes.* Albany: State University of New York Press.

Yablonsky, Lewis. 1968. *The Hippie Trip: A Firsthand Account of the Beliefs and Behaviors of Hippies in America by a Noted Sociologist.* New York: Pegasus.

Želvys, V. I. 1990. "Obscene Humor: What the Hell?" *Humor: International Journal of Humor Research* 3:323–332.

Zimmerman, Ann. 2001. "Leapin' Lizards! Service Animals Are Multiplying Like Doggone Rabbits." *Wall Street Journal,* February 24. http://online.wsj.com/article/SB10001424052748703652104576122 461180284204.html. Accessed August 6, 2011.

Zussman, Robert. 1996. "Autobiographical Occasions." *Contemporary Sociology* 25:143–148.

———. 2000. "Autobiographical Occasions: Introduction to the Special Issue." *Qualitative Sociology* 23:5–8.

Index

About the Book

A weary-looking man stands at an intersection, backpack at his feet. Curled up nearby is a mixed-breed dog, unfazed by the passing traffic. The man holds a sign that reads, "Two old dogs need help. God bless." What's happening here?

Leslie Irvine breaks new ground in the study of homelessness by investigating the frequently noticed, yet underexplored, role that animals play in the lives of homeless people. Irvine conducted interviews on street corners, in shelters, even at highway underpasses, to provide insights into the benefits and liabilities that animals have for the homeless. She also weighs the perspectives of social service workers, veterinarians, and local communities. Her work provides a new way of looking at both the meaning of animal companionship and the concept of home itself.

Leslie Irvine is associate professor of sociology at the University of Colorado at Boulder.